Monetary Unions

The Economic and Monetary Union (EMU) in which some members of the European Union (EU) have joined, has prompted much discussion of monetary union. Most of this discussion has focused on the immediate issues, such as prospects for the euro and the possibility of expanding the euro-zone. Few authors have stood back and considered either the relevant theory or what lessons might be drawn from other unions that have been formed in the past. Four of the chapters in this volume do this, and although the fifth does look directly at EMU, it does so with the aid of analytical tools not previously used on that subject.

In the second chapter Bennett McCallum reviews the extant theory of monetary unions. In the third, Michael D. Bordo and Lars Jonung look specifically at past experience for lessons that might be learned from previous unions for European monetary union, considering both national and multinational monetary unions. Discussion of the prospects for European monetary union has often focused on whether the European union is an optimal currency area and, if not, how long it might take to become one and whether there might be unacceptable costs to some part of the territory along the way. Hugh Rockoff considers these same questions in relation to the US experience, often cited as the most successful example of monetary union. Marc Flandreau adds a European historical perspective, with particular attention to the monetary union of Austria and Hungary. In the final chapter, Roland Vaubel applies public choice analysis to various institutional aspects of EMU, focusing on such critical questions as the prospects for inflation and for future enlargement of both EMU and the EU.

Forrest H. Capie is Professor of Economic History and **Geoffrey E. Wood** is Professor of Economics at City University Business School.

Routledge International Studies in Money and Banking

1 **Private Banking in Europe**
Lynn Bicker

2 **Bank Deregulation and Monetary Order**
George Selgin

3 **Money in Islam**
A study in Islamic political economy
Masudul Alam Choudhury

4 **The Future of European Financial Centres**
Kirsten Bindemann

5 **Payment Systems in Global Perspective**
Maxwell J. Fry, Isaak Kilato, Sandra Roger, Krzysztof Senderowicz, David Sheppard, Francisco Solis and John Trundle

6 **What is Money?**
John Smithin

7 **Finance**
A characteristics approach
Edited by David Blake

8 **Organisational Change and Retail Finance**
An ethnographic perspective
Richard Harper, Dave Randall and Mark Rouncefield

9 **The History of the Bundesbank**
Lessons for the European Central Bank
Jakob de Haan

10 **The Euro**
A challenge and opportunity for financial markets
Published on behalf of *Société Universitaire Européenne de Recherches Financières (SUERF)*
Edited by Michael Artis, Axel Weber and Elizabeth Hennessy

11 **Central Banking in Eastern Europe**
Nigel Healey

12 **Money, Credit and Prices Stability**
Paul Dalziel

13 **Monetary Policy, Capital Flows and Exchange Rates**
Essays in memory of Maxwell Fry
Edited by William Allen and David Dickinson

14 **Adapting to Financial Globalisation**
Published on behalf of *Société Universitaire Européenne de Recherches Financières (SUERF)*
Edited by Morten Balling, Eduard H. Hochreiter and Elizabeth Hennessy

15 **Monetary Macroeconomics**
A new approach
Alvaro Cencini

16 **Monetary Stability in Europe**
Stefan Collignon

17 **Technology and Finance**
Challenges for financial markets, business strategies and policy makers
Published on behalf of *Société Universitaire Européenne de Recherches Financières (SUERF)*
Edited by Morten Balling, Frank Lierman and Andrew Mullineux

18 **Monetary Unions**
Theory, history, public choice
Edited by Forrest H. Capie and Geoffrey E. Wood

Monetary Unions

Theory, history, public choice

Edited by Forrest H. Capie and Geoffrey E. Wood

Routledge
Taylor & Francis Group
LONDON AND NEW YORK

First published 2003
by Routledge
2 Park Square, Milton Park, Abingdon, Oxfordshire OX14 4RN

Simultaneously published in the USA and Canada
by Routledge
711 Third Avenue, New York, NY 10017

First issued in paperback 2014

Routledge is an imprint of the Taylor and Francis Group an informa company

Typeset in Baskerville by
BOOK NOW Ltd

British Library Cataloguing in Publication Data
A catalogue record for this book is available from the British Library

Library of Congress Cataloging in Publication Data
A catalog record for this book has been requested

ISBN 13: 978-0-415-30039-1 (hbk)
ISBN 13: 978-1-138-00868-7 (pbk)

Contents

List of figures vii
List of tables viii
List of contributors ix
Acknowledgements x

1 **Introduction** 1
FORREST H. CAPIE AND GEOFFREY E. WOOD

2 **Theoretical issues pertaining to monetary unions** 7
BENNETT T. McCALLUM

Comments by Peter Sinclair 26
Geoffrey E. Wood 36

3 **The future of EMU: what does the history of monetary unions tell us?** 42
MICHAEL D. BORDO AND LARS JONUNG

Comments by Tim Congdon 70
Charles Goodhart 73

4 **How long did it take the United States to become an optimal currency area?** 76
HUGH ROCKOFF

Comments by Ronald McKinnon 104
Anna J. Schwartz 108

5 **The bank, the states, and the market: an Austro-Hungarian tale for Euroland, 1867–1914** 111
MARC FLANDREAU

Comments by Luca Einaudi 142

6 The future of the euro: a public choice perspective **146**
ROLAND VAUBEL

Comments by Fabrizio Zampolli 182
Mark Salmon 189

Index 194

Figures

2.1 The relationship between monetary efficiency and economic integration for a country joining a fixed exchange rate area 39
2.2 The relationship between economic stability loss and economic integration for a country joining a fixed exchange rate area 39
2.3 The balance between losses and gains for a country joining a fixed exchange rate area 39
4.1 All bank deposits by region, 1875–96 87
4.2 National bank deposits by region, 1875–1900 89
4.3 All bank deposits by region, 1900–14 91
4.4 Deposits by Federal Reserve district, 1922–41 93
4.5 Deposits by Federal Reserve district: the first two years of the depression, 1929–31 94
4.6 Deposits by Federal Reserve district before the doubling of reserve ratios, 1934–6 95
5.1 The Austro-Hungarian budgetary structure 118
5.2 Deficits in Austria and Hungary, 1875–1912 120
5.3 Common budgets in Austria and Hungary, 1880–1912 121
5.4 Quinquennial estimates of the burden of public debts in Austria and Hungary, 1875–1910 122
5.5 Exchange rate in Vienna, 1881–99 126
5.6 Yields on Austro-Hungarian securities: gold vs. paper, 1882–9 131
5.7 The spread between paper- and gold-denominated currencies in Austria and Hungary, 1880–95 133
6.1 The central banker's calculus 155
6.2 Nominal and real D-Mark/US$ exchange rates 162
6.3 Effective exchange rates, EMU-11/US$ 164
6.4 Effective exchange rates, EMU-11/UK£ 166

Tables

3.1 The creation of some monetary unions in the nineteenth century 46
3.2 The dissolution of some monetary unions in the twentieth century 57
4.1 Agricultural prices and the NNP deflator, 1879–1900 83
4.2 A chronology of the US monetary union 99
5.1 Lesson from the past? 117
5.2 Debt burden and debt structure: Austria and Hungary 132
6.1 The inflation median in the Governing Council of the European Central Bank: consumer price index 148
6.2 Sensitivity to inflation, central bank independence, DM pegging and inflation in EMU-11, 1976–93 150
6.3 Cross-section analysis of inflation in EMU-11 (ln), 1976–93 151
6.4 Seigniorage gains and losses in EMU-11 154
6.5 Governments and the Central Bank Council in the EMU in May 2001 158
6.6 Prospective election dates, ECB coalitions and political business cycles in the EMU, 2000–6 159
6.7 Bilateral trade as a percentage of GDP, 1997 161
6.8 Real and nominal exchange rate trends, D-Mark per US$ 163
6.9 Real and nominal exchange rate trends, EMU-11 per US$ 163
6.10 Enlargement of EMU by present EU members 165
6.11 Real and nominal exchange rate trends, EMU-11 per UK£ 166
6.12 National minimum reserve requirements prior to EMU (end of 1994), sight liabilities or money market cash reserve 167
6.13 Openness and real exchange rate trends of Eastern European states vis-à-vis EMU-11 169
6.14 Taxonomy of optimal exchange rate arrangements for the Eastern European states 170
6.15 Actual and predicted central bank staff prior to EMU 172
6.16 Actual and predicted central bank staff in EMU-11 173

Contributors

Michael D. Bordo, Department of Economics, Rutgers University

Forrest H. Capie, Department of Banking and Finance, City Business School

Tim Congdon, Cardiff Business School

Luca Einaudi, Department of Economic Affairs, Prime Minister's Office, Rome and Centre for History and Economics, King's College, Cambridge

Marc Flandreau, Observatoire Français des Conjonctures Economiques

Charles Goodhart, London School of Economics and Political Science

Lars Jonung, European Commission, Economic and Financial Affairs, Directorate-General, formerly Stockholm School of Economics

Bennett T. McCallum, Graduate School of Industrial Administration, Carnegie Mellon University

Ronald McKinnon, Department of Economics, Stanford University

Hugh Rockoff, Department of Economics, Rutgers University

Mark Salmon, Financial Econometrics Research Centre, Department of Banking and Finance, City University Business School

Anna J. Schwartz, National Bureau of Economic Research

Peter Sinclair, Department of Economics, University of Birmingham

Roland Vaubel, Department of Economics, Universität Mannheim

Geoffrey E. Wood, Department of Banking and Finance, City Business School

Fabrizio Zampolli, Department of Economics, University of Warwick

Acknowledgements

One of the papers in this volume has only one discussant. Its other discussant, Morris Perlman, died before he was able to produce a written version of his comments. Morris was a fine economist, a perceptive scholar, and a good friend. He is a great loss.

We are greatly indebted to Wes Wadman and Amex Investment Bank for the financial support which made possible the conference necessary to produce this book.

Forrest H. Capie
Geoffrey E. Wood

1 Introduction

Forrest H. Capie and Geoffrey E. Wood

This book comprises the papers presented at a conference on monetary unions held at City University, London, in May 1999, along with the comments on them by their discussants at the conference. Monetary union was a much discussed subject at that time, of course prompted by the Economic and Monetary Union (EMU) in which some members of the European Union (EU) have joined, and has remained so since then. Most of the discussion, though, has been focused on that particular union. Few authors have stood back and considered either the relevant theory, whatever that might turn out to be, or what lessons might be drawn from other unions that have been formed, some durable, some not, in the past. It is the aim of four of the papers gathered together in this volume to address these issues; and although the fifth does look directly at EMU, it does so with the aid of analytical tools not previously used on that subject.

This short introductory essay provides a brief guide to the book, sets out the main points of each paper, and concludes by setting out the overall points to emerge from the conference as a whole.

The theory of monetary unions originated with a short but very well known paper by Robert Mundell (1961).[1] The paper draws attention to the problems of monetary union across a large, geographically diverse area (problems possibly exacerbated by an issue Mundell does not discuss, the area's encompassing several languages). In his paper, the one which opens this volume and which concentrates on analytical issues, Bennett McCallum considers Mundell's paper, as well as subsequent, but still pioneering, papers by McKinnon (1963) and Kenen (1969). McCallum also touches on the theory of currency crises, and an aspect of the connection between fiscal and monetary policy.

What emerges very strikingly is how little *that is operational* economic theory has to say on this subject. That certainly does not mean that it has no contribution to offer – only that it cannot be directly applied to answer, for example, whether a particular country should join EMU (or of course any other monetary union). What it very clearly can do is provide guidance on the questions to address to past episodes of monetary union. That is exactly how it is used in the papers by Michael Bordo and Lars Jonung, Hugh Rockoff and Marc Flandreau. One of these unions, the USA (studied by Hugh Rockoff) was certainly a success – at least by one criterion, which is discussed in the comment (on McCallum's paper) by Wood, and used by Anna

Schwartz in her remarks on the Rockoff paper. Bordo and Jonung seek to draw lessons for EMU from the study of a wide range of unions, and Flandreau from the experiences of a particular (pre-1914) union. Only Roland Vaubel looks directly at EMU, and, applying public choice analysis, makes predictions for its future inflation and business cycle behaviour, and considers the consequences of various still prospective members actually joining. His very striking results are discussed in a little more detail below.

We now move on to the papers, following in our discussion the order in which they appear in the book (and were presented at the conference).

The first paper in the volume, by Bennett McCallum, deals with some theoretical aspects of monetary union. As is well known, the most obvious and fundamental tool to use in this area, optimum currency area theory, has so far proved non-operational. In his paper, McCallum reviews this theory and concludes that it is still in that position. The original article, by Mundell (1961), and the subsequent additions by McKinnon (1963) and Kenen (1969) have provided a list of factors relevant when deciding whether an area is optimal, but have got no further. Later work by Bayoumi and Eichengreen (1996, 1997) has gone some way beyond this, but only by producing rankings of suitability for membership of a particular union; they do not provide any way of deciding on the optimality of a union.

McCallum also discusses the history of the subject, and provides an explanation for its developing only in the 1960s; his explanation turns largely on the existence of a consensus in favour of a worldwide fixed rate system until the attack on that consensus by Milton Friedman in 1953.

In view of the comparatively limited guidance optimum currency area theory can give, what other tools of economic analysis are useful in the area?

McCallum proposes two. He considers the comparatively recently developed theory of currency crises. (He notes that this, too, dated really from Milton Friedman's 1953 paper on flexible exchange rates.) This theory is relevant because it shows that a 'fixed but adjustable' exchange rate regime, such as the EU had for some years before going to EMU, is not viable in the long term. The reason is straightforward; so long as governments wish to retain the freedom to change their exchange rates, they by implication wish on some occasions to subordinate defending the rate to some other policy objective. Knowing this is in itself sufficient to expose the currency to attack. European countries, then, had to move from the ERM (exchange rate mechanism). (In which direction they moved, fixed or floating, was of course not preordained by that body of theory.)

The paper concludes with a brief appraisal of the fiscal theory of inflation – the theory which says that price level behaviour is determined by the stock of government bonds, quite independently of whatever the money supply is doing. McCallum rejects this theory, and thereby raises questions about the purpose of fiscal rules in EMU (or any other monetary union).

Bordo and Jonung look specifically at past experience for lessons that might be learned from previous unions for European monetary union. They first survey the experience of national monetary unions – that is, those involved in nation building – looking at three specifically: the United States, Italy and Germany. They then consider multinational monetary unions: the Latin Monetary Union and the Scandinavian Monetary Union. Some others that are noted are those that existed informally between Britain and some of its colonies in the nineteenth century. And then there are some close approximations to monetary union found in certain currency boards. These latter have become more common again recently, having been a popular institution in the nineteenth century. (The East Caribbean Currency Area is currently a multinational monetary union with a single monetary authority. Where formerly there was a currency board for the seven territories there is now a currency union.)

The strongest element in the formation of monetary unions in the past has been political. In the main they have been formed to facilitate political unification or in some cases the rationalisation of different currencies after political unification. Economic reasons can obviously play a part. Equally, the principal cause of the break-up of monetary unions (Soviet Union, Czechoslovakia, etc.) can also be found in political developments. It can be that within a political entity economic strains can develop between certain regions which can then result in the break-up of the political union.

From this survey of historical experience Bordo and Jonung draw some strong and important conclusions. The main one concerns whether or not EMU will be a national or multinational union. According to one view monetary union is being used to promote political union. Bordo and Jonung list a number of defects in EMU as it stands. These include the lack of a number of features normally found in a modern monetary system, such as lender of last resort, a central supervisory body, an accountable central bank and co-ordinated fiscal policies, and inconsistent requirements in monetary policy. They add that Europe is quite clearly not an optimum currency area. They judge, however, that EMU will move towards being a national monetary union. The likelihood is that when one region suffers a shock this will simply stimulate the moves for a larger central authority to carry out the necessary fiscal transfers to smooth the adjustment process. Their guess is that EMU will hold together and that based on historical experience it takes rather extreme circumstances such as war to break unions up.

That EMU is a political agenda rather than the economic agenda that is often presented has become more and more widely accepted. One discussant, Charles Goodhart both noted this, and was not so sanguine as Bordo and Jonung that the union would survive adverse shocks.

A major part of the economic analysis of monetary unions is concerned with whether or not the territories covered make, in the jargon, an optimum currency area. As noted in the opening paper this is not an easy concept to make operational. It is straightforward to list the basic requirements such as price flexibility, labour mobility, capital mobility and so on, but much more difficult to say at what stage the combined factors have defined an optimum currency area. The originator of the concept, Robert Mundell, has in fact come out in support of the idea that the different European states would certainly become an optimum currency area even if they are not one at present. There can perhaps be no denying that; but the questions would then be, how long would that take and might there be unacceptable costs to some parts of the territory along the way. This in fact is the question that Hugh Rockoff addresses in relation to the United States. The United States was a political union from an early date, and that would no doubt have smoothed the monetary experience. Nevertheless, the question can still be put – might some parts of the United States have been better off with their own currencies floating against the US dollar?

Rockoff traces US experience from the origins of the monetary union, which dates from the ratification of the constitution in 1788. Prior to that, currency varied among the different colonies. The central question that he puts is, might the United States have been better off if some of the regions had had their own currency? He shows that there were bitter disputes over the 150 years after ratification. Typically what happened was that one region would experience a shock – commonly a fall in demand for an agricultural product – and the local banking system would suffer, leading in turn to falling money supply and real income.

In the Civil War there were effectively three monetary regions: the East and the mid-West used greenbacks; the South had a confederate dollar; and the Pacific coast stayed on gold. But after the war there was a long struggle towards acceptance of reunification. Rockoff shows too that in terms of optimum currency area criteria some regions differed highly from others, and that in many ways they were separable currency areas.

The most extreme experience was the great depression of 1929–32. While the whole country suffered there were big differences. It was at that point, argues Rockoff, that important institutional changes were made such as the development of federally funded transfer programmes which 'redistributed reserves lost through interregional payments deficits'. These and the increasing integration of the labour market helped to bring the United States closer to an optimum currency area. But the answer to the question 'How long did it take the United States to become a optimum currency area?' is roughly 150 years.

Marc Flandreau is perhaps best known for his work on bimetallism and the working of the French monetary system in the middle of the nineteenth century; and that of course included the relationship with the Latin Monetary Union. He raises here the question as to how useful the study of historical experience can be for guidance on the sustainability of modern monetary unions. He points out, correctly in our view, that most of the arrangements that went under the name of 'monetary unions' can be found in the nineteenth century when most countries adhered to some form of metallic monetary standard. So unions such as the Latin Monetary Union or the Scandinavian Monetary Union turn out on closer examination not to be monetary unions of the kind we currently have in mind but, rather, simply currency unions. The countries involved simply agreed to accept each others' currency. Given that these were coins with specified metal content there was little to get excited about and much of the activity was already taking place without any formal agreement. These unions had no common monetary policy and no common central bank. There were other monetary unions. There were those of the Swiss states, the Italian Kingdoms and the German States. But these were of course essentially attempts at political union. The driving force was political union; and different currencies had to be rationalised in order to facilitate political union or as a sensible practice after political union was achieved, or some combination of both of these. Insofar as the European monetary union is supposed to be about separate states and not political union, these latter examples should be of little interest to us. And yet, as Charles Goodhart at this conference stressed, European monetary union is a political agenda and has been carried along with 'devilish cleverness by a politically astute clique intent on achieving their own ends'.

Be that as it may, Flandreau tried instead to find an experience which might fit our purposes more closely – a monetary union between separate independent states; this is found in the alliance between Austria and Hungary. This was an arrangement whereby both countries surrendered monetary sovereignty to a common central bank but retained fiscal sovereignty. The Habsburg monarchy operated without the kind of agreement that exists in Europe today to keep public expenditure within certain limits. There were great pressures to raise public spending in the nineteenth century to promote economic development and it was left to the capital market to discipline the fiscal authorities. The 'compromise of 1867' was the agreement struck between the two countries for a period of ten years and reviewed regularly until 1917. Flandreau traces the monetary and fiscal experience of this union. He shows how the two states were continuously concerned about their reputation in the market. There was some competition over reputation and as they standardised their debt instruments the market could better read the price signals.

This is an extremely interesting use of history which escapes from many of the limitations that apply to studies of other monetary unions.

In his penetrating paper (updated to June 2002) Roland Vaubel applies public choice analysis - in particular the median voter theorem, the theory of the political business cycle and the economic theory of bureaucracy - to various institutional aspects of EMU. He is concerned with the behaviour of EMU institutions rather than directly with EMU itself, although, of course, the behaviour of the institutions clearly has implications for EMU. The institutions he focuses on are the European Central Bank (ECB) and the EU's Council of Ministers. The results (to which Vaubel attaches a reminder that they are the mid-point of a confidence interval and not a precise forecast – a warning which of course all econometric work should carry) are striking. Whatever methods he uses produce significantly higher inflation than the current ECB target – the predicted rates all exceed 5 per cent pa. There will, as a result of the timing of elections, very likely be a boom between 2002 and 2004. The effects of the Euro on unemployment are ambiguous in sign but certainly distributed very unevenly across the area.

And what of EMU (and, of course, EU) enlargement? Vaubel considers both Eastern prospective members of the EU, and existing non-EMU countries in the EU. Here too the results are fascinating. Of the Eastern countries, only Slovenia and Hungary are well suited to EMU membership; and of all the current EU countries, the UK is the least suitable for membership. There are many more results in this fascinating paper. The two discussants express some reservations – as does Vaubel, who points out that 'The analysis of this article – like most empirical research – is merely suggestive'. Doubts are raised both about aspects of the econometrics and about the relevance of certain parts of public choice analysis. Nevertheless the paper is important, and remains so even should every one of its predictions be falsified. Its fundamental importance lies in showing how the tools of a particular, and very specialised, area of economics can be applied, and in showing how very important they are. For the rigour of the analysis demonstrates persuasively that simply hoping or asserting that matters will work out well for some institutional design is insufficient. Supporters of the design must argue their case before putting the model they have designed into operation. Faith, hope and trusting that men of goodwill will always produce good results is not enough. Quoting from the conclusion of this paper gives a striking and important example of the dangers lying in that 'blind optimism' approach. 'It is easy to agree on an inflation target and leave open how it might be attained. If it is not attained it might be attributed to factors other than monetary policy. After all, failure to attain the target will not be sanctioned.'

Conclusion

The papers that we have reviewed contain a great deal that is both interesting and enlightening on the subject of monetary unions. But the main general focus seems to be that there is as yet no body of analysis which can give guidance on the optimality of prospective unions. The theory is still, very much like the theory of customs unions, a collection of useful points and particular cases. Nevertheless, there is one point that runs through all the papers: the importance of the political dimension. The economic analysis of monetary unions, actual or prospective, is important; but carrying it out without consideration of political pressures and institutions would provide at best a partial and quite easily a misleading view.

Note

1 Mundell is sometimes hailed as the 'father of EMU'. But he surely receives this title not on the basis of the above cited paper, but on the result of a much less well known one, 'Some uncommon arguments for common currencies', published in 1973. This subsequent paper, which focused on the possibility that with flexible exchange rates uncertainty about the future course of rates could disrupt the international capital market, has suffered neglect (compared at least to his 1961 paper) and has yet to be followed up.

References

Bayoumi, T. and Eichengreen, B. (1996). 'Operationalising the Theory of Optimum Currency Areas', CEPR Discussion paper 1484.

Bayoumi, T. and Eichengreen, B. (1997). 'Exchange Market Pressure and Exchange Rate Management: Perspectives from the Theory of Optimum Currency Areas' in Blejer, M. I. *et al.*, eds, *Optimum Currency Areas: New Analytical and Policy Developments.* IMF, Washington, DC.

Friedman, M. (1953). *Essays in Positive Economics.* University of Chicago Press, Chicago.

Kenen, Peter B. (1969). 'The Theory of Optimum Currency Areas: An Eclectic View' in Mundell, R. A. and Swoboda, A. K., eds, *Monetary Problems of the International Economy,* Proceedings of the Conference on International Monetary Problems held September 1966. University of Chicago Press, Chicago.

McKinnon, Ronald (1963). 'Optimum Currency Areas', *American Economic Review, 53.*

Mundell, R. A. (1961). 'A Theory of Optimum Currency Areas', *American Economic Review 51.*

Mundell, R. A. (1973) 'Some Uncommon Arguments for Common Currencies' in Johnson, H. G. and Swoboda, A. K., eds, *The Economics of Common Currencies.* Allen and Unwin, London.

2 Theoretical issues pertaining to monetary unions

Bennett T. McCallum

Introduction

The purpose of this paper is to review the economic theory relevant to the subject of *monetary unions*, in principle to provide a background for the remainder of the conference. This is a difficult assignment, for there is only a small bit of theory that is directly and strongly relevant to the topic, whereas the amount of theory that is of possibly significant relevance is huge – too large to cover in a single paper of moderate length. Accordingly, I have had to make some difficult and debatable choices regarding content.

The one theoretical topic that is of clear and direct relevance is the theory of optimal currency areas, since the basic purpose of that analysis is to specify conditions under which it is (or is not) economically advantageous for a group of economies to adopt a single currency. But direct relevance does not imply that an extensive discussion of this topic is appropriate because, on the one hand, its central propositions are well known and, on the other hand, the essential concepts involved are perhaps so difficult to measure as to render the theory virtually non-operational. Accordingly, just one section of the paper, the next, will be devoted to the subject of optimal currency areas.

A second topic that seems worthy of some review is the recently prominent theory of exchange-rate (and other financial) crises. This topic is relevant because one of its main practical messages is, as I understand it, that with unregulated international financial flows the relevant choice for a group of economies is between currency union and floating exchange rates. In other words, the apparent intermediate option of a fixed but possibly adjustable exchange rate is actually close to infeasible. Accordingly, a short review of this literature is in order and will be attempted in the third section.

Third, the topic of monetary union envisions a single currency for economies that have distinct governments and thus, to some extent, potentially distinct fiscal authorities. Consequently, the subject of the relationship between fiscal and monetary policies arises. As a whole, this subject is too extensive to be reviewed here. A particular issue that has quite recently been the subject of considerable theoretical attention, however, is the so-called "fiscal theory of price level determination." This is a topic of fundamental importance that has been developed in a number of writings that are theoretically sophisticated and rather difficult to comprehend without extensive study. It is also a topic in which I have taken some prior interest. An exposition of the issues is therefore provided in the fourth section of the paper. It should be clearly stated at the outset that, due to my previous involvement, this presentation does not pretend to be a balanced, unbiased overview but is instead a partisan attempt to justify a particular position regarding this theory – the position that I consider to be most appropriate.

Finally, there is a short summary of the paper.

Optimal currency areas

The optimal currency area concept was introduced, as is well known, by Mundell (1961). Despite appearances, the foregoing should be regarded as a striking statement because it is surprising that such a basic idea would not have been developed previously. Nevertheless, the statement is, as well as I have been able to determine, correct. I will return to this point below, and will offer an explanation for the reason that the concept had not been developed previously, but for the moment let us continue the substantive theoretical discussion. The crucial tradeoff identified by Mundell is, according to my own textbook,[1] that "an extension of the area over which a single currency prevails enhances [microeconomic] efficiency but reduces the possibility of monetary policy responses to shocks [or conditions] that affect various subareas differently" (McCallum 1996: 258). The wider the area, that is, the greater are the efficiency benefits of possessing a single medium of exchange and medium of account,[2] but the smaller the area, the greater are the possibilities of tailoring monetary policy to (temporary) local needs. Somewhere between one currency for the entire world and one for each country (or for each city, or neighborhood, . . .) lies the optimum. The plot of net benefits versus number of currencies might be quite flat, of course, over a wide range that includes the optimum.

In a sense, the foregoing is all there is to be said in terms of pure theory, but most authors would discuss the topic at somewhat greater length. The recent and highly regarded graduate level textbook by Obstfeld and Rogoff (1996: 632–4) sustains the discussion for approximately two full pages by listing four main benefits and four main costs to a pair of countries from having a common currency. These are, in the words of Obstfeld and Rogoff, as follows, with benefits listed first.

- B1 Reduced transaction costs from currency conversion . . .
- B2 Reduced accounting costs and greater predictability of relative prices for firms doing business in both countries.
- B3 Insulation from monetary disturbances and speculative bubbles that might otherwise lead to temporary unnecessary fluctuations in real exchange rates. . . .
- B4 Less political pressure for trade protection because of sharp shifts in real exchange rates.

- C1 Individual regions in a currency union forgo the ability to use monetary policy to respond to region-specific macroeconomic disturbances. . . .

C2 Regions in a currency union give up the option to use inflation to reduce the real burden of public debt. . . .

C3 . . . Political and strategic problems arise in determining how member countries split seignorage revenues. . . .

C4 Avoiding speculative attacks in the transition from individual currencies to a common currency can be a major problem. . . .

Here it would appear that B1, B2, B3, C1, and C2 accord nicely with the simple statement expressed above whereas C4 represents only a transitional difficulty[3] and B4 and C3 are basically political rather than economic in nature. If I were making a list of the Obstfeld–Rogoff type, however, I would add another distinct benefit as follows: the existence of a common currency tends to bring a greater degree of integration to financial and non-financial markets in the two countries.

Merely stating that this optimization problem exists does nothing, obviously, to solve it for any two actual countries such as the UK and Germany. The relevant issue for the present paper is what theoretical writings have to say about the way in which the optimization problem should be handled in practice. In his original paper, Mundell (1961) emphasized factor mobility, especially labor mobility, as a crucial consideration. Subsequent contributions by McKinnon (1963), Kenen (1969), and others have proposed other criteria for consideration. In particular, McKinnon emphasized openness, measured by the share of tradable goods in a country's output, whereas Kenen focussed on the extent of product diversification in production. For an extensive review of this literature, including references to many additional authors, see Ishiyama (1975) or Tower and Willett (1976).

After reflecting on some of these writings, my own impression was that there is significant merit to several of the proposed criteria, in other words, that no one of them is itself sufficient. Furthermore, each of the criteria is extremely difficult to implement quantitatively. So when I began this paper, I found it difficult to avoid the conclusion that the optimal currency area (OCA) concept is, in practice, non-operational. Consequently, my first draft expressed the opinion that, although the concept reflects an important and interesting tradeoff, in actual practice one can not go far beyond the rather limp conclusion that currency unions 'will be relatively more attractive for small, open economies that engage in a large volume of international trade (relative to their size)' whereas 'floating rates . . . are more suitable for large and relatively self-contained economies' (McCallum 1996: 225).

Since writing the first draft, I have seen a pair of papers by Bayoumi and Eichengreen (1996, 1997) whose purpose is to operationalize the OCA concept. Their approach in the 1997 paper is to develop quantitative measures or proxies pertaining to size, trade linkages, and dissimilarity of aggregate shocks for different European countries each considered relative to Germany.[4] An index of unsuitability for membership in the contemplated currency area is constructed (for each country except Germany) by using coefficients obtained in a cross-section regression whose dependent variable is the variability of bilateral exchange rates with Germany. This index indicates that Austria, Belgium, Ireland, the Netherlands, and Switzerland would be relatively suitable for inclusion in the union, whereas Denmark, Finland,

Norway, Portugal, Spain, Sweden, and the United Kingdom would be relatively unsuitable. These groupings seem sensible enough that I would have to agree that Bayoumi and Eichengreen have made notable progress toward operationalization of the OCA theory.[5]

Nevertheless, it must be recognized that their approach yields only rankings of suitability, not actual cost–benefit measures that would indicate where the line separating included versus excluded currencies should be drawn. Accordingly, one could still argue that true operationality of the OCA concept has not been achieved. To emphasize this point, it might be argued that if there was ever a situation that cried out for application of the OCA calculus, it was the January 1999 creation of the European Monetary Union. But Bayoumi and Eichengreen's (1996) review of numerous studies indicates that they do not actually provide estimates indicating which countries should, and which should not, be members of the Euro area. The European Union publication *One Market, One Money* presented some worthwhile analysis – especially in its attempt to estimate the resource savings of a single currency rather than truly fixed exchange rates among national currencies – but all in all it too seems not to pass the test.[6]

Let us now return to questions relating to the history of the optimum currency area's crucial tradeoff concept. Was Mundell (1961) actually the first to express it clearly? Yeager (1976) mentions another publication of the same year, namely Balassa (1961: 263–8). But examination indicates that the latter gives consideration to the type of costs and benefits implied by the tradeoff, without ever posing the issue in terms of an 'optimal area' concept. Indeed, the same can be said for an earlier publication by Yeager himself (1959a). In addition, some other earlier writings of relevance are cited by Ishiyama (1975) and by Willett and Tower (1970). But even if one were to conclude that the concept had been clearly formulated by someone prior to Mundell, which is debatable, it would nevertheless be striking that its formulation did not occur until some date not long before 1961. So let us move on to the more interesting question, *why* did this recognition not come sooner?

To the latter question there is, I believe, a rather clear-cut (although conjectural) answer. It is that prior to the 1950s, the predominant position among international and monetary economists was that some metallic monetary standard should be adopted by all countries. The most common position was that the *same* monetary standard, typically the gold standard, should prevail everywhere.[7] Then, in the absence of restrictions on gold flows, there would be a unified monetary system; the fact that different units of account would be used in different countries would not negate the existence of a unified medium of exchange and medium of account.[8] Furthermore, even if different metals were used by some countries, there would be no scope for floating exchange rates or for the associated possibility of tailoring monetary policy to different conditions in different regions.

The great break with this orthodoxy came, of course, with the publication of Friedman's 'The Case for Flexible Exchange Rates' (1953). This, together with other pro-floating rate writings, including Lutz (1954), Sohmen (1957), and Yeager (1959b), altered the intellectual climate enough to permit the relevant issues to arise. In Friedman's essay there is no attempt to balance off the benefits and costs of floating rates, but that is so because the paper's task was to persuade analysts of the existence of benefits. But in this task the paper was successful enough that within a few years Mundell could take a more balanced perspective and look for an optimizing tradeoff.

Another development was necessary, furthermore, before Friedman's. Since the main benefit of a floating exchange rate is that it permits monetary policy to be different in different regions, and therefore to be usable for offsetting demand shocks that would have undesirable (albeit temporary) effects on output and employment, there needed to be professional recognition that monetary policy could be useful in this way. In other words, there needed to be recognition of the possibility of monetary stabilization policy of the type that we now call Keynesian. It is my own belief that Keynes's *General Theory* (1936) was largely unsuccessful as an undertaking in economic theory, but it succeeded spectacularly in calling the profession's attention to the importance of considering short-run issues. The point, from the perspective of the present discussion, is that the recognition of some role for monetary stabilization policy provides one potential benefit for floating exchange rates, i.e. for the possible optimality of more than a single worldwide currency. This particular role is not strictly necessary, for different countries could have different preferences regarding long-run average inflation rates – perhaps for public finance reasons – but the stabilization role is more prominent and would remain relevant even if average inflation preferences were the same everywhere.[9]

The discussion to this point has proceeded as if floating rates and currency unions were the only possibilities. In other words, we have not mentioned the possibility of countries with fixed but potentially adjustable exchange rates. Experiences during recent years – most prominently in Europe in 1992 and 1993, Mexico in 1994–5, and Asia in 1997–8 – have strengthened the belief that the fixed-but-adjustable arrangement is illusory for the reason that was spelled out so effectively by Friedman (1953). This reason, of course, is that fixed (but adjustable) rates tend to invite speculative attacks. In Friedman's words:

> Because the exchange rate is changed infrequently and only to meet substantial difficulties, a change tends to come well after the onset of difficulty, to be postponed as long as possible, and to be made only after substantial pressure on the exchange rate has accumulated. In consequence, there is seldom any doubt about the direction in which an exchange rate will be changed, if it is changed. In the interim between the suspicion of a possible change in the rate and its actual change, there is every incentive to sell the country's currency if a devaluation is expected . . . or to buy it if an appreciation is expected.
>
> (Friedman 1953: 164)

Friedman's argument is rather compelling and may seem more convincing now than ever before. Nevertheless, a more formal literature concerning speculative attacks on exchange rates has built up over the past 20 years, and deserves some attention in any review of theory relevant to the topic of monetary unification. To provide a brief review is the purpose of the next section of the paper. Comments on the currency-board possibility will be included toward the end of this next section.

The theory of currency crises

The currency crisis or speculative attack literature came to prominence with writings by Krugman (1979) and Flood and Garber (1984a). Extensive recent reviews of the theory by Flood and Marion (1998), Marion (1999), and Garber and Svensson (1995) indicate clearly, however, that the crucial ideas were present somewhat earlier in a comparatively neglected paper by Salant and Henderson (1978).[10]

The simplest and cleanest model is one developed by Flood and Garber (1984a). As a preliminary step, let us consider how a *floating* exchange rate would behave in a small open economy in which prices are highly flexible, so that employment and output are always close to their "natural rate" levels. The analytical framework typically utilized in the literature is normally described as also requiring uncovered interest parity, purchasing power parity, and constant values for output and the real interest rate in the home economy. The following presentation indicates how the latter three requirements can be dispensed with.

Let M_t be the stock of base money, P_t the price level, S_t the price of foreign exchange, Q_t the real exchange rate, Y_t the rate of output, and R_t the nominal interest rate. For all of these except the last, let lower case letters denote logarithms, e.g. $s_t = \log S_t$; for the last we have $r_t = R_t - E_t \Delta p_{t+1}$, the real interest rate. Also, let "*" denote a foreign or rest-of-world variable. Then we write the model as follows.

$$y_t = b_0 + E_t y_{t+1} + b_1 r_t + b_2(x_t - E_t x_{t+1}) + \eta_t \qquad b_1 < 0,\ b_2 > 0 \tag{2.1a}$$

$$m_t - p_t = c_0 + c_1 y_t + c_2 R_t + \varepsilon_t \qquad c_1 > 0,\ c_2 < 0 \tag{2.1b}$$

$$x_t = a_0 + a_1 q_t + a_2 y_t + a_3 y^*_t + \xi_t \qquad a_1, a_3 > 0,\ a_2 < 0 \tag{2.1c}$$

$$q_t = s_t - p_t + p^*_t \tag{2.1d}$$

$$R_t = R^*_t + E_t \Delta s_{t+1} + \zeta_t \tag{2.1e}$$

$$y_t = \bar{y}_t \tag{2.1f}$$

Here (2.1a) and (2.1b) reflect dynamic optimizing versions of relations of the IS and LM type that have been justified by McCallum and Nelson (1999), among others, with the former augmented by trade flows, x_t representing the log of exports minus the log of imports. The value of x_t is modelled in (2.1c) as depending on the real exchange rate and income levels at home and abroad. Equation (2.1d) is an identity; (2.1e) represents uncovered interest parity with a random, time-variable risk premium, and (2.1f) assumes that, with price flexibility, output equals its (exogenous) market-clearing natural rate value, $\bar{y}_t$. The terms η_t, ε_t, ξ_t, and ζ_t represent exogenous stochastic shocks.

Of course, we also have the identities

$$r_t = R_t - E_t \Delta p_{t+1} \tag{2.2}$$

$$r^*_t = R^*_t - E_t\Delta p^*_{t+1}, \tag{2.3}$$

so these plus (2.1d) permit us to rewrite (2.1e) as

$$r_t = r^*_t + E_t q_{t+1} - q_t + \zeta_t \tag{2.4}$$

Then it can be seen that relations (2.1a), (2.1c), (2.1f), and (2.4) comprise a subsystem that determines the dynamic behavior of y_t, q_t, x_t, and r_t given exogenous processes for η_t, ξ_t, ζ_t, $\bar{y}_t$, and all foreign variables. Consequently, we can substitute (2.1d) and (2.1e) into (2.1b) to obtain

$$m_t - (s_t + p^*_t - q_t) = c_0 + c_1\bar{y}_t + c_2(R^*_t + E_t\Delta s_{t+1} + \zeta_t) + \varepsilon_t \tag{2.5}$$

and the latter can be expressed as

$$m_t - s_t = \gamma + \alpha(E_t s_{t+1} - s_t) + v_t \qquad \alpha < 0, \tag{2.6}$$

where v_t is a highly composite stochastic term, with $Ev_t = 0$, that reflects the behavior of numerous variables, all of which are exogenous to s_t and m_t.

Thus we end up with equation (2.6) to describe the behavior of the exchange rate in a flexible-price economy. Because it is of the same form as the Cagan (1956) formula for money demand, except with s_t appearing where p_t usually appears, the behavior of the exchange rate in this setting is quite familiar. In particular we know that, on average over an extended period of time, the exchange rate will depreciate at the rate of growth of the money stock: if the money stock grows at the rate μ, then the exchange rate will depreciate at the rate μ. Crucially, we also know that the desired level of $m_t - s_t$ at any time will be negatively related to μ, since smaller real money holdings are desired when their expected depreciation rate is high. This simple and familiar model provides a convenient vehicle for the analysis in the currency crisis literature. To keep matters as simple as possible, while still making the basic points, the stochastic disturbance term v_t is often neglected, i.e. the case of perfect foresight is utilized. In what follows, we shall follow that common practice. Then we find, via simple rational expectations (RE) analysis, that with $m_t = m_{t-1} + \mu$ the exchange rate behaves as

$$s_t = -\gamma - \alpha\mu + m_t \tag{2.7}$$

After these preliminaries, let us now consider an economy with a fixed exchange rate. We have specified that s_t is the log of the exchange rate and now we suppose that its value is fixed at the value $\bar{s}$; i.e. we have the fixed rate $s_t = \bar{s}$. To maintain this value, the log of M_t must be kept constant at (say) $\bar{m}$. But suppose that the government of the economy in question engages in another activity besides exchange-rate fixing that requires positive growth at the rate μ of the domestic credit portion of the monetary base. (Let $M = \mathrm{DC} + \mathrm{FR}$, where M is the base, FR is the stock of foreign exchange reserves, and DC is the domestic credit portion of M.) To keep M_t constant while expanding DC_t, FR_t must fall as time passes. If the growth rate of DC_t is maintained permanently at μ, and log M_t is kept at $\bar{m}$, then eventually FR_t will fall to zero, at which point it would become impossible to maintain the fixed exchange rate.[11]

But with rational expectations – i.e. perfect foresight in the absence of shocks – the fixed exchange rate regime will collapse *before* FR_t falls to zero. For by the time that FR_t reaches zero, the exchange rate that would prevail in the absence of official intervention – i.e. with a floating rate – would be higher than the previously fixed value. Thus there would occur a discrete, abrupt depreciation at this time, a fall in value of the home country currency. But with rational expectations, market participants would know that this is going to happen, and when it will happen, so before then they would become unwilling to hold the domestic currency, since to do so would be to incur a capital loss that is anticipated. So, instead, they sell off the domestic currency in exchange for foreign exchange reserves earlier.

In the basic Flood–Garber (1984a) model, it is assumed that when the fixed-rate regime breaks down, a floating-rate regime takes its place and is maintained indefinitely thereafter.[12] Let $\tilde{s}_t$ be the "shadow exchange rate" that would prevail at time t if a floating-rate regime were to go into effect at t with $FR_t = 0$;

$$\tilde{s}_t = -(\gamma + \alpha\mu) + d_t \tag{2.8}$$

where $d_t = \log DC_t$. Then according to the basic model, a currency crisis occurs when $\tilde{s}_t$ rises to the level $\bar{s}$. There is then no discontinuity in s_t and thus no anticipated capital gain or loss; instead there is an abrupt fall in FR as market participants use their holdings of domestic currency to purchase foreign exchange from the central bank. In addition, there is an upward jump (from zero to μ) in the expected inflation rate, and therefore an upward jump in the nominal rate of interest – a jump that makes asset holders satisfied with the reduced stock of money. What about the possibility of an earlier attack? Such would not occur because prior to the point in time at which $\tilde{s}_t = \bar{s}$, the former would be the smaller so there would be capital losses to participants in a speculative attack against the currency if it were "successful." Thus there is no incentive for an earlier attack to occur.[13]

In sum, the basic model explains why there are abrupt losses of foreign exchange holdings by central banks, abrupt changes in interest rates, and a regime change to a floating rate at the time of a currency crisis, even though no major external triggering event happens at that time. It also explains (in principle) the time at which this collapse will occur, since the growth of m_t and therefore $\tilde{s}_t$ is a deterministic function of time.[14] In an important sense, however, the model does not actually *explain* the occurrence of a collapse, because the model begins with the *assumption* that the country's government is attempting to maintain a fixed exchange rate while conducting another policy activity that is incompatible with such maintenance of that fixed rate. In such a situation it is obvious that one of the two incompatible policy goals must eventually be given up, and the basic model just presumes that the other policy activity has precedence over keeping the exchange rate pegged at $\bar{s}$.

The literature contains several extensions of the basic model, however, that are more ambitious in this regard. Several notable examples have been developed and discussed by Obstfeld (1986, 1994, 1996), but we can outline the essential ingredients with a simple extension of the Flood–Garber model described above.[15] Accordingly, let us modify the basic model by assuming that (i) in the absence of a speculative attack, the rate of growth of domestic credit is zero, i.e. $\mu_0 = 0$, but (ii) if an attack occurs then DC_t grows thereafter at the positive rate μ_1. In addition, it is assumed that this value satisfies $\mu_1 > \log(M_0/DC_0)/(-\alpha)$.

In this situation, there are two RE (perfect foresight) equilibria. If there is no speculative attack, then with zero growth in domestic credit there is no literal inconsistency with the fixed exchange rate $s_t = \bar{s}$, so it can survive indefinitely. Alternatively, if there is an attack, then there will be an abrupt fall in reserves, a depreciation of the exchange rate to the value $\tilde{s}_t = -\gamma - \alpha\mu_1 + d_t$, and $\tilde{s}_t$ will henceforth grow indefinitely at the rate μ_1. Thus the fact that policy is not unconditionally dedicated to maintaining the fixed rate, but would in the face of a major attack surrender to speculators and thereafter pursue an alternative goal, implies that the fixed-rate policy is subject to attack.[16] There are several other models, described by Obstfeld (1996), that lead to similar conclusions.

What should one make of the foregoing, with regard to the feasibility of a fixed but potentially adjustable exchange rate? Garber and Svensson (1995: 1891) begin the relevant section of their prominent survey paper with the following statement: "A salient feature of fixed exchange rate regimes is their inevitable collapse into some other policy regime." Obstfeld and Rogoff (1995: 77–8), by contrast, state that "there are no insurmountable technical obstacles to fixing exchange rates. Most central banks have access to enough foreign exchange resources to beat down a speculative attack of *any* magnitude." Despite these apparently conflicting statements, however, there is actually no substantive disagreement between these two pairs of authors. In particular, Garber and Svensson (1995: 1892) recognize that "a central bank can always preserve a fixed exchange rate through a sustained high interest rate or, equivalently, through a sufficiently drastic contraction in [the] monetary base"; their inevitability of collapse stems from "the presumption that the adherence to a fixed exchange rate is a secondary policy – it is to be maintained only as long as it is compatible with policies that have priority." And for their part, Obstfeld and Rogoff (1995: 78) finish the incomplete sentence quoted above with the proviso, "provided they are willing to subordinate all the other goals of monetary policy." In fact, they continue as follows:

> If central banks virtually always have the resources to crush speculators, why do they suffer periodic humiliation by foreign exchange markets? The problem, of course, is that very few central banks will cling to an exchange-rate target without regard to what is happening in the rest of the economy. Domestic political realities simply will not allow it, even when agreements with foreign governments are at stake.
>
> (Obstfeld and Rogoff 1995: 79)

In sum, Obstfeld and Rogoff agree with the Garber–Svensson conclusion that, in practice, fixed (but adjustable) exchange-rate regimes are not a viable option for most economies, basically for the reasons identified by Friedman and developed in the currency-crisis literature.

What about the notion that creation of a *currency board* provides one way, short of monetary union, for an economy to maintain a fixed exchange rate? From the foregoing discussion, the answer seems reasonably clear. The creation of a currency board gives rise to an institution that is more difficult and costly to dismantle, when it interferes with some other policy objective, than a more conventional fixed-rate arrangement. But unless maintenance of the currency board arrangement has priority over all other macroeconomic objectives, eventually the currency board, too, will break down. The same might even be said for membership in a currency union, but the costs of departing from a union are presumably even greater than those from the termination of a currency board. The other members of the union might conceivably even go to war to prevent its breakup.

The fiscal theory of price level determination

During the past few years, a striking body of literature has appeared in which it is argued that general price level determination is essentially a fiscal, rather than a monetary, phenomenon. The most prominent papers to date are those of Woodford (1994, 1995, 1998), Sims (1994, 1998), and Cochrane (1998), but there are several others of significance.[17] If the theory expounded in these papers were valid empirically, there would be major implications for the manner in which fiscal and monetary policies are related in a monetary union, as Woodford (1996), Sims (1997), and Bergin (2000) emphasize. The purpose of the present section is to describe this theory and explain why I believe that it is not empirically valid, but instead is basically misleading.[18] For simplicity, the argument will be conducted in terms of a single closed economy, but if the theory is misleading in that case it will also be misleading regarding the relationship between monetary and fiscal policies in the more complex setting of a monetary union.

At the outset it should be emphasized just how drastically unorthodox or counter-traditional the fiscal theory of price level determination is.[19] Specifically, it does not merely suggest that fiscal as well as monetary policy stances are significant for price level behavior; instead it almost claims that only fiscal policy is relevant. In the prototype model to be sketched below, the price level moves over time in a manner that is very closely related to the path of government bonds outstanding and entirely unlike the path of the stock of high-powered money. Therefore it is not the case that the argument involves fiscal behavior that drives an accommodative monetary authority, as when rapid base money growth serves to finance a fiscal deficit.[20] Furthermore, the type of model typically utilized in the literature's analysis is not of the overlapping generations type, in which the Ricardian equivalence proposition is known to fail. Instead, the model is basically of the Sidrauski–Brock type, in which Ricardian equivalence results are normally obtained, i.e. results implying that bond-financial tax changes have no effect on the price level or other macroeconomic variables of primary interest.[21] In such a setting, fiscalist positions are truly startling.

As a background for illustrating these drastic results, let us begin with an orthodox analysis of price level determination in an extremely simple and transparent setting. Suppose that the (per capita) money demand function for a closed economy is of the textbook form

$$m_t - p_t = c_0 + c_1 y_t + c_2 R_t + v_t \qquad c_1 > 0,\ c_2 < 0, \tag{2.9}$$

where m_t, p_t, and y_t are logs of the (base) money stock, price level, and output (income) for period t, while R_t denotes a one-period nominal interest rate. The disturbance v_t is taken for simplicity to be white noise. It is well known that there are rigorous dynamic general equilibrium models with optimizing agents that will justify (2.9) as an approximation to a combination of implied Euler equations (first-order conditions).[22] The present exposition is intended to convey the essential features of a full optimizing analysis while ignoring some of the details.

Furthermore, let us assume that the economy is one in which output and the real rate of interest are constant over time. Then (2.9) collapses to

$$m_t - p_t = \gamma + \alpha\,(E_t p_{t+1} - p_t) + v_t \qquad \alpha = c_2 \tag{2.10}$$

which is the familiar Cagan specification for money demand. And let us consider cases in which the growth rate of the (base) money stock is kept constant by the central bank, so that

$$m_t = m_{t-1} + \mu \tag{2.11}$$

where μ is the growth rate of the money stock. These relations plus rational expectations determine the behavior of p_t and m_t for time periods $t = 1, 2, \ldots$ It is possible that the structure was different prior to period 1.

In this setting, the orthodox bubble-free or "fundamentals" rational expectations (RE) solution for p_t can be found by conjecturing that it is of the form

$$p_t = \phi_0 + \phi_1 \mu_{t-1} + \phi_2 v_t \tag{2.12}$$

since m_{t-1} and v_t are evidently the system's only state variables. In that case we have $E_t p_{t+1} = \phi_0 + \phi_1(m_{t-1} + \mu)$ so substitution of the latter, (2.11), and (2.12) into (2.10) yields

$$m_{t-1} + \mu = \gamma + \alpha\,[\phi_0 + \phi_1(m_{t-1} + \mu)] + (1-\alpha)\,(\phi_0 + \phi_1 m_{t-1} + \phi_2 v_t) + v_t \tag{2.13}$$

The latter implies that for (2.12) to be a solution, i.e. to hold for all realizations of v_t and m_{t-1}, we must have satisfaction of the undetermined-coefficient (UC) conditions

$$\begin{aligned}
1 &= \alpha\phi_1 + (1-\alpha)\phi_1 \\
0 &= (1-\alpha)\,\phi_2 + 1 \\
\mu &= \gamma + \alpha\phi_1\mu + (1-\alpha)\phi_0 + \alpha\phi_0
\end{aligned} \tag{2.14}$$

Thus we have that $\phi_1 = 1$, $\phi_2 = -1/(1-\alpha)$ and $\phi_0 = \mu - \gamma - \alpha\mu$, i.e. the solution is

$$\begin{aligned} p_t &= \mu(1-\alpha) - \gamma + m_{t-1} - 1/(1-\alpha)v_t \\ &= m_t - (\gamma + \alpha\mu) - v_t/(1-\alpha) \end{aligned} \tag{2.15}$$

Here we see that p_t grows one-for-one with m_t, i.e. the price level P_t moves on average in proportion to the money stock M_t, but fluctuates around this average position in response to realizations of v_t, with p_t being temporarily reduced by positive money demand shocks ($v_t > 0$) or boosted by negative shocks ($v_t < 0$). This is clearly an entirely traditional – one might even say "monetarist" – analysis of price level behavior in the economy in question.

Now for an even simpler special case, let us suppose that the money growth rate is zero, i.e. that $\mu = 0$ so that $m_t = m$. Then the solution for p_t is

$$p_t = m - \gamma - v_t/(1-\alpha) \tag{2.16}$$

And, finally, if money demand shocks were absent we would have $p_t = m - \gamma$.

It must be noted, however, that while (2.15) and its special case (2.16) give the well-behaved, orthodox, bubble-free RE solutions for this model, there are other expressions as well that satisfy the model (2.10)(2.11) with RE. For simplicity, let us consider the special case with constant $m_t = m$, but now conjecture a solution of the form

$$p_t = \psi_0 + \psi_1 p_{t-1} + \psi_2 v_t + \psi_3 v_{t-1} \tag{2.17}$$

instead of $p_t = \phi_0 + \phi_2 v_t$. Then working through the same type of analysis as before, one finds that the UC conditions analogous to (2.14) are

$$\begin{aligned} 0 &= \alpha\psi_1^2 + (1-\alpha)\psi_1 \\ 0 &= \alpha\psi_1\psi_2 + \alpha\psi_3 + (1-\alpha)\psi_2 + 1 \\ 0 &= \alpha\psi_1\psi_3 + (1-\alpha)\psi_3 \\ m &= \gamma + \alpha\psi_0 + \alpha\psi_1\psi_0 + (1-\alpha)\psi_0 \end{aligned} \tag{2.18}$$

We see, now, that the first of these has two roots $\psi_1^{(1)} = 0$ and $\psi_1^{(2)} = (\alpha-1)/\alpha$. If the former is the relevant root, then we find that $\psi_3 = 0$, $\psi_2 = -1/(1-\alpha)$, and $\psi_0 = m - \gamma$ so that the same expression as in (2.16) is obtained. But if $\psi_1^{(2)}$ is relevant, then $\psi_3 = -1/\alpha$ and $\psi_0 = (m-\gamma)/\alpha$ while *any* value of ψ_2 is possible. So an infinity of solution paths is consistent with the model. Note, however, that $\psi_1^{(2)} = (\alpha - 1)/\alpha > 1.0$, so most of these solution paths are explosive.

Of course there are other variables and conditions besides those discussed thus far in a fully articulated model of the economy under discussion. As for conditions, it is typically true that a fully specified optimizing analysis would require that

$$\lim_{j \to \infty} E_t \beta^j M_{t+j}/P_{t+j} = 0 \tag{2.19}$$

i.e. that a transversality condition pertaining to real money balances must be satisfied. Here β is a typical agent's discount factor, $\beta = 1/(1 + \rho)$, with $\rho > 0$ and therefore $0 < \beta < 1$. Similarly, if one of the economy's assets is government bonds, then another condition necessary for individual optimality would be

$$\lim_{j\to\infty} E_t \beta^j B_{t+j}/P_{t+j} = 0, \tag{2.20}$$

B_{t+1} being the number of bonds purchased by an agent at t for the price $1/(1 + R_t)$ and redeemed for one unit of money in $t + 1$.

We are now at last prepared to turn to the fiscalist theory. With government bonds recognized, we could write the consolidated[23] government budget constraint in per capita terms as

$$P_t (g_t - tx_t) = M_{t+1} - M_t + (1 + R_t)^{-1} B_{t+1} - B_t \tag{2.21}$$

where g_t and tx_t are real government purchases and (lump sum) tax collections, respectively, in per capita terms. In real terms, this constraint could then be written as

$$g_t - tx_t = (M_{t+1} - M_t)/P_t + (1 + R_t)^{-1} (P_{t+1}/P_t)\, b_{t+1} - b_t, \tag{2.22}$$

where $b_t = B_t/P_t$. Please note the mixed notation being utilized: $b_t = B_t/P_t$ whereas $m_t = \log M_t$ and $p_t = \log P_t$. Condition (2.22) obtains for $t = 1, 2, \ldots$.

Now consider the special case of the economy discussed above in which m_t and M_t are constant. Also let the random shock v_t be absent so that P_{t+1} is correctly anticipated in t. Then with the real rate of interest r_t defined by $1 + r_t = (1 + R_t)/(1 + \pi_t)$ where $\pi_t = (P_{t+1} - P_t)/P_t$, and with $r_t = \rho$ as would be implied by optimizing behavior in the absence of shocks,[24] the government budget constraint becomes

$$b_{t+1} = (1 + \rho) b_t + (1 + \rho)(g_t - tx_t) \qquad t = 1, 2, \ldots. \tag{2.23}$$

But since $1 + \rho > 1.0$, if $g_t - tx_t$ is stationary (e.g. constant), the latter reveals a strong tendency for b_t to explode as time passes. As t grows without limit, b_t grows at the rate ρ, i.e. behaves like $(1 + \rho)^t$. Thus the transversality condition (2.20) tends not to be satisfied since growth of b_t just precisely offsets the shrinkage of $\beta^t = 1/(1 + \rho)^t$, yielding a limit that is a positive constant.

In fact, in this case there are just two paths for b_t that, with $g_t - tx_t$ constant, will satisfy (2.23) and also (2.20) for $t = 1, 2, \ldots$. One of these obtains if the value b_1 equals $-(1 + \rho)(g - tx)/\rho$, for then (2.23) implies that

$$\begin{aligned} b_2 &= (1 + \rho)\,[-(1 + \rho)(g - tx)/\rho] + (1 + \rho)(g - tx) \\ &= (1 + \rho)(g - tx)\,[-(1 + \rho)/\rho + 1] = (1 + \rho)\,(tx - g)/\rho \end{aligned} \tag{2.24}$$

and that same value prevails in all succeeding periods. But $b_1 = B_1/P_1$, and B_1 is the number of nominal government bonds outstanding at the beginning of the initial period, $t = 1$. Thus if the price level in this first period, P_1, adjusts to equal the value $P_1 = B_1\rho/(1 + \rho)\ (tx - g)$, then condition (2.20) as well as (2.23) will be satisfied. Indeed, this is precisely what the fiscalist theory predicts: P_1 adjusts relative to B_1 and $g - tx$ so as to satisfy the individual agents' optimality condition (2.20).

But what about the necessary condition for money holdings, equation (2.10)? Well, the fiscalist answer is that although the path just described will not conform to the $p_t = m - \gamma$ fundamentals solution implied by (2.16), it can and will satisfy the alternative solution $p_t = [(\alpha - 1)/\alpha]\, p_{t-1} + (m - \gamma)/\alpha$ for all $t = 2, 3, \ldots$.[25] The price level P_1, and thus p_1, is determined by B_1 and the b_1 necessary to satisfy (2.20), and subsequent P_t, p_t values are given by (2.17) with $\psi_1 = (\alpha - 1)/\alpha$. The price level is exploding as time passes, despite the constant value of M_t, but all of the model's equilibrium conditions including RE are satisfied nevertheless. Since P_t and B_t are growing at the same (explosive) rate, while M_t is constant, the outcome is rightfully regarded as highly "fiscalist."[26]

Now let us consider the one other path of b_t that will, with $g_t - tx_t$ constant, satisfy (2.10) and also (2.20). It is that $b_{t+1} = 0$ for all $t = 1, 2, \ldots$. Clearly, this is satisfied with $B_{t+1} = 0$ and in that case places no constraint on P_t values. Thus these are free to obey $p_t = m - \gamma$, as in (2.16). Therefore this solution is the orthodox or monetarist solution.[27]

So we end up with two RE solutions that represent two competing hypotheses regarding price level behavior in the hypothetical economy under study. It is an economy in which the money stock is constant over time, all behavioral relations are constant, and there are no stochastic disturbances impinging upon its agents or productive processes. According to the monetarist hypothesis, the price level is constant through time at a value that is proportional to the magnitude of the money stock, and no government bonds are purchased by private agents.[28] By contrast, the fiscalist hypothesis implies that, despite the constant money stock, the bond stock and the price level both explode as time passes – but without violating any optimality condition for private agents because the initial price level adjusts relative to the initial bond stock so as to make the real bond stock equal the single non-zero value that will permit the stock of real bonds to remain constant and the transversality condition (2.20) to be satisfied. Under this latter hypothesis, the initial price level is proportional to the initial bond stock and the price level grows in tandem with the bond stock.

In the introduction to this section, it was stated that the section would include not only a description of the fiscal theory of the price level but also an explanation of why I believe it to be empirically invalid. The description that has been given pertains to only one special case, and therefore fails to do justice to the richness of the fiscal proponents' analysis. But the nature of this special case is such that I think no additional words are needed to explain why I find it basically the less plausible of the two hypotheses under consideration.[29]

Conclusions

Let us conclude with a brief overview of the paper's arguments. The optimal currency area concept is central to economic analysis of monetary unions, as it clearly identifies the relevant optimizing tradeoff: extension of the area over which a single currency is used enhances allocative efficiency but reduces the possibility of tailoring monetary policy to the needs of different areas. Empirical work has verified the importance of various features of economies that make them strong or weak candidates for a common currency arrangement, but existing studies do not permit actual quantification of costs and benefits of adopting a common currency. In that sense, the OCA concept remains less than fully operational.

Another relevant body of theory is that pertaining to currency crises. Formal models clarify various points concerning speculative attacks on fixed exchange rates, and show how abrupt reserve losses and depreciations can occur rationally at times when no major shocks are present. These formal models also support the notion that a fixed (but potentially adjustable) exchange regime is not a viable option for most nations, given today's mobility of financial capital. The reason, according to the theory, is that speculative attacks can succeed even if there is no current policy inconsistency if governments have other policy objectives that may at some date take priority over the support of a fixed exchange rate.

The third area discussed is the recently developed fiscal theory of price level determination. It is emphasized that this theory is drastically different than monetarist orthodoxy; it does not contend that fiscal behavior drives an accommodative monetary authority, but rather that the price level basically mimics the pattern of the government bond stock outstanding rather than base money when their paths differ drastically. An example is exposited in which there are two rational expectations solutions in an economy with a constant money supply. The monetarist solution is that the price level is also constant whereas the fiscalist theory implies that the bond stock and price level both explode as time passes (without violation of any private optimality conditions). These solutions may be viewed as competing hypotheses about the behavior of actual economies, and the paper suggests that the monetarist hypothesis is the more likely to prevail in actuality.

Notes

1 See McCallum (1996: 258–9 and 209–14).

2 For simplicity, I here assume that the two are the same. This is of course not logically necessary, but will usually be the case except in environments of very high inflation.

3 If transitional costs are to be considered, one should certainly count the resource and educational costs of conversion by one or more regions to the new common currency.

4 Some earlier work of this general type is reviewed and evaluated by Edison and Melvin (1990).

5 In my textbook, one end-of-chapter problem asks the student to consider "would it be more advantageous for Portugal or France to have fixed exchange rates with Spain?" (1996: 226). The Bayoumi and Eichengreen (1997: 768) results for selected bilateral comparisons indicate that "Portugal" is the correct answer, which is certainly what the textbook intended.

6 Certainly, actual decisions whether to participate were not based on optimal-currency-area analyses, but that is another matter. The issue here is whether there are any convincing economic studies.

7 Mill (1848) puts the matter very nicely, as he does so often, as follows: "Let us suppose

that all countries had the same currency, as in the progress of political improvement they one day will have" (Book III, Ch. XX, § 2).

8 If gold is the standard metal in various countries that have different coinage systems, one might regard gold as the common medium of account even though units of account would differ with different coinage systems.

9 For quite a few years, especially during the 1960s and 1970s, it was widely believed that different countries might desire different average inflation rates because of different preferences regarding output and employment relative to inflation, but in more recent time professional opinion has moved strongly toward the Friedman (1966)–Phelps (1967) position that there exists no long-run tradeoff.

10 On this, see especially Flood and Marion (1998: fn. 1).

11 Actually the situation is more complex in that the authorities could have a positive or negative level of reserves that they will maintain after collapse of the fixed rate. For expositional simplicity, that level is (as usual) taken to be zero.

12 Note that some assumption must be adopted regarding policy behavior after the breakdown, or the model will be incomplete. Various alternative assumptions are considered in the literature; one of these will be analysed below.

13 From the individual asset holder's viewpoint, there would be costs of holding more foreign exchange in their portfolio, costs that would outweigh the negligible effect to be had on the precipitation of a general speculative attack.

14 With the assumption that the post-collapse level of FR is zero, then $\tilde{s}_t = -\gamma - \alpha\mu + d_0 + \mu t$, where d_0 is the log of "initial" DC. Thus t at collapse time is $(\bar{s} + \gamma + \alpha\mu - d_0)/\mu$. We see that a lower μ or higher $\bar{s}$ will extend the life of the fixed-rate regime.

15 This extension was first proposed by Flood and Garber (1984b).

16 Note that in this variant of the model there is an abrupt depreciation at the time of attack, but in a manner that does not imply anticipated capital gains or losses.

17 Some of these are Leeper (1991), Bergin (2000), Dupor (1997), and Schmitt-Grohe and Uribe (1997).

18 My argument has been presented previously in McCallum (1998, 1999a); a somewhat similar and complementary position is taken by Buiter (1998), in a study that discusses several other issues as well.

19 In what follows, I shall for brevity often refer to the latter as the "fiscal" or "fiscalist" theory.

20 Thus the theory is quite different from that of Sargent and Wallace (1981).

21 For an analysis of this model, see McCallum (1984).

22 See, for example, Woodford (1995) or McCallum and Nelson (1999).

23 The government consists of a fiscal authority and a central bank.

24 See, for example, McCallum (1998).

25 It might be asked why this relation does not determine p_1 in relation to p_0. I believe the answer is that it determines the value of ψ_2.

26 There is a serious problem, however, with this solution: if $tx - g < 0$, then a negative price level would be required for satisfaction of (2.23) by the assumed value of b_1. This problem is stressed by Buiter (1998: 20) and McCallum (1998: 8).

27 It is not obvious how (2.23) is satisfied with $B_{t+1} = 0$ when $tx - g > 0$. But in this case the equilibrium condition $B^D{}_{t+1} \le B^S{}_{t+1}$ is satisfied where bond supply $b^S{}_{t+1}$ satisfies (2.20) and bond demand is $b^D{}_{t+1} = 0$. Buiter (1998: 17) argues that the fiscalist assumptions "violate the normal rules for constructing a well-posed general equilibrium model." Also see McCallum (1998: 8–9).

28 This does not necessarily imply that none are offered for sale by the government.

29 A brief but somewhat more general discussion of the interaction of monetary and fiscal policy strategies is included in McCallum (1999).

References

Balassa, B. (1961) *The Theory of Economic Integration*. Richard D. Irwin, Homewood, IL.

Bayoumi, T., and B. Eichengreen (1996) "Operationalizing the Theory of Optimum Currency Areas," CEPR Working Paper 1484.

—— and —— (1997) "Ever Closer to Heaven? An Optimum-Currency-Area Index for European Countries," *European Economic Review, 41.*

Bergin, P. R. (1997) "Fiscal Solvency and Price Level Determination in a Monetary Union," *Journal of Monetary Economics, 45.*

—— (2000) "Fiscal Solvency and Price Level Determination in a Monetary Union," *Journal of Monetary Economics, 45.*

Buiter, W. H. (1998) "The Young Person's Guide to Neutrality, Price Level Indeterminacy, Interest Rate Pegs, and Fiscal Theories of the Price Level," NBER Working Paper 6396.

Cagan, P. (1956) "The Monetary Dynamics of Hyperinflation," in Friedman, M., ed., *Studies in the Quantity Theory of Money*. University of Chicago Press, Chicago.

Cochrane, J. H. (1998) "A Frictionless View of US Inflation," *NBER Macroeconomics Annual 1998*. MIT Press, Cambridge, MA.

Commission of the European Communities (1990) "One Market, One Money," *European Economy, 44.*

Dupor, B. (2000) "Exchange Rates and the Fiscal Theory of the Price Level," *Journal of Monetary Economics, 45.*

Edison, H. J. and M. Melvin (1990) "The Determinants and Implications of the Choice of an Exchange Rate System," in Haraf, W. S. and T. D. Willett, eds, *Monetary Policy for a Volatile Global Economy*. AEI Press, Washington, DC.

Flood, R. P. and P. M. Garber (1984a) "Collapsing Exchange-Rate Regimes: Some Linear Examples," *Journal of International Economics, 17.*

—— and —— (1984b) "Gold Monetization and Gold Discipline," *Journal of Political Economy, 92.*

—— and N. Marion (1998) "Perspectives on the Recent Currency Crisis Literature," NBER Working Paper 6380.

Friedman, M. (1953) "The Case for Flexible Exchange Rates," in Friedman, M., *Essays in Positive Economics*. University of Chicago Press, Chicago.

—— (1996) "Comments," in Shultz, G. P. and R. Z. Aliber, eds, *Guidelines, Informal Controls, and the Marketplace*. University of Chicago Press, Chicago.

Garber, P. M. and L. E. O. Svensson (1995) "The Operation and Collapse of Fixed Exchange Rate Regimes," in Grossman, G. and K. Rogoff, eds, *Handbook of International Economics*, Vol. III. North Holland, Amsterdam.

Ishiyama, Y. (1975) "The Theory of Optimum Currency Areas: A Survey," *IMF Staff Papers, 22.*

Kenen, P. B. (1969) "The Theory of Optimum Currency Areas: An Eclectic View," in Mundell, R. A. and A. K. Swoboda, eds, *Monetary Problems of the International Economy*. University of Chicago Press, Chicago.

Keynes, J. M. (1936) *The General Theory of Employment, Interest, and Money*. Macmillan, London.

Krugman, P. R. (1979) "A Model of Balance of Payments Crises," *Journal of Money, Credit, and Banking, 11.*

Leeper, E. M. (1991) "Equilibria Under 'Active' and 'Passive' Monetary and Fiscal Policies," *Journal of Monetary Economics, 27.*

Lutz, F. A. (1954) "The Case for Flexible Exchange Rates," *Banca Nazionale del Lavaro Review, 7.*
McCallum, B. T. (1984) "Are Bond-Financed Deficits Inflationary? A Ricardian Analysis," *Journal of Political Economy, 92.*
—— (1996) *International Monetary Economics.* Oxford University Press, New York.
—— (1998) "Indeterminacy, Bubbles, and the Fiscal Theory of Price Level Determination," NBER Working Paper 6456 also (2001) *Journal of Monetary Economics, 47.*
—— (1999) "Issues in the Design of Monetary Policy Rules," in Taylor, J. B. and M. Woodford, eds, *Handbook in Macroeconomics.* North-Holland, Amsterdam.
—— and E. Nelson (1999) "An Optimizing IS-LM Specification for Monetary Policy and Business Cycle Analysis," *Journal of Money, Credit, and Banking, 31.*
McKinnon, R. I. (1963) "Optimum Currency Areas," *American Economic Review, 53.*
Marion, N. (1999) "Some Parallels Between Currency and Banking Crises," in Isard, P., A. Razin and A. Rose, eds, *International Finance and Financial Crises: Essays in Honor of Robert P. Flood, Jr.* International Monetary Fund and Kluwer Academic Publishers, 1999. Also in *International Tax and Public Finance, 6.*
Meade, J. E. (1957) "The Balance-of-Payments Problems of a European Free-Trade Area," *Economic Journal, 67.*
Mill, J. S.(1848) *Principles of Political Economy.* John W. Parker, London.
Mundell, R. A. (1961) "A Theory of Optimum Currency Areas," *American Economic Review, 51.*
Obstfeld, M. (1986) "Rational and Self-Fulfilling Balance of Payments Crises," *American Economic Review, 76.*
—— (1994) "The Logic of Currency Crises," *Bank of France Cahiers Economiques et Monetaires, 43.*
—— (1996) "Models of Currency Crises with Self-Fulfilling Features," *European Economic Review, 40.*
—— and K. Rogoff (1995) "The Mirage of Fixed Exchange Rates," *Journal of Economic Perspectives, 9.*
—— and —— (1996) *Foundations of International Macroeconomics.* MIT Press, Cambridge, MA.
Phelps, E. S. (1967) "Phillips Curves, Expectations of Inflation, and Optimal Unemployment over Time," *Economica, 34.*
Salant, S. W. and D. W. Henderson (1978) "Market Anticipations of Government Policies and the Price of Gold," *Journal of Political Economy, 86.*
Sargent, T. J. and N. Wallace (1981) "Some Unpleasant Monetarist Arithmetic," *Federal Reserve Bank of Minneapolis Quarterly Review, 5*(3).
Schmitt-Grohe, S. and M. Uribe (1997) "Price Level Determinacy and Monetary Policy Under a Balanced-Budget Requirement," FEDS Working Paper 1997–39.
Sims, C. A. (1994) "A Simple Model for the Study of the Determination of the Price Level and the Interaction of Monetary and Fiscal Policy," *Economic Theory, 4.*
—— (1997) "Fiscal Foundations of Price Stability in Open Economies," Working Paper, Yale University.
—— (1998) "Econometric Implications of the Government Budget Constraint," *Journal of Econometrics, 83.*
Sohmen, E. (1957) "Demand Elasticities and the Foreign-Exchange Market," *Journal of Political Economy, 65.*
Tower, E. and T. D. Willett (1976) *The Theory of Optimum Currency Areas and Exchange Rate Flexibility.* Special Studies in International Economics No. 11, Princeton International Finance Section, Princeton, NJ.

Willett, T. D. and E. Tower (1970) "The Concept of Optimum Currency Areas and the Choice Between Fixed and Flexible Exchange Rates," in Halm, G. N., ed., *Approaches to Greater Flexibility of Exchange Rates.* Princeton University Press, Princeton, NJ.

Woodford, M. (1994) "Monetary Policy and Price-Level Determinacy in a Cash-in-Advance Economy," *Economic Theory, 4.*

—— (1995) "Price-Level Determinacy Without Control of a Monetary Aggregate," *Carnegie-Rochester Conference Series on Public Policy, 43.*

—— (1996) "Control of the Public Debt: A Requirement for Price Stability?," NBER Working Paper 5684.

—— (1998) "Public Debt and the Price Level," Working Paper, Princeton University, Princeton, NJ.

Yeager, L. B. (1959a) "Exchange Rates Within a Common Market," *Social Research, 25.*

—— (1959b) "The Misconceived Problem of International Liquidity," *Journal of Finance, 14.*

—— (1976) *International Monetary Relations: Theory, History, and Policy.* Harper & Row, New York, 2nd edn.

Comments on Chapter 2 – Theoretical issues pertaining to monetary unions

Peter Sinclair

Bennett McCallum's analysis of the two issues that he examines (foreign exchange crises and the fiscalist theory of prices) is both cogent and profound. But some of their links to monetary unions are left implicit, and I shall try to bring them out. Before I turn to them, I should like to offer some opinions about the main benefits and costs of monetary union, on which he writes early on in his paper.

McCallum lists the four difficulties (C1 to C4) mentioned by Obstfeld and Rogoff (1996). The first of these is the fact that, in a monetary union, 'individual regions in a currency union forgo the ability to respond to region-specific macroeconomic disturbances'. My query here stems from the point that monetary policy surely does not just reduce to the short-term question of how best, if at all, to react to one-off shocks. There are also long term trends to consider. The key trend in this context is the average rate at which prices should change over time. On its own, under freely floating exchange rates, a country can choose its ideal rate of price inflation or deflation. In a union, it cannot: the choice of target inflation rate is a matter for the group as a whole, or for the central authority, if any, to which the task of selecting the target may have been delegated.

When the countries that form a currency union agree on their ideal, annual average inflation target rate, all well and good. Aside from any difficulties with C1–C4, at least, the union will now be free to enjoy its gains from the savings in currency conversion costs, and the benefits they bring to trade. If members' optimum inflation rates vary a little, but not too much, the union should still be beneficial. But too great a degree of diversity in national inflation targets must mean that some members, possibly all members, lose more in having to accept nationally suboptimal average inflation than they gain from currency conversion cost savings. At this point the currency union becomes an instrument of harm.

What does a country's optimum average inflation rate depend upon? Under ideal circumstances, it will equal minus the real rate of interest. It is here, and only here, that real money balances go untaxed in the steady state. Real money would be priced at its marginal cost, on the assumption that the creation of real money is costless at the margin, and Friedman's Optimum Quantity of Money (1969) would be attained. In a multi-country setting, real interest rates would be common if key parameters (such as those for population growth, time-preference, Harrod-neutral technological progress and relative risk-aversion, in a Ramsey set-up) happened to be common too – or if endogenous discounting permitted them (as in Brenton *et al.* 1997, for example) to be equalized by international capital movements.

Under second-best conditions, optimum inflation rates become more opaque. Menu costs raise them – towards zero when monopoly is not a feature, and above zero when it is (Diamond 1993). Phelps' public revenue argument (1973) for taxing money may also apply. Let us sketch a heterogeneous-agent version of it.

Suppose the authorities have just two independent financial policy instruments at their disposal, a tax on income (net of investment) and a tax on money balances. Each period, let us assume, these two taxes, together, have to finance a given level of government spending, and a transfer payment made to all. The transfer payment is a choice variable, but not an independent one. As in Mirrlees (1971), abilities to earn differ across the population, and truth-telling constraints block the first-best device of non-distorting taxes on ability. Everyone's utility depends on leisure and consumption. Real money is useful because it saves time. The task of a government is to set its two tax rates to maximize its perception of social welfare (which may be some amalgam of average, median and minimum utilities), given people's choices of labour supply and money demand. Monetary policy and tax policy are inextricably linked.

Examples of a system like this have been studied by Sinclair (1997). Given a sufficiently low government spending need, money will generally not be taxed. But if the State has a large enough revenue target, income tax may well need to be supplemented by seignorage. Interestingly, this model does not generally display a 'vertical Phillips curve'. Although there are other, indirect effects that could go either way, a higher rate of inflation squeezes real balances, so that more time has to be devoted to search, trade and transactions, and this squeezes the labour supply of those working, reducing aggregate output. Further, when the minimum level of ability is low enough, those with low ability drop out of the labour force, so that the rate of inflation can be linked to unemployment as well as output.

The optimum rate of tax on money, if any, is sensitive to social welfare weightings ('democracy', in the form of a larger weight on median welfare, interestingly tends to create a pro-inflation bias). It also varies with the shape of the money–time saving function (lower interest elasticity of money demand pointing to a higher tax on money). The dispersion of abilities and elasticities of consumption–marginal utilities matter too (with either low, the call for transfers weakens, and with it the need, if any, for taxing money). Again, the key issue is whether the currency union's members are sufficiently similar in these underlying characteristics. If they are, they will want to have similar inflation trends anyway, and might as well form a monetary union if this brings real resource savings. If they are not, those with most deviance from the group average in these characteristics are the prime candidates for losing out (unless the effects of deviance in two or more dimensions happen to cancel). Wide cross-country diversity in optimum inflation trends would also no doubt manifest itself in costly, acrimonious debate within the union. In extreme circumstances, this could even raise the spectre of possible break-up; more generally, it would generate additional uncertainty about future policy, with probably adverse knock-on effects, such as those on the risk-premium parameter in McCallum's nominal interest rate equation (2.1e).

The long-run optimum inflation question is obviously important. So it is a bit of a puzzle why the literatures on optimum currency areas, both old and new, focus so much more on the short-run. In fact, both must matter. Two countries might agree that 2 per cent annual inflation averages were best for both of them, but disagree quite strongly about monetary policy on a year-by-year basis. There are two possible reasons for this. Both countries could face similar shocks, with one preferring the price level to act as shock absorber, let us say, and the other something else (such as short-term interest rates). Or they could face different shocks, to which each would have responded the same way had they been similar and simultaneous. Alternatively, shocks could be similar in size and timing, as could the responses the two countries would prefer to make to them, but the countries could differ in their ideal long-run inflation targets for reasons explored above.

When reviewing the optimum currency area literatures, McCallum concentrates on the key tradeoff between asymmetric shock responses (best made within a one-money-per-country basis) and currency conversion costs (which by themselves argue for a currency union embracing the whole world). The general view, McCallum suggests, is that neither of these extremes, one-money-per-country or one-world-money, is likely to be ideal. The optimum currency area is pinpointed, it would seem, on a journey from the former towards the latter, where the marginal cost of impaired responses to country-specific shocks just balances the marginal benefits from lowering currency conversion costs.

It is not obvious that something intermediate between one money per country and one money for the world has to better than either. Consider the following case. Suppose there are *n* countries in the world, each endowed with the same supply of a unique good, except that one of the countries will face a sharp reduction in its endowment. All countries face the same risk of this. Citizens' preferences are everywhere symmetric CES, with an elasticity of substitution not less than unity, and additive separability, and utility displays a given coefficient of relative risk aversion to this aggregate. Anything imported from a different monetary area costs more, because of currency conversion (which acts like iceberg transport costs). Individuals cannot borrow or lend directly, nor can they insure themselves against the supply shocks. But the financial authority in each monetary area can do this, by giving each of the area's residents a positive transfer when the area, or a part of it, suffers a supply shock, financed by an interest-free loan from the rest of the world.

With one-money-per-country, perfect insurance can be provided, but all but home goods are needlessly expensive because of the currency conversion costs. With one-world-money, currency conversion costs vanish, but so does insurance. If currency conversion costs are rather large in relation to risk-aversion, substitution elasticities and the size of shocks, one-world-money will be best. Reverse this, and one-money-per-country should deliver the highest expected utility.

Parameters can be calibrated so that expected utility in these two extremes is the same. This means that the currency conversion costs are negligible if the elasticity of substitution is unitary – the value of the shocked country's exports will be perfectly insulated, because a given fraction of world income will be spent on them, whatever the supply shock and whether it happens or not. But they go up with the substitution elasticity to keep expected utility unchanged.

Now consider a set of m symmetric monetary unions, each with n/m members, setting transfers to local residents optimally in the event of an adverse intra-area supply shock. The larger the number of monetary unions, the bigger the waste from currency conversion costs, but the lower the cost of income-destabilization within the union. A bigger union provides unneeded extra income to residents of more areas unaffected by the supply shock, extra income that they have to spend then and there given the capital market imperfections, and less help to those within the area who are suffering from it. The upshot is this. First, scrutiny of various cases reveals that expected utility with $n > m > 1$ is often strictly less than expected utility with $m = 1$ (one-world-money) or $m = n$ (one-money-per-country). Second, when an intermediate case ($n > m > 1$) does outperform the extremes, an outcome that becomes more probable as n, the number of countries and products, shrinks, it appears that $m = 2$ is usually best.

In other words, expected utility often appears U-shaped when presented as a function of m, and this casts doubt upon the existence of an 'interior' optimum currency area larger than one country but smaller than the world as a whole. This particular shape is not inevitable, however, even when the two extremes are set so that countries will be indifferent between them ('extremal indifference'). An interior optimum is a possibility. To compensate for the ambiguity, it appears that an interior optimum, if it exists, prescribes that the optimum currency area may be half the world. This holds in many cases identified, given extremal indifference. For the optimum currency area to consist of anything but the whole world, half the world, or just the single country, it appears that extremal indifference has to be relaxed. The intuition for the 'half the world is best' result is that, for all integer values for m above unity, it minimizes the number of MRS/MRT ratios between pairs of goods and countries that suffer distortion from currency conversion costs.

The '$m = 2$ can be best' result testifies to the possible superiority of a half-way house between one-money-per-country, and one-world-money. McCallum explores another kind of half-way house – the adoption of fixed-but-adjustable parities between national countries' currencies. In the context of the European Union, McCallum is essentially evaluating the characteristics, and ultimate survival prospects, of something like the European Exchange Rate Mechanism (ERM), as an alternative to European Monetary Union (EMU). He adduces the literature on foreign exchange crises, particularly Flood and Garber (1984), and neatly encapsulates central features of it within an attractive, simple model. McCallum's overall verdict is sceptical: a system of the ERM type cannot survive, unless participants' monetary policies really are fully consistent and singlemindedly adhered to. As McCallum notes, this accords well with evidence of the ERM (Britain's eviction in September 1992, and the massive band-widenings of August 1993) as well as later crises in Mexico and South East Asia.

What do these conclusions imply for optimum currency areas, as an alternative? A monetary union disposes of currency conversion costs, which an exchange rate union – durable or doomed – can never do. But to last, an exchange rate union requires the kind of strict parallelism between participating countries' monetary policies that is really tantamount to a single monetary policy for the entire area. So the benefit–cost comparison seems clear: the monetary union is better than an exchange rate union designed to last indefinitely. But this does not quite exclude the case for a terminable exchange rate union. This preserves the option to float or revise parities. Of course a monetary union may not last for ever either. Many do not (witness the rapid collapse of the ex-USSR rouble area and the ex-Jugoslavian dinar area in the 1990s, and the slower, century-long break-up of the sterling area in the previous dozen or so decades). But the costs of dissolving a monetary union surely far outweigh those of revising an exchange rate parity.

A country should join a monetary union, this suggests, rather than a fixed-but-adjustable exchange rate area, unless the true social value of the option to change the parity is positive. One factor making for a positive option value is the greater flexibility it gives the country's policymakers – particularly in dealing with country-specific shocks. But the value could be negative: currency conversion costs imply this, at least for a worldwide monetary union where trade diversion cannot follow, and probably for smaller unions too.

There are of course also reputational issues to consider here. Holding inflation down to ideal levels might prove impossible for a country on its own, for familiar time-consistency reasons explored by Barro and Gordon (1983) and Kydland and Prescott (1977). A monetary union might deal with this difficulty, much like central bank independence or delegation to a conservative central banker are widely held to do. In that case, the value of the option to alter parities would be lowered further. But this begs the question of whether the monetary union is actually any better than the single country at removing the time-consistency inflationary bias problem. In practice, it may or may not. No generalization is possible. It is worth observing, however, that there is one reason for expecting a smaller area to be more proficient at avoiding temptations to inflate than a larger area. This is the phenomenon of currency substitution, which could well moderate the short-run seignorage gain from inflation more successfully in a small country, where residents have more rival national monies to switch into. Those managing a big monetary union, especially if prone to myopia, may observe that their residents' currency substitution opportunities are very limited.

McCallum's model for exploring foreign exchange crises is very neat. It has the outstanding merit of reconciling something close to the traditional ISLM open economy model with infinite-horizon optimizing. So, despite appearances, it is well micro-founded. But, as McCallum stresses, it cannot claim to be complete. For me, one omission of particular interest is the absence of any trade-off, even temporarily, between inflation and output. This makes it unable to handle Barro–Gordon issues, for example. It also prevents treatment of the subtler theme alluded to in C2 in McCallum's list of arguments for and against monetary unions, which is that surprise inflation cuts the real value of the State's unindexed debt, permitting a reduction in distortionary taxes to which welfare, and probably output, are vulnerable.

There is another reason for regretting the absence of an output–inflation trade-off. Let the log of natural output, call it η, be stationary. Suppose we replace the second term on the RHS of (2.1a), as (2.1f) will now permit. Then replace (2.1f) by

$$p_{t+1} - p_t = g(y_t - \eta). \tag{2.1f*}$$

(2.1f*) includes (2.1f) as a special case when $1/g$ vanishes. If g is low, so that home prices change slowly in the face of an output gap, the resulting system is saddle-stable under a free float. Stochastics-free perfect foresight paths can be found most conveniently for the two variables q and $m - p$, as Buiter and Miller show (1981). If g is really high, but finite, however, we encounter a rather worrying phenomenon. What had been a saddle-stable system, Buiter and Miller reveal, becomes globally unstable. The reasoning for the phenomenon is as follows. Expected inflation is the wedge between the nominal interest rate (which governs money demand in (2.1b)) and the real interest rate that influences aggregate demand (2.1a). So higher expected inflation raises the current level of real aggregate demand consistent with a given real money stock. But that means that prices must be expected to rise faster, from (2.1f*). So there is a positive feedback effect, which will make the system globally unstable if g is too big. The system can cope with a strictly vertical Phillips curve (the McCallum case of perfect price flexibility). It can also cope with a fairly flat one. But faced with a steep, yet not quite vertical Phillips curve, it will explode. This could be taken to imply less than full confidence in speculators' ability to single out a rational-expectations path for a free floating exchange rate. This would matter even more if the parameter g is not known for sure, but thought to be quite high (and maybe capable of increasing when inflation is rapid). If so, the basis for Friedman's sanguine views about the merits of free floating, which McCallum cites, might be placed in some doubt.

A final reflection on the currency-crisis section of McCallum's paper is this. The stochastic term in the uncovered interest parity equation, (2.1e), may be influenced by the country's stock of net claims on the rest of the world (call this z). Exports are permitted to deviate from imports, and there is no explicit term for net overseas asset income, so z can presumably change over time. These considerations could enable the model to address some aspects of the fiscal issues explored later in McCallum's paper. Higher government spending, for example, would presumably lead initially to real appreciation under a free float, but the resulting trade balance deterioration would cause z (if previously stationary) to keep sliding. The final state of rest would involve permanently higher real interest rates and lower real money at home and, at the same time, a permanently lower real exchange rate (needed to improve competitiveness enough to generate a trade surplus that balanced higher overseas debt charges). In a fixed exchange rate system, the fiscal expansion would trigger what would look like an ever-growing peso problem, if the trade deficit were financed by overseas borrowing. If not, there would presumably be an unsustainable fall in reserves, with expulsion from the fixed exchange rate at some point before they ran out, much as in McCallum's analysis of the effects of an exchange-rate-incompatible growth rate for domestic credit.

These last points are offered by way of a plea for not omitting fiscal variables from the exchange rate question. The final substantive part of McCallum's paper is devoted to exploring and assessing the fiscal theory of prices. This theory does not just try to incorporate budgetary variables into the model of price determination. It gives them centre stage, so much so that monetary variables become no more than 'noises off'.

McCallum is highly sceptical of this theory. So, I must confess, am I. McCallum's demonstration of its potential disobedience to transversality conditions is elegant and persuasive. My remarks about the theory fall into three groups. First, I shall raise some theoretical questions about it. Second, I shall offer a few observations on the empirical issue of the relative comovements of money, bonds and prices. Third, I shall try to draw some inferences about the theory's relevance to monetary unions.

First, the theory. What is to count as money is notoriously unclear. Consider the IMF's concept of quasi-money, or the Radcliffean or Tobinesque concept of near-money. Quasi-money includes a vast raft of financial instruments, typically interest-bearing, which are used to settle accounts as well as store value. For larger companies and financial institutions, Treasury Bills have a market value that is almost wholly insensitive to interest rates. They can also be liquidated at negligible cost. For Radcliffe, defining money called for an arbitrary incision into a continuum of assets; government debt about to mature was a prime example of an asset that was to all intents and purposes 'as good as money' from the standpoint of most of its holders. In his 1965 model, Tobin's 'money' is government debt with bearing non-negative nominal interest. The type of bonds examined in the fiscal theory of price determination that McCallum explores is indeed just like Treasury Bills. They bear no explicit interest coupon, and they will mature for sure in the 'next period'. Bonds are future money. If we rewrote the model in continuous time, so that the duration of the interval of time between periods vanished, the distinction between money and these bonds would all but disappear. We could in principle amalgamate the two into a composite, and call it liquid government debt. It would be a simple matter to rewrite our theory of price level determination in terms of this aggregate. That would be uncontroversial; and those who maintained that prices were really governed by just one of these two components of liquid government debt, either the pure money or the bills on their own, would court derision. The budget deficit – which would determine the growth of liquid government debt, assuming no transactions in any longer-term bonds – would seem the ultimate source of inflation.

Even these steps are, however, open to objections. There are transactions in longer-dated debt, open market operations as well as sales to fund the deficit. There are powerful reasons for not detaching debt about to mature from less ripe bonds. The term structure of interest rates on all bonds, including implicit yields on bills, is glued together by present expectations of future short and long rates. To an economist, these expectations may not be divorced from forecast trajectories for inflation and Ramsey's cast list of variables that govern the evolution of the marginal product of capital. And if the definition of money has to be widened, why not to inside money, created by financial intermediaries? Or at least some weighted aggregate, such as Divisia money? And are bonds, strictly speaking, future money, money 'with a time fuse'? In the fiscal model, bonds are not really future money at all – they are future bonds!

Further, the exponents of the fiscal theory of prices – the claim that bond paths govern price paths, and that 'money' is irrelevant – run into other difficulties. For example, many countries now issue indexed bonds. Where do they fit in? What would happen if all bonds were indexed, and old nominal bonds disappeared? In that event, surely a legitimate possibility, the fiscal theory would have to be false. Perhaps a deeper objection turns on the fact that it is real money that people seek to hold, either because they like it for its own sake, or because of cash-in-advance constraints, or for its time-saving characteristics. In the second and third of these respects, and possibly all three, bonds simply fail to cut the mustard. (Extra real bonds, by contrast, are balanced in present value by the stream of extra real taxes levied to finance them.) Here lies the ultimate source of the link between nominal money and the price level. And even if some financial institutions emerge to provide such 'liquidity' services from deposits backed by bonds, they will still want some (real) cash inventory, and their cash ratio cannot be kept falling at an arbitrary rate, independent of the pattern of financial innovation.

Then there is the question of taxes. Typically, bonds bear coupons, financed by distorting taxes. We saw that this underlay one argument for inflation-bias, with potential relevance to the monetary union issue. To this extent, they must impinge on output, and a one-to-one link with prices could not strictly follow, at least outside the steady state. Furthermore, one of these distorting taxes is the tax on money, which yields seignorage. The absence of bond coupons and seignorage from (2.20) is striking.

When the nominal money supply is constant, McCallum shows that, in the simplest case, only two steady states can obtain. In one, the bond stock is retired in full in the following period, and prices end up constant. In the other, bonds and prices keep rising, at a common rate in the steady state, and real money eventually shrivels up to nothing (the fiscalist case). There are of course other possibilities: the stocks of money and bonds could grow at a common rate, for example, with prices eventually rising in parallel. In that case, if π is the rate of inflation, and κ the ratio of money to bonds, I find that the long run ratio of B to P will be given by

$$B/P = (tx_t - g_t)(1 + \rho)/[\rho - \kappa\pi(1 + \rho)]$$

if the budget surplus is constant. The presence of seignorage now implies that the economy can afford the burden of a higher real bond stock to service. Bonds and money coexist indefinitely, in necessarily fixed proportions in a steady state, and it makes no sense to say that the price level path is 'determined' by only one of them. By extension, if money and bonds grow at different but constant rates, inflation will ultimately be 'determined', presumably, by the rate of expansion of whichever grows faster.

On empirical evidence, there are periods when nominal government debt and nominal income both outpace narrow money. The United States from the start of Nixon's Presidency to the end of Reagan's is one such. The 1910s, for Britain and several other belligerents, are another. But nominal debt far outpaces nominal income in these cases, and money velocity rose with increased inflation expectations. There are also fascinating periods when nominal income and prices move in the opposite direction to nominal debt. Britain in the decade from 1985 is one such. And then there is the century after Waterloo, which saw the ratios of bonds to narrow money and national income fall by over three-quarters, with prices broadly trendless. At least on the basis of this cursory evidence, a claim that bonds should display a one-to-one link with prices, irrespective of the path of the money supply, appears empirically unfounded.

Lastly, what does the fiscal theory of prices imply for monetary unions? Unfortunately the models examined by McCallum relate only to the closed economy. So what matters for prices in the fiscalist case – (a) the value of government bonds domestic residents hold, or (b) the stock of bond claims outstanding against its government? Budget deficit equations tell us about how the latter evolves, but McCallum's observations on transversality relate to the former. The traditional, monetary view is quite plain here: unless sterilized, bonds to finance budget deficits inflate the home money supply automatically, threatening inflation, if they are sold to foreigners. But the answer to the question carries very different implications for a monetary union. In case (b), the union's central financial authority must presumably keep the summed liabilities of all union public authorities growing at the desired rate of growth of nominal income, with each national component rising in parallel to stop relative price levels falling out of line. Case (a), by contrast, would call, one imagines, for common target growth rates for bond holdings, of any provenance, within each member country. Inflation targets might also be needed, but currency would be a sideshow.

This seems like cloud-cuckoo-land. But the nugget of truth to be gleaned is presumably this: the bond stock must in the end determine the price level, if it persistently outpaces the supply of money. In this light, the European Union's Growth and Stability Pact ceilings on Eurozone participants' deficits and debt can be seen as adjuncts to the European Central Bank's monetary policy, to help ensure that that does not happen. If national governments' liabilities were to keep growing at different rates, and particularly if more indebted countries' government bonds grew faster than the average, the strains in the system could become insupportable. More generally, monetary and fiscal policies cannot be split off from each other, in or out of a monetary union.

Too much rigidity, and policymakers will be unable to plug gaps in credit and insurance markets by supporting consumption in areas in temporary hard times. Too much laxity, and the integrity of monetary policy may be violated by incompatible objectives (and eventual exchange rate depreciation, or monetary break-up) or by the budgetary machinations of myopic, vote-hunting or even debt-racing local politicians. How to draw and tread the thin line between these two is a challenge for any jurisdiction, national or supranational. McCallum's penetrating observations enable us to think more clearly about important aspects of this key issue.

References

Barro, R. J. and D. Gordon (1983) 'A Positive Theory of Monetary Policy in a Natural Rate Model', *Journal of Political Economy*, *91*.

Brenton, P. A., H. G. Scott and P. J. N. Sinclair (1997) *International Trade*. Oxford University Press, Oxford.

Buiter, W. H. and M. Miller (1981) 'Monetary Policy and International Competitiveness: the Problems of Adjustment', Oxford Economic Papers, and in Eltis, W. A. and P. J. N. Sinclair, eds, *The Money Supply and the Exchange Rate*. Oxford University Press, Oxford.

Diamond, P. A. (1993) 'Search, Sticky Prices and Inflation', *Review of Economic Studies, 60.*

Flood, R. P. and P. M. Garber (1984) 'Collapsing Exchange-Rate Regimes: Some Linear Examples', *Journal of International Economics*, 1–13.

Friedman, M. (1969) 'The Optimum Quantity of Money', in Friedman, M., *The Optimum Quantity of Money and Other Essays*. University of Chicago Press, Chicago.

Kydland, F. and E. C. Prescott (1977) 'Rules rather than Discretion: the Inconsistency of Optimal Plans', *Journal of Political Economy, 85.*

Mirrlees, J. A. (1971) 'An Exploration in the Theory of Optimum Income Taxation', *Review of Economic Studies, 38.*

Obstfeld, M. and K. Rogoff (1996) *Foundations of International Macroeconomics*, MIT Press, Cambridge, MA.

Phelps, E. S. (1973) 'Inflation in the Theory of Public Finance', *Swedish Journal of Economics, 75.*

Sinclair, P. J. N. (1997) 'Optimum Tax and Monetary Arrangements in the Open Economy', in Milner, C. and J. Borkakoti, eds, *International Trade and Labour Markets*, Macmillan, London.

Tobin, J. (1965) 'Money and Economic Growth', *Econometrica, 33.*

Comments on Chapter 2 – Theoretical issues pertaining to monetary unions

Geoffrey E. Wood

Introduction

The paper Professor McCallum has written is imaginative, thorough and useful. That is no surprise. It deals with four aspects of the theory of optimal currency areas. These are, first, traditional optimum currency area theory and second, the history of that body of theory. Examination of these issues is followed by consideration of what choice of exchange rate regime faces countries when they eschew exchange controls over capital movements and, finally, by an examination of the fiscal theory of inflation. These comments touch on all four topics, very briefly on the first and fourth and in a little more detail on the other two.

History of thought

McCallum dates the theory from Robert Mundell's 1961 article. That is surely correct. There were precursors, but Mundell's was the first to view the choice of currency domain as an optimising problem. This comparatively recent development is, McCallum suggests, due to two factors. Before Milton Friedman's (1953) 'Case for Flexible Exchange Rates', the 'most common position [among international monetary economists] was that the same monetary standard, typically the gold standard, should prevail everywhere'. The theory could not develop until Friedman had changed that view, even though Keynes's 'General Theory' had in 1936 raised the possibility of using monetary policy for short run stabilisation.

The theory's recent development is in my view much more puzzling than the paper suggests; for the intellectual climate was suitable for it in the 1880s and 1890s. Writers on economics have been aware of short run price stickiness, and the consequent effects of price level or monetary shocks on output, since David Hume's 'Of Money' (1752). Marshall's 'Pure Theory of Foreign Trade and Domestic Values', which appeared in 1879, showed (inter alia) how terms of trade changes would affect prices. Accordingly, even though it seemed desirable to aim for a worldwide monetary standard, it surely remains surprising that there was no discussion of the optimal area which might from time to time suspend gold convertibility in the face of a shock. After all, national boundaries were still fluid, and currency unions being formed and broken. Economists had, then, perhaps fifty more years than McCallum suggests to formulate the optimum currency area concept.

The fiscal theory of inflation

McCallum discusses this theory and rejects it. Two quite notable episodes in British economic history support him in this conclusion. First there was the currency debasement under Henry VIII. No government debt was issued, and prices rose with the nominal quality of money. Later, from 1688 to 1788, the public debt to national income ratio rose from around zero to over 100 per cent. There was no even approximately matching rise in the price level. Price indices from so far in the past must be treated with even greater caution than their present-day counterparts; and price level comparisons over long periods are always no more than suggestive. But for what these data are worth, they are decisively inconsistent with the fiscal theory of inflation.

That is a pity in the present context. For the theory would provide a compelling rationale for the Maastricht 'Stability Pact', which limits debt to income ratios for EMU member governments, and would provide a clear prediction of the consequences should there be failure to adhere to that pact.

But as the theory is far from analytically robust and is not well supported by the data, it must be dispensed with in the present discussion, despite its apparent relevance.

Exchange rate regimes

Writing in 1953 Milton Friedman (op. cit.) displayed (even by his standards) remarkable intellectual penetration when he argued that without exchange controls only truly fixed or freely floating exchange rates are viable, for there had been essentially no experience of intermediate regimes without controls which might have suggested either the question or the conclusion. The conclusion, though, is well supported by both subsequent experience and subsequent theoretical developments. This has led some, even some economists, to argue for the reimposition of some form of exchange control. The arguments are worth taking seriously; they are politically attractive and are, indeed, supported by that notable advocate of free trade in goods, Jagdish Bhagwati (e.g. 1998). Bhagwati makes two arguments. No-one, he says, has shown by calculating them that there are gains from capital mobility, although such gains have been measured for trade in goods. Second, whatever these gains may be, there is, he asserts, a tremendous downside risk. As an example of that risk he cites the turmoil in South-East Asian currency markets and economies in the late 1990s.

Measuring the gains from international capital mobility is well beyond the scope of a comment, but a simple and well-known example is very suggestive. Between 1869 and 1878 the US ran, on average, a current account deficit of around 1 per cent of GDP every year. The deficit then continued, at a lower average level, for a further ten years. A substantial excess of domestic investment over domestic saving was thereby permitted for some 20 years. How long would the US have taken to develop without that? The loss in income to the US would surely have been substantial.

Further, a measure of that loss alone would understate the loss to the world as a whole. For the development of the US raised real wages very substantially in the UK and, indeed, throughout a good part of Europe, by lowering the price of grain. That benefit, too, would have been foregone without capital mobility. It is quite clear that international capital mobility can bring substantial welfare improvements.

What of the downside risks? South East Asia is certainly not a persuasive example of these. Capital mobility was not at fault there. The blame surely lies very clearly with banking systems implicitly guaranteed by governments, and which (perhaps the price of these guarantees) often made loans on political rather than economic criteria. Claims that western banks were 'herd like' or irrational in that episode are hard to support. In view of the precedent, established by the IMF's Mexican bailout, that banks would lose little if things went wrong, it would have been irrational of them not to lend.[1]

The case for capital controls really is weak; and countries should, as McCallum concludes, choose between a rigidly fixed exchange rate and a free float.

Optimum currency area theory

After reviewing this body of theory, which sets out various criteria by which we may decide whether or not an area is an optimum currency area, McCallum concludes that (with the partial exception of two recent papers) the literature draws attention to some relevant issues, but provides neither clear-cut answers nor methods of reaching such answers. He is surely right. The same point is made implicitly in a recent textbook by Krugman and Obstfeld (1994: 611–17). In the course of a very clear exposition of optimum currency theory they construct a diagram. The construction is in three stages.

In Figure 1.1 the upward sloping GG schedule shows that a country's monetary efficiency gain from joining a fixed exchange rate area rises as the country's economic integration with the area rises. In Figure 1.2 the downward sloping LL schedule shows that a country's economic stability loss from joining a fixed exchange rate area falls as the country's economic integration with the area rises. And finally, in Figure 1.3 the intersection of GG and LL at point 1 determines a critical level of economic integration 0 between a fixed exchange rate area and a country considering whether to join. At any level of integration above 0, the decision to join yields positive net economic benefits to the joining country.

The analysis shows the relevant issues: but a reading of the labelling of the axis shows how far the theory is from being operational. It may therefore be appropriate to approach the concept of an optimum currency area in a different way.

Rather than starting by listing the conditions which make a currency area optimal, and seeing which areas satisfy these conditions, we should start with the following definition. 'The basic definition of a currency area of optimum size is that it can maintain itself indefinitely in competition with currency areas of other sizes.' That definition may seem somehow familiar. Familiarity would not be surprising. The definition is taken, with one modification, from the fourth (1987) edition of George Stigler's *The Theory of Price*. The change is that 'currency area' has been substitute for 'firm'. Stigler produced that definition on the basis of concluding that 'the theory of

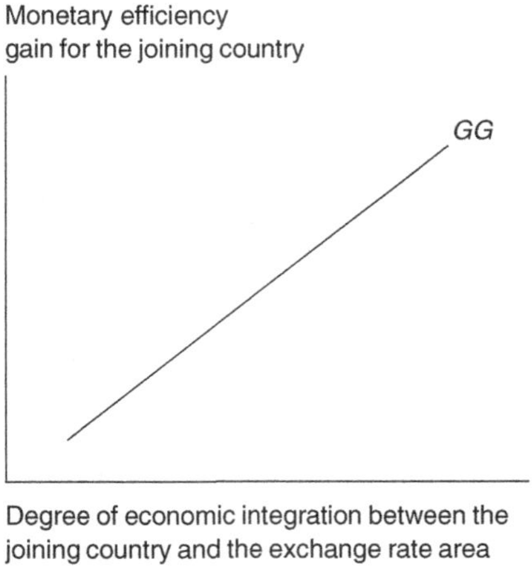

Figure 2.1 The relationship between monetary efficiency and economic integration for a country joining a fixed exchange rate area.

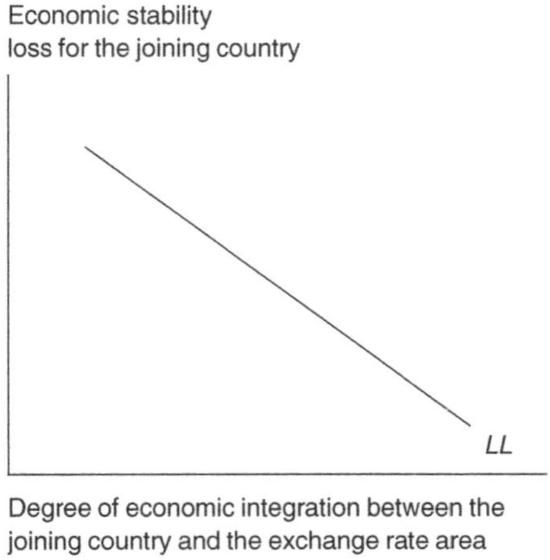

Figure 2.2 The relationship between economic stability loss and economic integration for a country joining a fixed exchange rate area.

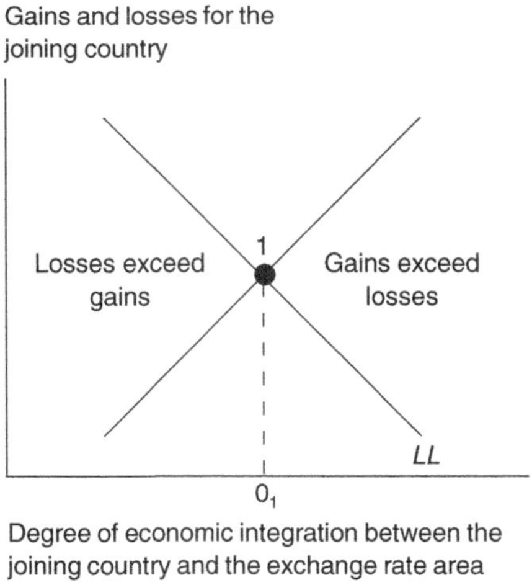

Figure 2.3 The balance between losses and gains for a country joining a fixed exchange rate area.

the economies of scale has never achieved scientific prosperity' (1958: 4). He went on, 'A large cause of its poverty is that the central concept of the theory – the firm of optimum size – has eluded confident measurement' (1958: 14). He then argued that we should judge the optimum size by whether firms survive or not. Trying that led him to find a wide range of optimum sizes. We see the same when we look at currency areas which have survived without the protection of exchange controls.[2] What can we do with this concept? We can borrow from Stigler again; and look at various factors popularly said to contribute to currency area size, as he did for firm size. (For example he looked and rejected advertising expenditure.) We could look at labour mobility; at price stability; at commodity composition of output. Given the reluctance of governments to abandon national currencies, we could focus on how competition led them to adopt policies necessary for their currencies' survival.

When this approach is taken it becomes much harder to defend the claim that the clear association between the abolition of exchange controls and the downward trend in inflation as seen over the past two decades is just a coincidence. The theory also has an immediate application in considering EMU. We can consider any proposed currency area and ask if it falls within the range of existing optimum areas. If, as the Euro area does, the answer is not quite, we can then compare it with a successful currency area of almost the same size (considering both economic and geographical dimensions) and ask if it has the same attributes. The obvious comparison is with the USA. The answer from that comparison would appear to be that some factors are lacking, and, if optimality develops over time (as Hugh Rokoff suggests that it does in his paper in this book) the road to it could be bumpy.

Conclusion

McCallum has written a careful paper with which one can have no serious disagreements. His suggestion as to why the optimum currency area concept emerged in the 1960s is plausible; but why did the concept not emerge in the 1880s, when conditions were as favourable? His rejection of the fiscal theory of inflation can be bolstered by some items of evidence, and his conclusion that countries must, in the absence of exchange controls, chose between really fixed rates and a free float is bolstered by some observations suggesting countries are wise to dispense with exchange controls.

And finally, as the optimum currency area concept is, as he has concluded, still not operational, a concluding suggestion is that we borrow from George Stigler's approach to the optimal size of firm. The 'survivor' technique was fruitful there. It may well be useful in optimum currency area work also, and help us make productive a concept that has for almost four decades remained interesting but troublingly non-operational.

Notes

1 See Goodhart and Delargy (1998) or Wood (1999).
2 It also prompts questions such as 'what is an area?'. Is it an economic concept (measured, say, by GNP) or a geographic area? How big a currency area is Australia?

References

Bhagwati, Jagdish (1998) 'The Capital Myth: the Difference between Trade in Widgets and in Dollars', *Foreign Affairs*, 7(3) May/June.

Friedman, Milton (1953) 'The Case for Flexible Exchange Rates', in Friedman, M., *Essays in Positive Economics*. University of Chicago Press, Chicago.

Goodhart, C. A. E. and P. J. R. Delargy (1998) 'Financial Crises: Plus ça change, plus c'est la même chose', *International Finance*, *1*(2).

Hume, D., ([1752] 1955) Excerpts from *Essays, Moral Political and Literary*, Vol 1, Longmans Green London, in Eugene Rotwein, ed., *Writings on Economics*. Nelson, London; University of Wisconsin Press, Madison.

Keynes, J. M. (1936) *The General Theory of Employment, Interest, and Money*. Macmillan, London.

Krugman, P. and M. Obstfeld (1994) *International Economics*. HarperCollins, New York.

Marshall, Alfred (1879), reprinted 1930, 'The Pure Theory of Foreign Trade and the Pure Theory of Domestic Values', in *Series of Reprints of Scarce Tracts in Economic and Political Science*, No. 1, London School of Economic and Political Science, London. (Privately printed in 1879.)

Mundell, Robert (1961) 'A Theory of Optimum Currency Areas', *American Economic Review*, *51*.

Stigler, G. J. (1987) *The Theory of Price*. Macmillan, New York; Collier Macmillan, London.

Stigler, G. J. (1958) 'The Economies of Scale', *Journal of Law and Economics*, *1*.

Wood, G. E. (1999) 'Great Crashes in History: Have they Lessons for Today?', *Oxford Review of Economic Policy*, *15*(3).

3 The future of EMU

What does the history of monetary unions tell us?

Michael D. Bordo and Lars Jonung

Introduction

On 1 January 1999 the exchange rates of eleven members of the European Union were locked to each other at irrevocably fixed rates. This was a major step towards the establishment of the European Monetary Union (EMU) and the European Central Bank (ECB). The eleven domestic currencies has been replaced by one single currency, the euro. It circulates in an economic region probably larger than that of any other currency area. 1 January 1999 marks an important transition not only in the history of Europe but in the history of the global monetary system.

The creation of EMU and the ECB has triggered a discussion of the future of EMU. Independent observers have pointed to a number of shortcomings, 'flaws' or 'hazard areas' in the construction and workings of EMU. These include (1) the absence of a central lender of last resort function for EMU, (2) the lack of a central authority supervising the financial systems of EMU, (3) weak democratic control (accountability) of the ECB, (4) unclear and inconsistent policy directives for the ECB, (5) the absence of central co-ordination of fiscal policies within EMU combined with unduly strict criteria for domestic debt and deficits as set out in the Maastricht rules and the Stability Pact in the face of asymmetric shocks, and (6) Euroland is not an 'optimal' currency area. The list can be lengthened.

Do these shortcomings represent major threats to the future of EMU? Will they eventually spell the demise and break-up of EMU? Or will they be handled by the European policy authorities in a successful way, leading to a lasting and prosperous EMU?

We answer these questions by examining the historical record of a number of unions that have turned out to be lasting as well as some unions that have been dissolved. Our aim is to extract the key conditions for the establishment and survival of monetary unions. Our interpretation of the historical record serves as the basis for our forecast for the future of EMU, although we are well aware that there is no clear precedent to EMU. While by now the literature on monetary unions and European monetary co-operation is voluminous, there are few systematic studies dealing with the stability or sustainability of monetary unions and monetary integration.[2]

The paper is organized as follows. First, the most commonly asserted shortcomings of EMU and of the ECB in the present debate are listed to serve as a guide for the examination of the historical record. Next, we investigate why monetary unions were created, focusing upon five major monetary unions established in the nineteenth century. Then we examine the break-up of monetary unions in the twentieth century. Finally, we confront our account of monetary union performance with forecasts for the future of EMU and evaluate the destabilizing effects of several shortcomings in the construction of EMU.[1]

Much of recent analysis of monetary unions by economists is based on the framework suggested by the literature on optimal currency areas. This approach is not well suited for the analysis of the history of monetary unions. It is too static and ahistorical. Instead, our approach is an evolutionary one, since we examine a long stretch of time and the character of the processes causing the appearance and dissolution of monetary co-operation and unification.

The shortcomings of EMU

The economics profession has in general been sceptical of a European monetary union. Economists have pointed to a large number of pitfalls on the road to a common European currency. Indeed, the road so far has been a rocky one.

The ERM crisis in the early 1990s severely threatened the EMU project. The last-minute effort in May 1998 to put a Frenchman in charge of the ECB as well as various attempts in the early spring of 1999 by the German minister of finance to press for a lowering of the euro-rate damaged credibility. The transition from stage two to stage three, when the exchange rates of the first set of countries to join EMU were permanently fixed, was once regarded as highly risky, potentially provoking speculative attacks. No such attacks materialized, however. The transition went smoothly at the turn of the new year of 1999. Now after January 1st 1999, the creation of EMU and the ECB has triggered a discussion of the future of EMU since it seems to have passed the major hurdles of the long transition stage that started in the 1970s.[2]

Economists have pointed to a number of shortcomings, also termed 'deficiencies', 'flaws' or 'potential fault lines' in the construction of EMU. There are by now about half a dozen such 'hazard areas'.[3] We list the most common ones below, focusing on those pertaining to the euro-area once it was established but ignore 'deficiencies' pertaining to the transition stages before the common currency is introduced into circulation within Euroland. We thus concentrate our discussion on the long run 'steady-state' of EMU, assuming that it will successfully pass through the remaining transition.[4]

1 EMU lacks a central lender of last resort. The ECB has not been granted power by the Maastricht Treaty to serve this function. This stands in sharp contrast with modern central banks, which exercise lender of last resort responsibilities to guarantee the liquidity and functioning of the payments system.[5] In the face of a liquidity crisis, the absence of a lender of last resort may undermine the existence of EMU.
2 EMU lacks a central authority to supervise the financial systems, including the

commercial banks, of Euroland. The Maastricht Treaty gives the ECB some supervisory functions but they are primarily the task of the union members. This state of affairs portends that a future pan-European financial crisis may not be efficiently resolved, consequently threatening the stability of the Eurosystem.[6]

3. The ECB lacks democratic control and accountability. The ECB will be subject to political attacks and controversies that damage the legitimacy of EMU and erode popular support for the euro. The role of the European parliament in monitoring the ECB is unclear at this point as well. Should major economic problems arise within a single member of EMU, populist political movements may use them to attack EMU and the ECB.[7]
4. The policy directives for the ECB are inconsistent, unclear, and badly designed. Although the ECB is to carry out 'domestic' monetary policy within Euroland, according to the Maastricht Treaty, exchange rate policy for EMU is set by the Council of the European Union, that is by the Council of finance ministers of EMU.[8] This will result in political discussion, tensions and political pressure on the monetary policy of the ECB.
5. The absence of central co-ordination of fiscal policies within EMU in combination with unduly strict criteria for domestic debt and deficits, as set out in the Maastricht rules and the Stability Pact, implies that EMU will not be able to respond to asymmetric shocks and disturbances in a satisfactory way.[9] For example, presently (summer 1999) the booming Irish economy is in need of a tighter monetary policy yet the ECB has lowered interest rates in Euroland making monetary policy in Ireland more expansionary.[10]
6. Europe is too large a geographical area to form a well-functioning monetary union. In other words, Euroland with its present eleven member states is not an optimal currency area (OCA). This point, which dates from the analysis of optimal currency areas initiated by Mundell (1961), has been debated continuously since the announcement of the plans for a monetary union in Europe. Most empirical work on this issue reaches the conclusion that EMU is not an optimal monetary union, at least it is less optimal than the US monetary union.[11] The efficiency gains from increased trade do not outweigh the costs of surrendering control over national monetary policies.

The costs of that surrender will depend on the incidence of asymmetric or idiosyncratic macroeconomic disturbances across Euroland, the degree of flexibility of wages and prices, the mobility of factors of production within Euroland, and the extent to which fiscal policies, either on a national or on a pan-European level, can serve as a substitute for changes in the exchange rate and the interest rate of the domestic currency.

European labour markets are commonly described as rigid and labour mobility within the EMU members as limited. Under these circumstances an asymmetric shock will set off an adjustment process that will be slower and more costly within EMU than otherwise. Rising unemployment, and requests for fiscal transfers and for protection, will undermine the credibility of EMU and the political cohesion required for a well-functioning monetary union.[12]

This point is probably the major objection to EMU. The abolition of domestic currencies and thus of the ability to adjust nominal exchange rates and domestic interest rates when faced with asymmetric or country-specific shocks, in the opinion of most economists, threatens the stability of EMU.[13]

This list of shortcomings or objections is substantial,[14] but will they turn out to be important in the future. How have monetary unions in the past dealt with the issues we have listed? Below we study the historical record, first to examine the process of creation and maintenance of monetary unions, then the process of their dissolution.

The creation of monetary unions

There is a historical record of monetary unions within which the same currency served as a unit of account, medium of exchange and store of value. Thus, a monetary union had one exchange rate towards the rest of the world. In our view, the history of monetary unions is best understood by distinguishing between national monetary unions and multinational monetary unions.[15]

In a national monetary union political and monetary sovereignty go hand in hand. Roughly speaking, the borders of the nation-state are the borders of the monetary area. For example, within the British monetary union comprising England, Scotland, Wales and Northern Ireland, Scottish commercial banks still issue bank notes. These notes are perfectly interchangeable for Bank of England notes. In the United States each of the Federal Reserve Banks issues dollar bills perfectly acceptable in every reserve district – a five dollar bill issued by the Federal Reserve Bank of Richmond is always perfectly interchangeable with a five dollar bill issued by any other Federal Reserve Bank. A national monetary union has as a rule one single monetary authority, commonly a central bank.

In a multinational monetary union international monetary co-operation between a number of independent countries is based on permanently fixed exchange rates between their currencies. Multinational monetary unions emerge when independent nation states link their monies together through a fixed exchange rate so that one country's money is perfectly exchangeable for that of another member country's at a fixed price. An extreme example is such that all member states use the same currency.

There is as a rule no common monetary authority in a multinational monetary union. An example of such a union is the Scandinavian monetary union, which had one common unit of account, the Scandinavian *krona*, and three members: Sweden, Norway and Denmark. Each member maintained its own central bank and issued its own *krona* currency, which circulated freely within the other countries as long as the union existed. The exchange rate of the Swedish, Danish and Norwegian currency units remained one to one to one during the existence of the Scandinavian monetary union.

We emphasize the distinction between a national and a multinational monetary union because we believe that the survival prospects of a monetary union depend crucially on whether it is organized as a national or a multinational union. The future of the EMU thus depends on whether EMU will more closely resemble a national or a multinational monetary union.

Table 3.1 The creation of some monetary unions in the nineteenth century

Monetary area	*Time of creation*
National monetary unions	
United States	1789–92
Italy	1861
Germany	1875
Multinational monetary unions	
Latin monetary union	1865
Scandinavian monetary union	1873–5

Source: Bordo and Jonung (1997) and Vanthoor (1996).

We first examine the establishment of three national monetary unions, those of the US, Italy and Germany, and next two multinational unions, the Latin and the Scandinavian unions, and finally the emergence of other forms of monetary unification. Here we deal primarily with the monetary experience of the late eighteenth century and the nineteenth century (Table 3.1).

National monetary unions

The United States monetary union[16]

The American revolutionary war was largely financed by the issue of fiat money both by the Congress (the continentals) and by the States (bills of credit). During the War of Independence (1776–83) paper money issues at the rate of 50 per cent per year in the first five years of the war generated a very rapid inflation rate of over 65 per cent per year and rapid depreciation of the exchange rate. The inflation ended after a currency reform in 1780 under which the federal government stopped issuing continentals, and the states agreed to accept outstanding issues in payment of taxes at 40 dollars to 1 in specie (a value much lower than the exchange rate of 1780) until 1783. After that date the continentals were to become worthless.

After the war the States continued to issue bills of credit during the Confederation period (1783–9), only some of which were credibly backed by future taxes. Consequently, problems emerged of excessive volatility of exchange rates that lead to exchange rate risk, high transactions costs, and competitive seigniorage.

The US monetary union was created with the signing of the Constitution in 1789. The constitution gave the Congress the sole power to 'coin money' and 'regulate the value thereof'. Moreover, the Coinage Act of 1792 defined the US dollar in terms of fixed weights of gold and silver coins, placing the country on a bimetallic standard. Finally, establishment of a national mint in Philadelphia in 1792 secured the foundations for an effective currency area.

While the Congress was given the exclusive power to coin money, the States were allowed to charter commercial banks and to regulate their note issue. All bank notes had to be convertible into specie. In the early decades of the nineteenth century, the quality of bank notes varied considerably and various bank notes circulated at a discount.

The movement to a complete monetary union with a more uniform nationwide price level was aided by the practices of the First Bank of the United States (1791–1811) and the Second Bank of the United States (1816–36). Neither Bank was designed as a modern central bank but as a public bank. Both banks were sufficiently well capitalized to be able to provide the government with medium-term bridge loans to finance shortfalls in government tax receipts. Both were also authorized to provide loans to the private sector to spur economic development. Finally, it was deemed imperative that they hold sufficient specie reserves to maintain convertibility of their notes. One of the practices of both Banks was to enforce the convertibility of state bank note issues and to transfer specie between regions.

After the demise of the Second Bank of the United States in 1836, the United States had no formal central bank until the establishment of the Federal Reserve System in 1914. However, the US Treasury served as a monetary authority and maintained specie convertibility.

Although banking instability characterized the nineteenth century, the monetary union remained intact with the exception of the Civil War period 1861–5 when the Confederate States issued their own fiduciary inconvertible currency denominated in dollars. In the face of great difficulties in raising tax revenues and in selling debt both at home and abroad, the Confederate government also expanded its money issues at an ever-increasing rate. By the end of the Civil War a hyperinflation vastly reduced the value of Confederate notes. Upon Union victory in April 1865, Confederate notes were declared illegal in the United States (Lerner 1956).

Monetary unification of the US was thus not completed until long after its political unification. The US did not establish a central bank with a lender of last resort function until this century. However, State bank regulation was undertaken by State banking inspectors well before the Civil War and national bank regulations by the Comptroller of the Currency beginning in 1863. These institutions evolved at a considerably later stage than the monetary unification.[17]

The Italian monetary union[18]

The main reason for the establishment of a currency union on the Apennine peninsula in the 1860s was political unification of the area now known as Italy.[19] The unification process, led by the Kingdom of Sardinia, was completed in 1861. Prior to 1861, disparate kinds of money circulated among the various small Italian states. In 1859, as many as 90 different metallic currencies were legal tender. In addition, major banks in the small states issued bank notes that served as legal tender in their respective regions. The existence of a plethora of different currencies was commonly regarded as a barrier to trade. In order to achieve more than a *de jure* politically unified Italy, measures were taken to turn the country into a monetary union as well.

The issue of coins was quickly resolved. During a brief transition period, only four currencies were acceptable and the others were exchanged for these four. Finally, in 1862, a new, unified coinage system was introduced based on the lira of

Sardinia. All pre-unification coins and paper monies were abolished and exchanged for coins denominated in the new lira, equal in value to the French franc. A bimetallic currency standard was chosen, primarily to conform to the monetary system of Italy's major trading partners and to accommodate the dominance of silver coins in southern Italy.[20] The currency ratio between silver and gold was set at the European standard of 15.5.

When Italy introduced the lira, the price of gold was falling, creating a shortage of silver coins. The legislators acted by lowering the silver content of coins to 83.5 per cent instead of the customary 90 per cent. This led to an export of silver coins, a phenomenon that the suspension of convertibility a few years later encouraged.[21]

The monetary unification of Italy was not accompanied by immediate action to establish a single monetary authority. Several regional banks were issuing notes as well as performing central bank functions. The *Banca Nazionale nel Regno d'Italia* (BNR), which was formed by the previous national bank of Sardinia and absorbed some other state banks in the process, held a dominant position in part because it was the largest bank in operation, in part because it was the bank of the state that led the political unification process.

Italian monetary research does not clearly explain why a single monetary authority was not created after unification. Apparently opposition to monetary unification was not the reason. Given that Sardinia imposed her system on the rest of the country in a wide range of matters, neglecting the preferences of other states, had she wanted why did she not establish the BNR as the central bank of Italy?

Several explanations have been offered. One is the general belief at the time that Italy would gain from competition between issuing banks, since banking was like any other industry, just as competition in other industries was considered beneficial. Also, prior to unification, the general concept of Italian banking was to combine the two functions of regional commercial banks that were credit institutions as well as note issuers. Money was created in the form of bank notes in response to demands for credit. The creation of one central bank, the central government might have concluded, would destroy, or severely impair, the functioning of commercial banks at the local level and the costs would exceed the benefits of control of the supply of paper money by a central bank.

When Italian monetary unification took place in 1862, almost the entire money stock consisted of coins. Since the supply of coinage was regulated by the supply of gold and silver, fluctuations in the Italian money stock followed the international pattern. The share of coins in the money supply remained stable until the mid-1860s, an indication that as long as bank notes were convertible into specie, the multiplicity of issuing banks did not create a problem.

When the central government's fiscal deficit rose sharply in the first half of the 1860s, it worsened the strain already put on public finances by its assuming the debt of the member states. Italian bond prices fell abroad, driving specie out of Italy and leaving the reserves of the commercial banks dangerously low. Their ability to lend to the government declined. To come to terms with the new situation, the government declared bank notes inconvertible into specie in 1866, *corso forzoso* in the language of the day.[22] After this step, the government received a large loan in notes from the BNR. In return, the position of the BNR was strengthened. The notes of other banks were made legal tender and at the same time convertible into BNR notes. BNR notes, however, were not convertible into other banks' notes. Consequently, BNR notes served as reserves for other banks.

The *corso forzoso* ended in 1884. Convertibility was resumed and the lira returned to gold parity. The notes of the six remaining note-issuing banks exchanged for each other at a one-to-one basis, although the parity was not stipulated by law. As a consequence of the *de facto* fixed exchange rate between the notes, each bank had an incentive to increase its stock of notes. The risk of the government discovering an over-issue was small. Furthermore, deteriorating government finances increased the likelihood that any illegal over-issue of notes would be legalized.

In 1891, a liquidity crisis due to the low levels of reserves relative to outstanding notes was pending. The government, as expected, responded by legalizing the total volume of notes in circulation by lowering reserve requirements. An ensuing enquiry into the state of the banking system completed in 1893 led to a major restructuring of the banking system. The *Banca d'Italia* was formed as an amalgamation between the BNR and the two remaining note-issuing Tuscan banks. The three other note-issuing banks were put under direct state supervision.[23] Despite these measures, specie continued to flow out of Italy. The lira depreciated, mainly as a result of the failure to reduce the excess issue of notes. The outflow triggered another liquidity crisis, and in 1894, bank notes once again were declared inconvertible into specie.

As part of the 1893 reshaping of the banking system, the government and the banks agreed to restrict the note issue to three times the volume of specie. In the long run this proved successful, in no small part due to the fact that the *Banca d'Italia* was established as the leading note-issuer with 75 per cent of total circulation. Fiscal discipline contributed to making the period up until World War I one of monetary stability with an appreciating lira.

The formation of the Italian monetary union, as in the case of the US monetary union, took place after political unification. Similar to the US case, the creation of Italian monetary unity was a time-consuming process.

The German monetary union

The German monetary – as well as political – unification process proceeded stepwise. Thus, scholars do not agree when the most important step towards monetary unification occurred. Holtfrerich (1993) suggests that the unification of coinage in 1857 represents the major, though not the final, achievement towards a monetary union. Others like Kindleberger (1981) are of the opinion that the creation of the *Reichsbank* in 1875 was the most important step. The disagreement has important implications: in the former case monetary unification preceded political unification and in the latter case vice versa. We believe that the most important step towards monetary unification was taken *after* the establishment of the Reich, so that Germany followed the same pattern as the US and Italy.

Prior to German monetary unification, each principality and free town issued its own coins and, in some cases, paper money. Since many of the principalities were quite small, it was inevitable that their coins spread across their borders as an accompaniment of the free flow of migration within the *Deutscher Bund*. In addition, many foreign coins, not least of French origin, circulated within Germany. Money exchanges were common and profitable.

The diversity of coins was a great nuisance. Merchants and industrialists, often with a liberal orientation, became the main proponents of unified economic and monetary conditions to reduce transaction costs emanating from the monetary disarray. The governments of the principalities resisted, safeguarding their seigniorage gains.

In 1834, all internal customs barriers were removed. This agreement, known as the *Zollverein*, also proposed that the various coinage systems should be integrated into a common standard as was done in 1857. In the 1860s voices were raised to continue the process of monetary unification. In 1870, the North German Federation, founded in 1867, prohibited new issues of state paper money and fixed the volume of note issues for most banks. These measures left the control of the future growth of paper money in the hands of the Prussian Bank.

The establishment in 1871 of the new unified German Reich following the Franco-Prussian war led to further steps. The coinage acts of 1871 and 1873 unified coinage throughout the Reich and introduced the *Mark* as the unit of account, based on the decimal system. In order to link the German currency to the British pound, at the time the leading international currency, the gold standard was adopted, with silver being reduced to use in coins of small denominations with less metal content than their face value.[24] In 1875, a new banking act transformed the Prussian Bank into the *Reichsbank* and forced most other banks to opt for ordinary banking business.[25] The *Reichsbank* was designated the central bank for the new Germany. From the 1870s till the outbreak of the First World War, Germany was part of the international gold standard.

Political unification, epitomized by the creation of the German Reich, was followed by three major changes in the German monetary system: the conversion of the currency standard from silver to gold, the replacement of the *Thaler* with the Mark as the unit of account, and the formation of a single central bank that, in practice, monopolized the issue of paper money. With political unification Germany also established a central bank that could function as a lender of last resort. Political unification was also a prerequisite for a common fiscal policy – as it emerged during the First World War.

These changes meant that Germany after a long process became a fully-fledged national monetary union. Again, in our opinion, monetary unification followed political unification.

Multinational monetary unions

The Latin and the Scandinavian monetary unions were created in the nineteenth century as multinational monetary unions. They were based on a standardized coinage across the union while each member country retained its central bank.

The Latin monetary union[26]

Prior to the establishment of the Latin Monetary Union in 1865, France, Belgium, Switzerland and, to some extent, Italy had a history of recognizing each other's currencies as means of payment. The basis of this arrangement was the French bimetallic system, in operation since 1803, which stipulated the fineness of each coin, regardless of whether it was a gold or a silver coin, at 90 per cent and fixed the relative value between gold and silver to 15.5.

In the 1850s, a fall in the market price of gold relative to the price of silver made gold coins overvalued at the mint. Consequently, it became profitable to melt silver coins and sell silver for gold at the market rate. As the price of gold continued to fall, even worn coins with low silver content started to disappear. The process left bimetallic countries virtually with a gold standard currency since gold was the only medium of exchange that remained in circulation. However, with no silver coins there was a lack of small-denomination monies to use in minor transactions.

Upon monetary unification, as noted above, Italy decided to lower the silver content of every coin smaller than 1 franc to 83.5 per cent. The result of the actions of Italy and similar ones by Switzerland was that debased silver coins from the neighbouring countries flooded mainly France but also Belgium, creating seigniorage gains for the issuers. France reacted in 1864 by reducing the silver content of every silver coin, except the 5-franc coin, to Italy's 83.5 per cent and by suspending the acceptance of Swiss coins by her customs offices.

The acute shortage of small denomination coins constituted a hindrance to trade both within and between countries and forced the countries into action to remedy the problem. The unilateral response by individual countries created an additional problem in the form of one country reaping seigniorage benefits at the expense of the others. To deal with this situation, Belgium proposed a joint monetary conference, held at the end of 1865, that created the Latin Monetary Union.

The main issues at the conference in 1865 were to secure and standardize the supply of subsidiary coinage for smaller transactions and the formal adoption of gold as the currency standard. The first issue was unanimously resolved by deciding that all silver coins of lower value than the 5-franc coin were to be token coins of 83.5 per cent silver fineness. State treasuries had to accept token coins, regardless of the country of origin, as payment up to 100 francs. Each state treasury was obliged to exchange the other state treasuries' existing holdings of its token coins into gold or silver 5-franc coins at par. The figure 83.5 per cent was chosen because of the dominant share of French and Italian token coins of that fineness already in circulation. The total value of token coins that each country was permitted to mint was restricted to 6 francs per capita. Due to strong French opposition and despite the fact that the other countries favoured such a move, the adoption of a gold standard was rejected in favour of retaining the bimetallic standard.[27]

The existing currencies continued to be in use virtually unchanged as parallel currencies. Each state treasury remained ultimately responsible for the redemption of its own coins. Apart from solving the problem of the scarcity of small-denomination coins, the purpose of the standardization of the dimension and metal content of the coins was to eliminate the possibility of seigniorage gains through the minting of debased coins. While aiming to restrict the amount of money in circulation, the conference failed to consider restrictions to prevent the member countries from issuing other forms of money – a failure that the issue of paper notes exploited. Consequently, the members still had considerable monetary independence.

Initially, the Latin monetary union achieved its objectives. However, two problems soon emerged. After the inauguration of the union, the price of gold started to rise. Silver 5-franc coins returned to circulation while gold coins were melted or exported. At the same time, France and Italy began to issue inconvertible paper money. In the case of France, it was a temporary measure due to the 1870–1 war with Germany. Italy's chronic government deficit maintained inconvertibility of the lira until 1881 and restored it again in 1894. The increased money supply in Italy led to a depreciation of the lira. Consequently, Italian silver coins were exported to the other member countries where they were legal tender. Obviously, this enabled the Italian government to finance part of her deficits with seigniorage, the cost of which was shared by all four countries, that is, Italy, France, Belgium and Switzerland.

In response to the problems facing the union, a conference by the members in 1874 decided to maintain the bimetallic standard but restrict the minting of silver 5-franc coins. In 1878 the members agreed to cease issuing 5-franc silver coins although those already in circulation were to remain legal tender. This arrangement established the 'limping gold standard'. In the discussions preceding the decision of 1874, both Belgium and Switzerland were originally in favour of terminating the union and the Belgian delegates argued for adoption of a gold standard. France and Italy, however, were against both proposals, probably because the Bank of France as well as the Italian government feared the huge costs of redeeming in gold all the 5-franc silver coins in circulation. The other three nations feared as well that a termination of the union might lead to Italy refusing to redeem the other countries' large holdings of Italian token coins. Instead, Italy had to agree to withdraw her token coins from international circulation for as long as she retained inconvertible paper money.

The union remained intact until the outbreak of the First World War, each member country with its own central bank. The main task of the union was to maintain a system of standardized coinage.

The Scandinavian monetary union[28]

Prior to the formation of the Scandinavian monetary union in 1873, the three Scandinavian countries were all on a silver standard.[29] Indeed, in the years leading up to the 1870s, all of them used the *riksdaler* as the unit of account. One Norwegian *specierigsdaler* was roughly equal to two Danish *rigsdaler* which in turn was roughly equal to four Swedish *riksdaler*. A considerable share of the coin circulation in each of the three countries consisted of coins minted in the other two. The difference in value separating these simple exchange rates from the exchange rates based on the currencies' values in silver was small for the Danish and Norwegian currencies. Any profit that could have arisen from arbitrage was negligible.

This was not the case for the Swedish currency, however. Its value exceeded 0.5 Danish or 0.25 Norwegian *rigsdaler*. The amount was sufficiently large to produce an inflow of Danish and Norwegian coins into Sweden, for which it was a nuisance.[30]

This currency flow was by no means the only reason, not even an important one, for aiming at a unified coinage. In all the Scandinavian countries, a lively debate regarding the most suitable specie standard - gold or silver - and regarding the merits of the decimal system for dividing the unit of account, created an intellectual climate in favour of adopting a common gold standard based on the decimal system for the Nordic currencies.[31] The decimal system was favoured on grounds of rationality. A currency based on the gold standard was deemed appropriate since Scandinavia's leading trading partners, the United Kingdom and Germany, were on gold. In addition, nationalistic sentiments running through Europe in the latter half of the nineteenth century took the form of Scandinavism in Scandinavia, a social and political willingness to bring the Nordic countries closer together.

All of these factors - the disequilibrium in currency flows, the perceived superiority of the gold standard and the decimal system and the political climate of the day - contributed to the creation by Sweden, Denmark and Norway of a common currency union in 1873. Although Norway did not formally sign the agreement until 1875, in practice her monetary standard was altered in 1873.[32]

The formation of the Scandinavian monetary union replaced the old unit of account, the *riksdaler*, with a new one, the Scandinavian *krona*. The value of a Scandinavian *krona* was specified in terms of gold and to be equal in all three countries where the new gold coin was minted. Subsidiary coins were to be minted in silver and copper with a fineness of 80 per cent and no restrictions were placed on the amount of such coins each country was allowed to mint. All coins were given legal tender status throughout the three Scandinavian countries. The state treasuries accepted unlimited amounts of coins irrespective of their country of origin. The only restrictions were a maximum amount stipulated for the settlement of private debts.

Because of the larger denominations of the gold coins compared to that of bank notes, notes remained in wide use in Sweden. Inter-country circulation consisted of notes and subsidiary coins. This caused some dissatisfaction since notes were not covered by the union agreement and thus did not always circulate at par. However, this shortcoming was eventually to be remedied.

The first enlargement of the Scandinavian monetary union occurred in 1885. The three central banks decided to establish inter-country drawing rights. Transactions between the central banks were made free of interest and other charges. It is unlikely that the central banks would have entered such an agreement if they felt that intra-Scandinavian currency flows would create permanent disadvantages. Consequently, the 1885 agreement indicates that no country sought to gain seigniorage benefits at the expense of the others. The smooth functioning of the union led Sweden and Norway to further extend the scope of the union in 1894 by accepting each other's notes at par without restrictions. The Danish central bank did not join the new agreement until 1901.[33]

No particular economic and political strains to the union appeared before the First World War - except for the political separation of Norway and Sweden in 1905 which caused some uncertainty for a brief period. The gold standard, by requiring convertibility into gold, ensured stability in the money supply. All three countries avoided issuing excessive amounts of subsidiary coins.[34] The money supply in the member countries expanded in line with economic growth. Inflation rates and interest rates exhibited identical patterns in Scandinavia during the union.

Other monetary unions[35]

In the nineteenth century, currency boards developed as a common monetary arrangement in many colonies, in particular in British colonies. A typical currency board issued notes and coins at least fully backed by reserves denominated in the currency of the colonial power. Currency boards were a method of economizing on the use of notes and coins of the colonial power.[36] A currency board represented a form of monetary union, more precisely an exchange rate union, between the colony and the home country.

Most colonies abolished their currency boards and established central banks of their own when they gained independence in the 1950s and 1960s. In a few cases the currency board system was maintained and managed, such as Hong Kong, Singapore, the East African Currency Area, emanating from British colonial rule but dissolved in 1977, and the East Caribbean Currency Area consisting of seven small island nations.[37]

The currency board institution has experienced a renaissance in the 1990s as Argentina, Estonia, Lithuania, Bulgaria and Bosnia have recently adopted currency boards. So far these experiments appear to have worked well in terms of establishing monetary stability and credibility relative to alternative monetary arrangements. However, it remains to be seen how well they will function in the long run.

A number of monetary unions were established in the twentieth century. One example is the CFA Franc Zone, formed in 1959 by former French colonies in west and central Africa, which actually has much in common with a currency board arrangement.[38] The zone is in practice two monetary unions covered by the same arrangement, with each union having its own monetary authority. Each union uses a unit of account called the CFA franc which in 1948 was set equal to 1/50 of a French franc.[39] The CFA francs are legal tender within their respective monetary unions and are convertible into French francs. France's influence over monetary policy in the region is substantial. The CFA Franc Zone has provided lower inflation rates than in neighbouring African countries, primarily by limiting credit to national governments. The union is still in operation.

The East Caribbean Currency Area is an example of a multinational monetary union with a single monetary authority. The East Caribbean Currency Area comprises seven small countries in the Caribbean Ocean that were previously British colonies.[40] Under British rule, monetary matters were controlled by the British Caribbean Currency Board, which has since evolved into the East Caribbean Central Bank. It is the sole issuer of a single currency for the union, the Caribbean dollar, which is legal tender in the seven member states. The seven member countries also co-operate in other matters, for instance through the East Caribbean Common Market. The union is still in operation.

Some unions deal with the case of a very small country adopting the monetary system of a large country, most commonly a close neighbour, for example Luxembourg–Belgium, Andorra–France, Monaco–France, the Vatican City–Italy, San Marino–Italy and Liechtenstein–Switzerland. In each of these cases, monetary authority is exercised entirely by the larger country.

There are a few cases of a small country that unilaterally adopts the monetary system of a country far away. Examples include Liberia where the Liberian dollar was fixed to the US dollar at a one-to-one rate and US bank notes were made legal tender in 1944 and Panama which, one year after the country was formed, in 1904 fixed the exchange rate of the domestic currency, the *balboa*, to the US dollar and made the US dollar legal tender.

The monetary union between Ireland and Britain formed after Irish Home Rule in 1922 represented a currency board institution.[41] When Ireland was part of Britain, sterling was used in Ireland. This arrangement was temporarily prolonged in 1922. With Britain as the largest trading partner of Ireland, the Irish government by taking no action to change the monetary system clearly indicated that the advantages of maintaining close monetary links to Britain outweighed the advantages of monetary sovereignty. In 1925, a new unit of account, the Irish pound, was introduced. The Irish pound was explicitly linked to sterling. It had to be backed by gold or sterling assets one-to-one and sterling remained legal tender. The union was not ended until 1979 when, due to the strong inflationary tendencies of the British economy, Ireland decided to join the newly formed EMS instead.

The dissolution of monetary unions

Several monetary unions were dissolved in the twentieth century. We first discuss the break-up of the two multinational unions considered above, and next the collapse of some national monetary unions.

Multinational monetary unions

The outbreak of the First World War signalled the end of the Latin and the Scandinavian monetary unions. The main cause of the break-up of the Latin Monetary Union was the First World War. The sharp increase in military expenditures left its members with no choice but to issue paper money.[42] Large quantities of paper money issued during the war remained in circulation after the end of hostilities. As paper money was not recognized as legal means of payment in any country other than the issuing one, the union was in effect terminated. During the war, silver coins were melted or exported. Remaining coins constituted a small share of the total money supply.

Belgium was the first member to act formally, declaring in 1925 that she would leave the union at the start of 1927. The other countries followed and the Latin monetary union was dissolved. The process was easy to carry out as each member had a central bank and a domestic currency of its own. The monetary separation did not create any major problems. It had *de facto* dissolved during the First World War.

Like the Latin monetary union, the Scandinavian monetary union's collapse was a result of the First World War. At the outbreak of war, Scandinavian notes were declared inconvertible into gold. At the same time, in order to prevent an outflow of gold, the export of gold was prohibited. The growth of the money supply thereby ceased to be tied to the supply of gold and the basis for the exchange of Scandinavian notes at par was eliminated.

Monetary policy was more expansive in Denmark and Norway than in Sweden. In 1915, the official exchange rates changed accordingly with one Swedish *krona* buying more than one Danish or Norwegian *krona*. The dissolution of the Scandinavian monetary union was a gradual one. It occurred in several steps: first, Scandinavian notes were not traded at par, then Scandinavian gold coins were prevented from circulating freely within Scandinavia, and finally coins were not traded at the one-to-one rate.[43] The union was officially terminated in the early 1920s although the political desire to maintain the union accounted for proposals to resurrect the Scandinavian monetary union later on.[44] Each member of the two multinational unions examined, the Latin and the Scandinavian one, continued to maintain a domestic monetary authority which facilitated the break-up of the union once it was subject to large disturbances.[45]

Other multinational unions were also dissolved in the twentieth century in Europe. The British–Irish currency board arrangement – which was a form of multinational monetary union – was terminated in the 1970s. Luxembourg established a central bank when it joined the European Central Bank system, ending the monetary union with Belgium that had lasted since the 1920s. These break-ups occurred with no major political tensions or repercussions.

To sum up, the dissolution of multinational monetary unions has been easy to carry out when each member country maintained a central bank of its own during the monetary union. The central banks of the nation states could rapidly re-establish the domestic 'national' monetary union.

National monetary unions

Several national monetary unions were terminated in the twentieth century and divided into smaller monetary areas. The two world wars contributed to the demise of some monetary unions: the Austro-Hungarian empire[46] and the Russian empire after the First World War; and the creation of new ones: the German monetary union after the Second World War splitting into two parts, one covered by Western and the other by Eastern Germany.

In the 1990s the national monetary unions of Soviet Union, Yugoslavia and Czechoslovakia broke up. The Ruble zone disintegrated in a lengthy process during the first half of the 1990s ending in a large number of new currency areas.[47] The Yugoslav monetary union in the face of a civil war collapsed into several new monetary unions – each associated with a new nation state and a new currency.[48]

The Czechs and Slovaks decided to form two nation states out of Czechoslovakia due to differences on politics and economics, but to remain in a monetary union until a later stage. The political break-up occurred on January 1st 1993 when the Czech republic and Slovakia separated. Political separation initiated expectations of a

Table 3.2 The dissolution of some monetary unions in the twentieth century

Monetary union	*Time of dissolution*	*Causes of dissolution*
National monetary unions		
Austria	1919–27	Defeat at war, creation of several new nation states
Russia	1918–20	Creation of several new nation states
Soviet Union	1992–4	Political unrest, creation of several new nation states
Yugoslavia	1991–4	Political unrest, civil war, rise of new states
Czechoslovakia	1993	Political divergences, rise of new nation states
Multinational monetary unions		
Latin monetary union	1914–27	Divergent monetary policies
Scandinavian monetary union	1914–24	Divergent monetary policies

Sources: Bordo and Jonung (1997), Garber and Spencer (1994: 36–7) and Goodhart (1995).

monetary separation, creating a divergence between the exchange rates of the new currencies. These expectations brought about monetary separation by February 1993, although so early a step had not been contemplated by the authorities.[49]

The common cause of these break-ups is found in the political process, not in the monetary union by itself nor in 'economic' forces. War and/or political disunity have brought about the dissolution of nation states. As a consequence of political separation monetary divorce followed. See Table 3.2 for a list of national monetary unions dissolved in the twentieth century.

The typical collapse has followed two paths. The first path was accompanied by fiscal and monetary turmoil and high inflation in some or all of the new monetary areas. This was the case of the dissolution of three European empires in the twentieth century, Austria-Hungary, Russia and the Soviet Union, as well as the dissolution of Yugoslavia. The second path was a more peaceful and orderly one. The dissolution of the monetary union of Czechoslovakia was an orderly affair, not accompanied by huge fiscal deficits and high inflation.

To sum up, when far-reaching political events cause the break-up of existing nation states into smaller nation states, monetary separation and divorce follows in almost all the cases we have studied.[50]

Summary: why are monetary unions created and dissolved?

According to our account of the establishment of monetary unions, the most important reason is that a national monetary union generally follows as part of the process of political unification. There are few examples in history of nation states, which are not a unified monetary area with a national currency unit of their own – and these have generally been very small states like Monaco, Andorra and Luxembourg.

Second are economic reasons, including a reduction in transaction costs by standardizing the coinage, gains from trade, access to wider markets and harmonization of policies. Third and finally, non-economic reasons besides political unification, including a common history, a common language, culture and religion have contributed to monetary unification. This is in particular the case with multinational monetary unions.

The causes of the break-up of national monetary unions are foremost found in political developments. Political unity is the glue that holds a monetary union together. Once that dissolves, it is most likely that the monetary union will dissolve.

Although we have argued that national monetary unity follows from political unity, we do not want to make a watertight separation between political and economic factors. They are closely interlinked. Political unity is based partially on economic conditions. As long as the economic gains from political unification outweigh the benefits from separation, the nation state will be a viable alternative, not running the risk of falling apart.

Within the nation state, political tensions created by economic differences between various regions and ethnic groups can result in the demise of the unity necessary for keeping the nation state together. The US civil war and the recent break-up of Czechoslovakia are examples of economic tensions that undermined political unity and hence monetary unity.

Most nation states have created – or create when deemed necessary – institutions and mechanisms to resolve domestic economic and political conflicts. Differences in economic outcomes are commonly alleviated by transfer payments. Tensions due to language, religion and culture can be reduced within the nation state through constitutional designs that allow a high degree of sovereignty for minority groups. Switzerland is an example of a nation state, as well as a monetary union, with widespread local political power to allow diversity in religion, language and culture. Most modern nation states, even federal ones, require substantial redistribution of income. Such redistribution may not be enough: fundamental differences between members, for example, due to religion and ethnicity, combined with political and/or economic shocks may produce break-ups of nation states and consequently of national monetary unions. Yugoslavia, Czechoslovakia and the Soviet Union are examples in the 1990s.

Our reading of the historical record, giving prominence to the 'political will' to explain the rise and fall of monetary unions, is consistent with the conclusions of other researchers. Cohen (1993: 190) argues from six case studies of monetary co-operation 'that political conditions are most instrumental in determining the sustainability of monetary cooperation among sovereign governments'. The term 'political conditions' covers the presence of a strong local hegemon or a dense network of institutional linkages. Cohen (1993: 188) concludes that 'Economic and organizational factors matter, but interstate politics appears to matter most of all.'[51]

The future of EMU: the lessons from history

Our history of monetary unions is based on a crucial distinction between national and multinational unions. When considering the future of EMU, we first should ask whether EMU will emerge as a national or a multinational monetary union? The answer is not obvious. The EMU-project is unique in the history of monetary unions. We have not found any clear and unambiguous historical precedent to EMU, where a group of monetarily and politically independent countries surrendered their national currencies to form a common monetary union based on a new unit of account under the leadership of a common monetary authority – while still retaining political independence. Monetary unification has heretofore followed political unification – not the other way around.

Political unity as a rule also entailed to some extent a centrally co-ordinated tax and expenditure system, thus allowing for central fiscal policies.[52] EMU is unique in the sense that monetary co-ordination within Euroland will be stronger than political and fiscal co-ordination.[53]

We are inclined to view EMU as closer to a national monetary union than to a multinational union for several reasons. EMU will have one common central bank, the ECB. It will eventually issue the only circulating money in Euroland. The previous central banks of the members of EMU will diminish in power and importance according to the Maastricht Treaty. They will most likely resemble the regional reserve banks of the Federal Reserve System of the US. This analogy suggests that they will not formulate a common European monetary policy. Monetary policy will be centralized on a pan-European level under the ECB. Furthermore, membership in EMU and the adoption of the Euro are regarded as permanent. There are no escape clauses. The Maastricht Treaty gives no country the right to leave EMU.[54]

This implies that, when forecasting the future of EMU, our conclusions derived from the history of national monetary unions are more relevant than those from the experience of multinational unions.[55] EMU involves considerably stronger monetary integration than was the case for the multinational unions of the past. We believe the closest historical parallel to EMU to be the national monetary unions of the United States, Italy and Germany.[56] These cases demonstrate how a complete monetary union, that is, the use of the same money as well as a common monetary policy across all jurisdictions, evolved over time. Initially all the institutions required for successful monetary policy, according to the conventional monetary policy wisdom of today, did not exist.

Starting from our critical assumption that EMU will be close to a national monetary union, we distil the following from the historical record.

(1) *EMU will be a flexible monetary union.* First of all, the history of monetary unification suggests that national monetary unions are permanent and flexible. They evolve over time in response to political and economic events. Their durability and flexibility is a consequence of the political process that once established monetary unity. EMU has been created by a strong will for political unity, despite a number of primarily 'economic' objections to the project. This political determination will likely design mechanisms and institutions to overcome the shortcomings of EMU that the initial set of rules and treaties embodied in the Eurosystem impose.

We initially listed several shortcomings, such as the absence of a lender of last resort and of a central authority supervising the financial system, lack of democratic control and accountability for the ECB, inconsistent policy directives for the ECB, lack of a central fiscal policy-making authority and Euroland not being an optimal currency area.

Seen from an evolutionary perspective, these shortcomings will likely be met by various solutions, emerging over time – just as they have emerged in national monetary unions. Thus, we do not regard this list per se as a major threat to the future of EMU. Indeed, current criticism by economists concerning the shortcomings of the Eurosystem lays the groundwork for future improvement. Policymakers will eventually respond where the critique is found deserving – a pattern that holds for general policy-making in an open society.

Let us briefly illustrate our interpretation by considering how shortcomings in the US monetary union were dealt with. A unified economy was created in the Constitutional Convention of 1789, which gave the Congress the power to coin and regulate the currency. It took another seven decades to create a complete uniform currency with the National Currency Act of 1863. The process involved two failed attempts to establish a central bank and the instability associated with state regulation of bank notes.

Establishment of a unified currency did not resolve the endemic problem in the nineteenth-century US financial system of periodic banking panics. Private mechanisms to provide emergency currency through the clearing houses and occasional interventions by the US Treasury were only successful in allaying several minor panics.

Major crises in 1893 and 1907 in which many banks failed and monetary contraction led to depression, were instrumental in the successful campaign to create a national lender of last resort and central bank by the Federal Reserve Act of 1913. Although the Federal Reserve System was empowered to act as a lender of last resort, it failed miserably in meeting banking panics in the early 1930s, thereby converting a not unusual contraction into the Great Depression. As a consequence of that experience the US developed an extensive financial regulatory network including deposit insurance, and the Federal Reserve Board finally evolved into an effective lender of last resort.

Moreover, the mechanisms to transfer fiscal resources from the federal government to the states in the face of shocks, were developed only many years after the monetary union was created. It took the shock of the Great Depression to devise an effective means for the federal government to transfer resources to the states.[57]

Our argument that institutions evolve in response to changing circumstances and requirements can be supported by the fact that European policy authorities have already displayed substantial flexibility in interpreting and adjusting to economic and political realities. The Maastricht criteria are tough on paper. In reality they have already been stretched incredibly in various ways, for example by allowing Belgium, Italy and others into the EMU in spite of their debt to GDP and deficit to GDP ratios being 'too' high.[58] Political desiderata have already overruled the rules of the Eurosystem.

The appointment of the first head of the ECB was something of a political farce but it was eventually solved by political will and flexibility. Regularly the financial press reports various proposals to adjust the statutes and structure of the EMU-system in response to different challenges. The system thus appears open to changes and revisions that will likely reduce its initial weakness and shortcomings.[59]

Of course, there is no guarantee that the Eurosystem will survive all future shocks, only that the system allows for mechanisms of self-correction and adjustment that increase its prospects for survival. Besides, we are not aware of any case in history in which a monetary union commenced with all the institutions required to function as prescribed by the modern view on monetary policy. Such institutions develop over time.

(2) *EMU will be hit by major shocks.* History shows that exceptional shocks and crises will eventually hit any monetary area. Countries like the US, Canada and Italy have been the subjects of asymmetric or region-specific shocks and structural shifts that have left permanent scars. The maritime provinces of Canada and Southern Italy have been struggling for long with comparative stagnation. In spite of transfers to these poor regions, their problems have not been solved. However, they have not led to the breakdown of political unity, splitting up the nation state, and thus the monetary union.

Major idiosyncratic disturbances and crises will hit EMU sooner or later. Judging from the record, national monetary unions survive such events except in the case of a collapse of the political unity underlying monetary unity. If EMU were to break-up, we conjecture that the initial cause would be a major exogenous shock that hits the members of the EMU asymmetrically. In addition political will may be lacking on the part of one or a group of EMU-countries to adjust to the common policy of the EMU. Here only fantasy limits the list of possible events or processes that could start a collapse of the EMU.[60]

(3) *EMU will be based on political unity.* Monetary unions of the past were in two important respects different from the present process leading to the common European currency. First, the national monetary unification of the eighteenth and nineteenth century followed *after* political unification and, second, they were based on specie. Consequently, monetary unification was a much simpler process than in the case of Euroland, thus also politically easier to carry through.

Countries that have joined the EMU today are on a fiat – not a specie – standard. Present European monetary unification is based on a commonly accepted politically decided commitment mechanism as opposed to the metallic standard of yesterday that had gold convertibility as a common focal point and commitment mechanism. The statutes of the ECB set out price stability as its 'principal objective'. A pre-condition for the EMU to succeed and be stable in the future is that the individual members of the EMU must display forever a similar commitment to this common goal, as did the advanced nations to the gold standard rule more than a century ago. This is most likely the major challenge facing EMU.

It is unclear how well EMU will succeed in maintaining such a convergence in policy preferences in the future. The process so far suggests that the political effort spent on creating EMU is probably greater compared to the political resources required to create the national monetary unions of the past. This demonstrates that EMU is basically a political project, reflecting a strong will to eventually create political unity within Europe.

The sequencing of events is reversed compared to the national unions of the past. Monetary unification has been used as a means of accomplishing the final aim of political unification. Political backing and support for EMU may be substantial at present but has to remain so in the future as well. The political imperative may remain strong as a result of the huge investment already made in the monetary unification process. However, we are reluctant to present any forecast on this matter. Political forces may turn and twist rapidly in the future.

The political economy of past national monetary unions also suggests that such arrangements are dominated by one or a few major economic powers in the centre, not by countries or members in the periphery. In the US, within the Federal Reserve system established in 1914, the Federal Reserve Bank of New York plays by tradition the most important role, in Italy the *Banca Nazionale nel Regno d'Italia* emerged eventually into the central bank and in Germany the state Bank of Prussia was the major element in the new *Reichsbank*, set up in 1875.[61]

This centre–periphery pattern has implications for the future working of the EMU, more specifically for the relationship between the major and minor member countries in the EMU. An obvious compensation for the loss of monetary sovereignty for a small or minor country from joining EMU is that it will take part in policy formation within the ECB. Judging from monetary history we should not, however, expect a peripheral country and thus a minor voice, to have a major influence on the decision-making process.

The political economy of the EMU will primarily be determined by the major powers among the members of the monetary union. If there were to be tension between for example Germany and France, the risk for the EMU to become unstable would increase. The EMU requires one dominating player or a strong coalition to function well.

(4) *EMU will not be an 'optimal' currency area.* A major objection of the economics profession to EMU is that it is not now and will not be an optimal currency area. History shows that the creation, reign and dissolution of national monetary unions have hardly any connection with the criteria spelled out in the literature on optimal currency area (OCA) inspired by the work of Mundell, McKinnon and Kenen. Instead, they have developed in a historical context as a result of the political process. The historical record suggests that the OCA-theory is not well suited to analyse the evolution of monetary unions as it lacks important political and historical dimensions. Thus it is not a promising concept for considering the future of EMU either.[62]

On this point see the succinct summary by Goodhart:

> The evidence therefore suggests that the theory of optimum currency areas has relatively little predictive power. Virtually all independent sovereign states have separate currencies, and changes in sovereign status lead rapidly to accompanying adjustments in monetary autonomy. The boundaries of states rarely coincide exactly with optimum currency areas, and changes in boundaries causing changes in currency domains rarely reflects shifts in optimum currency areas.
> (1995: 452)

To sum up, our emphasis on the political process as the major determinant of the future of the EMU is consistent with the views put forth by many researchers: see for example Cohen (1993, 1998), Corden (1972), Goodhart (1998) and Obstfeld (1998).

Conclusions

EMU is a unique construction without any clear precedent in monetary history. This suggests great caution when forecasting the future of EMU. However, we know that EMU will function as a national monetary union with one central bank and one common currency circulating within the union. We are therefore able to apply some forecasts based on the record of national monetary unions.

The major driving forces behind the establishment of national monetary unions as well as behind their dissolution are political ones. The 'economic' shortcomings noted by economists concerning the workings of the EMU need not spell disaster. They can be overcome by political forces as well as by market-based adjustment mechanisms.

The EMU and the ECB will be subject to major shocks in the future – just as is the case with any monetary area and its central bank. Monetary deficiencies or monetary problems that can be solved within the nation state should be solvable in a monetary union covering many nation states, given that the union is organized as a national monetary union with one type of money circulating within the whole union and with one central bank.

A major lesson from history is that monetary unification is an evolutionary process. EMU will evolve in the future in a way different from the existing plans for the EMU. This process, allowing the EMU to adapt and adjust to future disturbances, should properly be regarded as a policy learning process, where policy makers learn to cope with the shortcomings that emerge.[63] This process will continue as long as the political will to maintain the union is present. Once it disappears, the EMU may break apart. Judging from the history of national monetary unions such an outcome appears likely only under extreme circumstances.

Acknowledgements

This report builds upon and extends our previous work on the history of monetary unions, see Bordo and Jonung (1997). Anna Schwartz has generously helped us improve our arguments. We are greatly indebted to Pontus Hansson for research support and to Anders Bornefalk, Benjamin Cohen and Kurt Schuler for helpful suggestions.

Notes

1 Exceptions are Cohen (1993, 1998), Goodhart (1995) and Graboyes (1990).
2 For the history of the EMU-project see Gros and Thygesen (1997).
3 The shortcomings of the EMU have given rise to a flowering field of synonyms: 'sources of concern' (Eichengreen 1990), 'hazard area', 'weakness', 'potential fault lines' (Obstfeld 1998).

4 From a historical point of view, the sequencing of EMU, that is the lengthy step-by-step process involving ERM and the fulfilment of the Maastricht criteria etc., is without precedent. As we discuss below, monetary unions in the past have as a rule been introduced in a fairly rapid way without prior monetary and fiscal coordination.
5 This argument is set forth by *inter alia* Prati and Schinasi (1999).
6 See *inter alia* Prati and Schinasi (1999) and Obstfeld (1998).
7 See for example Feldstein (1997).
8 Monetary policy issues of the eurosystem are critically assessed by *inter alia* Begg *et al.* (1998), Buiter (1999) and Svensson (1999).
9 On the effects of the stability pact, see *inter alia* Eichengreen and Wyplosz (1998) and Flandreau, Le Cacheux and Zumer (1998). The counter-argument states that once EMU is created private agents will adjust to the new rules of the game and smooth shocks through other channels than through fiscal and monetary policies. See e.g. Melitz and Zumer (1998). See *inter alia* Alesina and Wacziarg (1998) on the weakness of the institutions of the EU.
10 The case of Ireland illustrates how monetary policy within a monetary union is determined by the centre, not the periphery.
11 See for example Eichengreen (1997).
12 See for example Obstfeld and Peri (1998) for a critical view of the effects of relatively low labour mobility within Europe.
13 See for example the discussion in Feldstein (1997). A more optimistic view is given by Wyplosz (1997).
14 The above list can be made longer. It could include the threat that election or political cycles within Europe may pose. When a majority of the EMU members face elections the same year, this will increase the risk of domestic expansive policies, threatening the EMU.
15 This argument is developed in Bordo and Jonung (1997).
16 The account of US monetary unification rests on *inter alia* the following contributions: McCallum (1992), Perkins (1994), Rolnick, Smith and Weber (1994) and Fraas (1974).
17 The legal tender status of a number of foreign currencies was abolished by the US Congress as late as in the 1850s. Cohen (1998: 34).
18 The account of the monetary unification of Italy is based on *inter alia* Fratianni and Spinelli (1985) and Sannucci (1989).
19 Venetia was incorporated in 1866 after Italy had participated on the Prussian side in her war against Austria. The Papal States were incorporated in 1870 when France, that until then had acted as a protector of the sovereignty of the Papal States, was engaged in war with Prussia.
20 See also the section on the Latin Monetary Union.
21 For an account of the fineness of coins, see the section on the Latin Monetary Union.
22 *Corso forzoso* translates broadly as 'forced circulation'.
23 The newly created *Banca d'Italia*, the *Banca di Napoli* and the *Banca di Sicilia*. The *Banca Romana* went into liquidation in 1893. Its business was taken over by the BNR.
24 There was an exception to the rule, however, as outstanding silver *Thalers* remained legal tender.
25 The termination of other banks' right to issue notes was not as straightforward as simply enacting a law forbidding it. Instead, the government allowed other state banks to continue to issue notes but to stipulate stringent rules concerning the denominations of the notes and the total amount issued. Private banks were forced to choose between issuing notes valid only in the region of the bank or performing their business nationwide.
26 This section is based on Griffiths (1991) and Redish (1993).
27 Of two possible explanations for the French resistance, one, mainly political, suggests that Napoleon III was planning a world monetary conference in 1867 where he hoped to be able to exchange French willingness to adopt the gold standard for universal adoption of the French monetary standard. He was thus unwilling to convert to a gold standard at this

stage. According to the other explanation, the Bank of France was concerned with the cost of redeeming outstanding silver coins in gold. This would stretch the Bank's reserves to the limit and Napoleon III, dependent on the Bank for loans, had to follow the Bank on this account.

28 This section is based on Jonung (1984) and Bergman, Gerlach and Jonung (1993).

29 Finland was at the time a grand-duchy of Russia. Iceland was governed by Denmark. Norway was formally part of a political union with Sweden but enjoyed far-reaching political independence.

30 The law proposed in the Swedish parliament in 1873 specifically mentioned the permanent costs emanating from the inflow of Danish and Norwegian silver coins.

31 The issue was debated at three meetings of Scandinavian economists: in 1863 in Gothenburg, in 1865 in Stockholm and in 1872 in Copenhagen.

32 The reasons for Norway's initial refusal to join the monetary union are not entirely clear. In any case, Norway joined the union two years later and, in doing so, accepted all the terms of the agreement. This was not particularly surprising since she had already introduced in 1873 all measures except the grant of legal tender status to Swedish and Danish coins.

33 The comparatively less widespread note circulation in Denmark may have induced the Danish central bank to treat the issue as less urgent. Notes represented 26 per cent of the circulation in Denmark, 41 per cent in Norway and 57 per cent in Sweden according to Henriksen, Kærgård and Sörensen (1994).

34 One event, however, suggests underlying political strains. In 1905, the Swedish central bank cancelled its participation in the 1885 agreement. However, a new renegotiated agreement quickly followed which allowed each central bank to charge the other banks when selling drawing rights. This option was not used for five years, and then by Norway and Denmark. The action of the Swedish central bank in 1905 may have been motivated by a desire to show its resentment that Norway had secured independence from Sweden that year.

35 This section is based on Cohen (1993) and Graboyes (1990).

36 For a description of the workings and history of currency boards, see Hanke, Jonung and Schuler (1993) and Schwartz (1992).

37 Cohen (1993) and appendix C in Hanke, Jonung and Schuler (1993).

38 More specifically, the members are Benin, Burkina Faso, Cameroon, Central African Republic, Chad, Congo, Equatorial Guinea, Gabon, Ivory Coast, Mali, Niger, Senegal and Togo.

39 In 1994, though, the CFA franc was devalued by 50 per cent.

40 The members are Anguilla, Antigua and Barbuda, Dominica, Grenada, St Kitts-Nevis, St Lucia and St Vincent and the Grenadines.

41 The section on the monetary union between Ireland and Britain is based on Bradley and Whelan (1992).

42 See Bordo and Jonung (1998) for an account of the international experience of the interaction of monetary and fiscal policies since the 1880s.

43 See the account of Bergman, Gerlach and Jonung (1993) and of Bergman (1999).

44 Recently, as a response to the creation of EMU, a Finnish–Swedish monetary union has been proposed as an alternative to Finnish and Swedish membership in the EMU. See Jonung and Sjöholm (1999).

45 The existence of a domestic central bank was an important prerequisite for the expansionary fiscal policies carried out during the First World War. Central banks in belligerent countries monetized the huge budget deficits emerging as a result of the financing of the war effort. See Bordo and Jonung (1998).

46 See Garber and Spencer (1994) and Dornbusch (1992).

47 This account is based on Bornefalk (1998).

48 This account is based on Kraft (1995) and Wyzan (1993).

49 See Fidrmuc and Horváth (1998) and Garber and Spencer (1994).

50 The independence of Norway from Sweden in 1905 and Ireland from the United Kingdom in the 1920s are exceptions in the sense that the monetary co-operation between the various countries continued *after* political separation.

51 Cohen (1993) examines the record of six multinational unions. He does not deal with the case of any national monetary union as defined by us. His conclusions concerning the role of political factors would most likely be strengthened if had also considered national monetary unions.

52 See also Goodhart (1995: 465): 'The domain of a single currency has generally had the same boundaries as its central political and fiscal system, and areas with independent currencies have likewise had separate political and fiscal centres.'

53 EMU is often regarded as a method for accomplishing political and fiscal unification. Once Europe has a common currency, it will rapidly move towards a federal state according to a common interpretation.

54 The Scandinavian monetary union had an explicit right for any member to leave the union. See Jonung (1999a).

55 However, we are aware that to some extent EMU will resemble a multinational monetary union. There is not complete central co-ordination of the political and fiscal systems of the member states. Monetary centralization goes before political and fiscal centralization. However, in our opinion EMU still is closer to the workings of a national monetary union than to a multinational union.

56 The US currency union is commonly used as a benchmark by economists when examining various issues of the process of European monetary unification.

57 See Wallis and Oates (1998)

58 See Obstfeld (1998: 24) and others.

59 On this point see for example the analysis of von Hagen and Fratianni (1993: 184) who conclude that 'The Maastricht agreement leaves many options to design the monetary and financial market institutions of the EMU.' Tietmeyer (1999) stressed the options that will be available for the Eurosystem in case of future disturbances.

60 For one account for potential causes of dissolution of the EMU, stressing the interplay between politics and economics, see Feldstein (1997).

61 The history of international exchange rate regimes suggests a similar pattern with the center having a strong influence on monetary policies: the United Kingdom was the hegemon of the classical gold standard, sometimes working in co-operation with France and Germany. The short-lived inter-war gold standard was dominated by the actions of the United Kingdom, the US and France. The United States played the key role in the Bretton Woods system. The ERM-arrangement that failed in 1992–3 was based on the policies of the *Bundesbank*.

62 Similar conclusions concerning the OCA-approach are found in Cohen (1993: 200). Goodhart (1998) examines two alternative concepts of money, concluding that the 'cartalist' approach has a firmer empirical foundation than the monetary theory underlying OCA-theory.

63 The learning process of US policy-makers was recently analysed by Sargent (1998) and of Swedish policy makers by Jonung (1999b).

References

Alesina, A. and R. Wacziarg (1998) 'Is Europe Going to Far?', paper prepared for the Carnegie-Rochester Conference on Public Policy, November 1998.

Begg, D., P. Grauwe, F. Giavazzi, H. Uhlig and C. Wyplosz (1998) 'The ECB: Safe at any speed?', *Monitoring the European Central Bank*, *1*(1). CEPR.

Bergman, M. (1999) 'Do Monetary Unions Make Economic Sense? Evidence from the Scandinavian Currency Unions 1873–1913', mimeo, University of Lund, *Scandinavian Journal of Economics, 101.*

Bergman, M., S. Gerlach and L. Jonung (1993) 'The Rise and Fall of the Scandinavian Currency Union 1873–1920', *European Economic Review*, *37*.

Bordo, M. D. and L. Jonung (1997) 'The history of monetary regimes – some lessons for Sweden and the EMU', *Swedish Economic Policy Review*, *4*.

Bordo, M. D. and L. Jonung (1998) 'A Return to the Convertibility Principle? Monetary and Fiscal Regimes in Historical Perspective. The International Evidence,' in Leijonhufvud, A., ed., *Monetary Theory as a Basis for Monetary Policy*. Macmillan, London.

Bornefalk, A. (1998) 'The Break-up of the Ruble Zone. The Political Economy of a Collapsing Monetary Union', Working Paper, Stockholm School of Economics, Stockholm.

Bradley, J. and K. Whelan (1992) 'Irish Experience of Monetary Linkages with the United Kingdom and Developments since joining the EMS', in Barrell, R., ed., *Economic Convergence and Monetary Union in Europe*. Sage, London.

Buiter, W. B. (1999) 'Alice in Euroland', Working Paper, Faculty of Economics and Politics, Cambridge, *Journal of Common Market Studies*, *37*.

Cohen, B. J. (1993) 'Beyond EMU: the Problem of Sustainability', *Economics and Politics*, *5*.

Cohen, B. J. (1998) *The Geography of Money*. Cornell University Press, Ithaca, NJ, and London.

Corden, W. M. (1972) 'Monetary Integration', *Essays in International Finance*, No. 93, April. Princeton, NJ.

Dornbusch, R. (1992) 'Monetary Problems of Post-Communism: Lessons from the End of the Austro-Hungarian Empire', *Weltwirtschaftliches Archiv*, pp. 391–424.

Eichengreen, B. (1990) 'One Money for Europe? Lessons from the US Currency Union', *Economic Policy*, *5*.

—— (1996) 'Déjà vu All Over Again: Lessons from the Gold Standard for European Monetary Unification', in Bayoumi, T., B. Eichengreen and M. Taylor, eds, *Modern Perspectives on the Gold Standard*. Cambridge University Press, Cambridge.

—— (1997) 'Is Europe an Optimum Currency Area?', in Eichengreen, B., *European Monetary Unification: Theory, Practice, and Analysis*. MIT Press, Cambridge, MA.

—— and C. Wyplosz (1998) 'The Stability Pact: More than a Minor Nuisance?', in Begg, D. *et al.*, eds, *EMU: Prospects and Challenges for the Euro*, special issue of *Economic Policy*. Blackwell, Oxford.

Feldstein, M. (1997) 'The Political Economy of the European Economic and Monetary Union: Political Sources of an Economic Liability', *Journal of Economic Perspectives*, *11*.

Fidrmuc, J. and Horváth, J. (1998) 'Stability of Monetary Unions: Lessons from the Break-up of Czechoslovakia', Working Paper from Center for Economic Research, Tilburg University.

Flandreau, M., J. Le Cacheux and F. Zumer (1998) 'Stability Without a Pact? Lessons from the European Gold Standard, 1880–1914', in Begg, D. *et al.*, eds, *EMU: Prospects and Challenges for the Euro*, special issue of *Economic Policy*, Blackwell, Oxford.

Fraas, A. (1974) 'The Second Bank of the United States: An Instrument for Interregional Monetary Union', *Journal of Economic History*, *34*.

Fratianni, M. and F. Spinelli (1985) 'Currency Competition, Fiscal Policy and the Money Supply Process in Italy from Unification to World War I', *Journal of European Economic History*, *14*(3).

Garber, P. and Spencer, M. (1994) 'The Dissolution of the Austro-Hungarian Empire: Lessons for Currency Reform', *Essays in International Finance*, No. 191, February.

Goodhart, C. A. E. (1995) 'The Political Economy of Monetary Union', in Kenen, P., ed., *Understanding Interdependence. The Macroeconomics of the Open Economy*. Princeton University Press, Princeton, NJ.

——(1998) 'The Two Concepts of Money: Implications for the Analysis of Optimal Currency Areas', *European Journal of Political Economy, 14.*

Graboyes, R. F. (1990) 'The EMU: Forerunners and Durability', *Federal Reserve Bank of Richmond Economic Review, 16* (July/August).

Griffiths, M. L. (1991) 'Monetary Union in Europe: Lessons from the Nineteenth Century', Workshop Paper, Virginia Polytechnic Institute and State University.

Gros, D. and N. Thygesen (1997) *European Monetary Integration. From the European Monetary System to European Monetary Union.* Longman, London.

von Hagen, J. and M. Fratianni (1993) 'The Transition to European Monetary Union', *Economics and Politics, 5.*

Hanke, S., L. Jonung and K. Schuler (1993) *Russian Currency and Finance. A Currency Board Approach to Reform.* Routledge, London.

Henriksen, I., N. Kærgård and C. Sörensen (1994) 'Den skandinaviske möntunion', *Den jyske historiker, 69–70.*

Holtfrerich, C.-L. (1993) 'Did Monetary Unification Precede or Follow Political Unification of Germany in the 19th Century', *European Economic Review, 37.*

Jonung, L. (1984) 'Swedish Experience Under the Classical Gold Standard 1873–1913', in Bordo M. D. and A. Schwartz, eds, *The Classical Gold Standard in Retrospective.* University of Chicago Press/National Bureau of Economic Research.

——(1999a) 'Den skandinaviska myntunionen 1875–1920. Vad säger den om EMU idag?', mimeo, Stockholm School of Economics.

——(1999b) *Looking Ahead Through the Rear-View Mirror. Swedish Stabilization Policy as a Learning Process, 1970–1995. A Summary.* Ministry of Finance, Stockholm.

—— and F. Sjöholm (1999) 'Should Finland and Sweden Form a Monetary Union?', *The World Economy, 22*(5).

Kindleberger, C. P. (1981b) *A Financial History of Western Europe.* George Allen & Unwin, London.

Kraft, E. (1995) 'Stabilising Inflation in Slovenia, Croatia and Macedonia: How Independence Has Affected Macroeconomic Policy Outcomes', *Europe-Asia Studies, 47.*

Lerner, E. M. (1956) 'Inflation in the Confederacy, 1861–65', in Friedman, M., ed., *Studies in the Quantity Theory of Money.* University of Chicago Press, Chicago.

McCallum, B. T. (1992) 'Money and Prices in Colonial America: a New Test of Competing Theories', *Journal of Political Economy, 100.*

Melitz, J. and F. Zumer (1998) 'Interregional and International Risk Sharing and Lessons for EMU', paper prepared for the Carnegie-Rochester Conference, November 1998.

Mundell, R. (1961) 'A Theory of Optimum Currency Areas', *American Economic Review, 51.*

Obstfeld, M. (1998) 'EMU: Ready, or not?', *NBER Working Papers series*, no 6682, August 1998.

Obstfeld, M. and G. Peri (1998) 'Regional Non-Adjustment and Fiscal Policy', in Begg, D. *et al.*, eds, *EMU: Prospects and Challenges for the Euro*, special issue of *Economic Policy*. Blackwell, Oxford.

Perkins, E. J. (1994) *American Public Finance and Financial Services, 1700–1815.* Ohio State University Press, Columbus, OH.

Prati, A. and G. Schinasi (1999) 'Financial Stability in European Economic and Monetary Union', *IMF Working Paper*, IMF, Washington DC, December 1998.

Redish, A. (1993) 'The Latin Monetary Union and the Emergence of the International Gold Standard', in Bordo, M. D., and F. Capie, eds, *Monetary Regimes in Transition.* Cambridge University Press, Cambridge.

Rolnick, A. J., B. D. Smith and W. E. Weber (1994) 'The Origins of the Monetary Union in the United States', in Siklos, P., ed., *Varieties of Monetary Experiences.* Kluwer, Boston, MA.

Sannucci, V. (1989) 'The Establishment of a Central Bank: Italy in the Nineteenth Century', in De Cecco, M. and A. Giovannini, eds, *A European Central Bank*. Cambridge University Press, Cambridge.

Sargent, T. (1998) *The Conquest of American Inflation*. Manuscript, Stanford University.

Schwartz, A. (1992) *Do Currency Boards Have a Future?* Institute of Economic Affairs Occasional Paper 88, London.

Svensson, L. (1999) 'Monetary Policy Issues for the Eurosystem', Working Paper, IIES, Stockholm.

Tietmeyer, H. (1999) 'The Eurosystem's Approach to Monetary Stability'. Lecture delivered to the Swedish Economic Association in Stockholm, 12 April 1999.

Vanthoor, W. (1996) *European Monetary Union Since 1848. A Political and Historical Analysis*. Edward Elgar, Cheltenham.

Wallis, J. J. and W. E. Oates (1998) 'The Impact of the New Deal on American Federalism', in Bordo, M. D., C. Goldin and E. White, eds, *The Defining Moment: the Great Depression and the American Economy in the Twentieth Century*. University of Chicago Press, Chicago.

Wyplosz, C. (1997) 'EMU: Why and How It Might Happen', *Journal of Economic Perspectives, 11*.

Wyzan, M. (1993) 'Monetary Independence and Macroeconomic Stabilization in Macedonia: An Initial Assessment', *Communist Economies and Economic Transformation, 5*.

Comments on Chapter 3 – The future of EMU

Tim Congdon

Bordo and Jonung have written a fascinating paper, which combines topicality with an impressive historical sweep. They differentiate national from multi-national monetary unions, and emphasize the interconnections between national monetary integration and political union. Arguably their most important conclusion is that, 'Political unity is the glue that holds a monetary union together. Once that dissolves, it is most likely that the monetary union will dissolve.' They go on to observe that European economic and monetary union is 'unique', because they could not find any precedent for politically independent nations surrendering 'their national currencies to form a common monetary union based on a new unit of account under the leadership of a common monetary authority'.

In the light of this uniqueness, their decision to categorize EMU as a national monetary union (rather than a multi-national union) is perhaps surprising. They justify the decision by noting that the European single currency area is to have only one central bank issuing the 'only circulating money'. They further suggest that the existing national central banks 'will most likely resemble the regional reserve banks of the Federal Reserve System' of the USA. Their views may be right, but some significant differences between the American and European arrangements need to be highlighted. Whereas in the USA the Federal Reserve Board in Washington is undoubtedly the dominant institution, several of the national central banks in the euro-zone at present have larger budgets and staffs than the European Central Bank itself. With the national central banks understandably feeling themselves threatened, they have preserved such important functions as banking supervision and hindered the ECB's attempts to take control of all the traditional central bank roles.

More fundamentally, the USA has a Federal government with extensive tax-raising powers, and prerogatives and duties that are far greater than any of the 50 state governments. By contrast, the nation states in the euro-zone remain largely in control of tax and public expenditure, and have resisted extensions of the European Union's right to tax revenue much beyond 1½ per cent of gross domestic product. Of course, fiscal and monetary structures interact in several ways. As the Maastricht Treaty recognized, constraints have to be placed on nations' budget deficits and governments' ability to borrow from the central bank in order to stop the over-issue of base money. It remains to be seen whether Europe's governments will tolerate these constraints in the long run. A fair comment is that – if the euro-zone is 'a national monetary union' – it is a far less complete example of such a union than the USA.

Also important are the level and distribution of seigniorage, which may be understood generally as the profits that accrue from money issue.[1] As Bordo and Jonung note, one of the obstacles to monetary union in early nineteenth-century Germany was that the principalities wanted to safeguard 'their seigniorage gains', which would be eliminated if a monetary union were formed and they lost the right to issue coins. Again, after 1870 the integrity of the Latin Monetary Union was undermined by the Italian government's tendency to run an excessive budget deficit. This led to the devaluation of the lira and the export of Italian silver coins, which were legal tender in other members of the union. 'Obviously, this enabled the Italian government to finance part of her deficits with seigniorage, the cost of which was shared by all four countries, that is, Italy, France, Belgium and Switzerland.' In view of these historical warnings, it is worrying that the seigniorage key in the Maastricht Treaty has not yet become operational. The key was originally intended to become effective with the legal introduction of the euro, but has been suspended until euro-denominated notes and coin start circulating.[2]

Bordo and Jonung's discussion of the development, and occasional breakdown, of previous monetary unions is thought-provoking. However, it suffers at times from too much hindsight. From an historical standpoint, it is a misunderstanding to equate monetary unification with the establishment of a well-defined central bank. When the new constitution of the USA took effect in 1789, the words 'central bank' had not been used in their modern sense. (Sir Francis Baring, writing in a pamphlet of 1797, was the first banker to characterize the Bank of England as *le dernier resort* in a crisis.) During the process of Italian political unification from 1859 to 1870, the directors of the Bank of England denied that their institution differed in essential respects from other privately owned banks in the United Kingdom. They would have rejected the notion that they ran 'a central bank', even if they had recognized the phrase. It was as late as 1866 that Hankey repudiated

> the most mischievous doctrine ever broached in the monetary and Banking world in this country; viz., that it is one of the proper functions of the Bank of England to keep ready money available at all times to supply the demands of Bankers who have rendered their own assets unavailable.[3]

The absence of a centralized note issue from the USA and Italy at an early stage in their nation building therefore does not imply that – by the standards of their times – they had backward currency systems or incomplete monetary unions. The centralization of the note issue occurred in association with and depended upon the emergence of central banks, but that did not happen anywhere in the world until the late nineteenth century. Most historians would regard England as a meaningful monetary union from at least the seventeenth century, if not earlier. But – if England was a monetary union in the eighteenth century despite having a multiplicity of note issues – the USA was also a monetary union in the early nineteenth century and Italy was a monetary union in the 1870s. The essence of union was the recognition of a common unit of account and a more or less satisfactory standardization of the coinage. The processes of centralizing the note issue and inter-bank clearing undoubtedly make a monetary union better integrated and more efficient, but they should not be confused with the process of monetary unification itself.

Notes

1 The term 'seigniorage' is surprisingly ambiguous. Its general meaning is clear enough, 'the profit accruing to the state from the issue of money', but the details are not. In a commodity money world this could be equated with the difference between the face value of coins and the intrinsic value of the metal content; in a paper money world it became much larger, because of the gap between the face value of notes and their printing costs. However, central banks also make a profit by earning a higher interest return on their assets than on their liabilities, while sometimes the proceeds of the inflation tax are deemed to be part of seigniorage. In the context of European currency unification, the preferred term has been 'monetary income', but this also has been an elusive concept. Disagreements have arisen between the ECB and the national central banks, and indeed between the different NCBs, about the exact meaning of 'monetary income'.

2 'Dispute over ESCB profits', *Central Banking*, spring 1997 and 'Tug-of-war over ESCB profits', *Central Banking*, August 1998. Central Banking Publications, London.

3 Hankey, Thomas (1876/1993) 'Banking in Connection with the Currency and the Bank of England', in *The Principles of Banking*, 3rd edn, reprinted in Collins, Michael, ed., *Central Banking in History*. Edward Elgar, Aldershot.

Comments on Chapter 3 – The future of EMU

Charles Goodhart

The main lesson of history, which Bordo and Jonung stress, is that the record of monetary unions tells us that the success, or failure, of monetary unions is basically determined by the political cohesion of the members of that union. Political issues are centre-stage, and economic developments influence the outcome largely in so far as they affect the political attitudes of the members of the union. In my view, the authors are absolutely right in this respect. It is, of course, a thesis which Professor B. J. Cohen has argued for several years; and also one which I have supported. I have no criticisms whatsoever to make of their historical sections, which form the greater part of the paper; and I recommend it to all those interested in the EMU process.

As they say towards the end of their paper, 'EMU is basically a political project, reflecting a strong will to create eventually political unity within Europe.' Yes, indeed, but whose strong will has been driving the EMU process forward? I would argue that this process has represented the triumph of the political elite over the conservative masses, who continue to exhibit a considerable inertia. I would assert that the elite in all the major northern countries, certainly in France, Germany, and to some considerable extent in the UK also, have been in favour of the Euro.

In Germany, however, if opinion polls are to be trusted, there has always been a majority of the public against giving up the DM, and opposed to its substitution by the Euro. No referendum on the issue was ever attempted in Germany. Attempts by a few politicians to use the unpopularity of the Euro to bolster their own political position were undermined by the seductive syllogism (often attributed to Kohl) that, 'A vote against the Euro is a vote for nationalism, and a vote for nationalism is a vote for'. In France, majority support for the Euro, despite the backing of virtually all the elite, was slight as shown in the referendum where there was a '*petit oui*'. And in the UK, of course, opinion polls have consistently shown the public to be opposed. Much the same has been true in Scandinavia.

Support for the Euro is, however, rock-solid in the Mediterranean countries, particularly where entry to the Euro is seen as equivalent to playing in the premier league of Europe. Again, support is very strong in the smaller states, and in those which are large recipients of Euro transfers from Brussels. Nevertheless, if one takes the major north-central European countries, it is arguable whether there really is a strong, common desire by the common people, as contrasted with the elite, to join the Euro. Whether this lukewarm political support, at least so far, will matter for the future development of the European Monetary Union, if the economic going should get rough, has yet to be seen.

In this respect, I must also applaud the brilliant sequencing strategy of those who brought about the founding of EMU, notably Delors, Kohl and Mitterrand. As far as the ordinary person on the street is concerned, the main change affecting her will occur when the Euro notes and coins are substituted for their national currency. Those of you old enough to remember will have recalled how unpopular the shift to decimalization in the UK was over twenty years ago. But that change did not involve the main unit, the pound, and many of the coins remained unchanged and identical; moreover it was a change from a complex system to a much simpler and easier system to understand. Nevertheless there was, at the time at least, widespread disaffection, belief that the change led to prices being rounded up and general unhappiness. Moreover, most currency reforms elsewhere have represented decimal shifts, knocking several zeros off an overinflated currency. Even these were, certainly at the time, generally unpopular, as in the shift from old to new francs. Moreover the difficulties of doing such a reform can be appreciated by the fact that neither Italy, where the basic unit is 1000 lira, nor Japan, where the basic unit is effectively 100 yen, have felt able to make such a simple and obvious currency reform. In the case of the Euro, however, the change is not going to be a simple decimal shift, but a change that will involve five significant places, a truly barbarous fraction, in moving from Euro to national currency, or back again. When it happens, it will be, I expect, deeply unpopular. It was, as I have already claimed, a master stroke, to leave this shift in national currencies into Euro notes and coins for several years, until the operation of Euro wholesale markets and the central monetary and macro institutions for the ESCB had already fully bedded down. The Euro, in effect, would be a fait accompli, before the implications of the change would seriously affect the ordinary person in the street. A master stroke of sequencing by the elite in command of the EMU process, which one must salute and admire!

Towards the end of their paper, the authors argue that the EMU will be a very flexible monetary union; and, in particular, that there will be substantial flexibility in interpreting and adjusting to economic and political realities.

> The Maastricht criteria are tough on paper. In reality they have already been stretched incredibly in various ways, for example by allowing Belgium, Italy and others into the EMU in spite of their debt to GDP and deficit to GDP ratios being 'too' high.

The authors, therefore, appear to believe that the Maastricht criteria, and presumably also the Stability and Growth Pact fiscal constraints, will be overturned, and are becoming a dead letter. It is true, I believe, that the limits on the debt ratio have been effectively abandoned. But the same is not the case, at any rate not yet, for the deficit ratio, which forms the centrepiece of the Stability and Growth Pact.

There is, indeed, a need, in my view, for some limitations on possible fiscal over-expansion by countries within the Eurozone, particularly now that the implications for interest rates and exchange rates would initially, at any rate, be much more muted. The precise nature of the constraints included in the Stability and Growth Pact, and the original Maastricht Treaty, were not, in my view, optimal. Nevertheless, they do provide an underpinning, and a degree of safety, for financial markets within the Eurozone. At the moment, markets are treating the bond issues of the respective governments within the Eurozone as effectively identical with respect to credit risk. If the Stability Pact should be openly flouted and thrown aside, it would remain to be seen how markets and governments would then react. It would be very interesting to observe.

Indeed, the whole EMU process is both fascinating and unique; never before in history have a number of separate national, sovereign countries agreed to pool their sovereign control over money within the adoption of a single federal monetary system. While this experiment has been driven by the strong political will and desire of the elite in the member countries, I, for one, have fears that it may prove fragile against adverse shocks, so long as the enthusiasm of the elite is not shared by a much larger proportion of their ordinary countrymen.

Let me finally try to tie this together with the discussion of fiscalism, which arose in the discussion of Professor B. McCallum's first paper on 'Theoretical Issues Pertaining to Monetary Union'. Under 'The Fiscal Theory of Price Level Determination', there are only two allowed methods for paying off debt. The first is by raising net tax revenues, relative to expenditures; the second is through a form of inflation tax. Consequently, under this theory, if there is no political will to raise the primary surplus, then the inevitable way in which the existing debt is effectively reduced must be through an inflation tax. Even when the money stock is tightly controlled, equilibrium can only be achieved by reducing the level of debt, to that which people are prepared to hold, through some measure of inflation. So, inflation has to be the equilibrium outcome.

The key assumption, however, is to rule out any possibility of another way of dealing with excessive debt, which is direct default. Given the lack of will in certain cases to raise the primary surplus, the decision whether to default, or to allow a massive inflationary tax, would not necessarily go in favour of the latter. Moreover, markets, faced with the prospect of either being defrauded by inflation or by direct default, would raise interest rates in advance of either event so rapidly and so fiercely that governments would rapidly be faced with the impossibility of raising more debt on such markets, and should monetary growth still be controlled, (as it would be by the ECB in EMU), would then be forced into default. The market process would seem much more likely to drive excessive deficit countries within the Eurozone into default than into hyperinflation, given the inability to control monetary growth for such a debt-raising government body. It is against this background that the limitations on the ability of member countries within the Eurozone to increase their debt without limit by raising deficits above 3 per cent of GDP should be seen.

4 How long did it take the United States to become an optimal currency area?

Hugh Rockoff

The troubled history of the American monetary union

The US monetary union began with the ratification of the Constitution in 1788. It has remained intact, with the exception of the Civil War years, ever since. And the United States has grown and prospered during that time. But it does not follow that the United States has grown and prospered because it has had a monetary union. The benefits of the monetary union – the relative ease with which interregional movements of capital, labor, and final products could take place – are evident. The costs of the monetary union, that I intend to focus upon here, are less evident, but nonetheless important.

Throughout the first 150 years of the US monetary union, at least, the United States was wracked repeatedly by bitter regional disputes over monetary policies and institutions. On more than one occasion, those disputes contributed to uncertainty about the future of policies and institutions that exacerbated economic disturbances, and contributed to mistakes in national monetary policy. Regional disputes over monetary policy arose because of real differences in regional interests: What was good monetary policy from the point of view of one region, was sometimes bad policy from the point of view of another. The most bitter disputes arose when adverse monetary reactions occurred in a region already suffering from a real shock. A decline in the demand for agricultural products, for example, would depress incomes, leading in turn to a round of bank failures and bank runs, and declining regional money supplies, that reinforced the effect of the initial shock. In short, an economic historian who is looking for illustrations of the cost of relinquishing monetary autonomy can find them in abundance in the monetary history of the United States.

Before turning to the history, however, I want to briefly summarize the theory of optimum currency areas to provide the necessary background for the remainder of the paper.

The theory of optimal currency areas

The optimum currency area hypothesis grew out of the debate over fixed vs. flexible exchange rates. Milton Friedman (1953), Leland Yeager (1959), and others had argued that a country could be better off by allowing its currency to float, and reserving domestic monetary policy for price or employment stability. The advocates of flexible exchange rates had recognized that a country could be too small to profit from flexible rates. But it was Robert Mundell, who first used the term "Optimum Currency Area" in a famous paper published in 1961, who clarified the circumstances under which a region or country would benefit from joining a monetary union.[1] On the one hand, Mundell argued, there were advantages for a region that joined a monetary union derived from minimizing transaction costs. On the other hand there were disadvantages derived from giving up the exchange rate, and changes in the stock of money, as policy tools. Whether a particular region constituted an optimal currency area or whether it would be better off as part of a larger monetary union depended on the net sum of these costs and benefits.

The benefits of a larger monetary union are usually fairly easy to see, although measuring them can be difficult. People can travel from one part of the country to another without having to convert their money; prices of products sold in distant regions can be compared without having to search for information or perform calculations, and interregional investments can be made without the risk of currency fluctuations.

The costs of joining a monetary union are less obvious, and will depend on a number of factors. Consider first the case in which economic activity is distributed randomly throughout the monetary union. Then the monetary authority need pay little attention to regions. What is optimal for one part of the country will be optimal for another. But suppose that the monetary union is divided into two regions, say East and West, that specialize in producing different goods, say steel and wheat. Now it is possible for there to be significant shifts in demand between the regions. The demand for steel might go up, while the demand for wheat is going down. To use the modern jargon, the country might be subject to asymmetric shocks. The West will run a balance of payments deficit with the East. Reserves will flow from West to East, and the stock of money in the West will fall, aggravating the recession caused by the decline in the demand for wheat. The stock of money in the East will rise, adding to the boom caused by the increase in the demand for steel. It is no longer clear that what is good for one region is good for all. The West might be better off with a national monetary policy that aimed to restore full employment, while the East might want a policy directed toward price stability.

If labor and capital are mobile across regions, then the impact of asymmetric shocks will be limited. Labor, for example, will respond to the shift in demand by moving from West to East, from wheat production and into steel production. The monetary authority will be able to neglect the problem of unemployment and focus on price stability. But now suppose that barriers to labor and capital mobility exist among regions, and assume further that monetary policy can affect real magnitudes in the short-run, say because certain prices or wages are sticky. Then the monetary authority faces a real dilemma. If the monetary authority follows a policy consistent with price stability in the East, it might aggravate the recession in the West; if it tilts full against the recession in the West, it might produce inflation in the East.

The East and West, to put it slightly differently, would be better off with separate currencies, and floating or at least adjustable rates between them. When demand shifted from the West to the East, the western currency would depreciate, mitigating the effects of the decline in demand. Meanwhile the monetary authority in the East could follow a policy aimed at price stability.

This is essentially the theory as originally developed by Mundell. The story depends on imperfections in capital and labor markets, and price and wage stickiness. As we move from the world of Keynesian or classic Monetarist economics, where monetary policy has important short-run effects, to assumptions of perfect labor and capital mobility and ineffective monetary policy, the case for subdividing economic regions into separate currency areas weakens. Nevertheless, as a number of writers have argued, a case for separate currencies may remain (Willett and Wihlborg 1999). For example, even if all factor markets cleared, a separate currency area could be justified if non-optimal policies were being followed outside the area. A flexible exchange rate then would prevent the importation of non-optimal price level movements.

One must also distinguish between the initial conditions and the long-run equilibrium. As Mundell (1973) has noted, the formation of a monetary union will set in motion forces that tend to create a more perfect monetary union. The question is how long will it take for a unified currency area to become an optimal currency area? I believe, as I will try to show below, that American monetary history offers important historical examples of regional monetary trends exacerbating the effects of asymmetric real shocks, and that it took a long time for the United States to become an optimal currency area. Before turning to the examples of problems within the American monetary union, I want to briefly recount the origins of the American monetary union.

Union

Prior to the Revolution the currency of the United States varied from colony to colony. The British pound, and other forms of hard currency such as the Spanish peso were accepted everywhere. But individual colonies also tried to make their own paper currencies legal tenders in order to provide revenues or to aid debtors. Under the Articles of Confederation (during the interregnum between the end of the Revolution and the Constitution) opinion, especially among the politically sophisticated, turned against paper money. The Constitution prohibited the states from issuing "bills of credit" (paper money) and gave to Congress the exclusive right to "coin money" and "establish the value thereof", thus creating a monetary union based on specie.

Part of the opposition to paper money was based on the experience of the very high rates of inflation under the fiat paper money regime of the Revolution. Tom Paine, for example, went from being an advocate of paper money to an opponent (Schweitzer 1989: 315) after witnessing the Revolutionary inflation. Opposition to paper money was increased by the development of fractional reserve banking, and the hope that bank notes would provide the convenience of government issued paper without the risk of over-issue.

There was also an important regional dimension to the opposition to state issued paper money. Rapid deflation after the Revolution had left farmers with heavy debt burdens. In the western counties of many states, where agriculture predominated, demands for debt and tax relief became insistent. States attempted to handle the problem in various ways. Some, such as Massachusetts, followed a get-tough policy with farmers who refused to pay. In many of these states farmers took up arms. The most serious outbreak of violence was in Massachusetts where Shays' Rebellion was crushed in 1787. Other states, such as Rhode Island, tried to help farmers by issuing legal-tender paper money and insisting that creditors accept it, even if they were residents of other states. While such policies pacified western farmers, they increased tensions among the states. It is conceivable that interstate tensions, such as those that arose between Rhode Island and its neighbors, could have been resolved by a clause in the Constitution requiring states to keep their currencies at par. But this would still leave room for some states to increase their seignorage by expanding their currencies and allowing them to circulate outside their own borders. Thus, a monetary union was viewed as a prerequisite for a political union (Rolnick, Smith, and Weber 1993).

The Constitution appeared to settle the debate between those states that would have used monetary policy to help western farmers and those that would not. But the issue reemerged in the debates over the First and Second Banks of the United States. The First Bank of the United States was chartered in 1791. It was part of Alexander Hamilton's plan for reorganizing the finances of the new government. Modeled to some extent on the Bank of England, it was intended to be a large bank, with a national branching system, that would help manage the new government's finances, and issue a paper money of uniform value (in part because it would be a legal tender for taxes) in all parts of the country. The term of the charter was limited to twenty years. When the charter came up for renewal in 1811 there was substantial opposition. Most of the opposition to the Bank, at least measured by the formal arguments against it, centered on the constitutionality of the Bank. The upshot was that the attempt to renew the charter failed, and the Bank was forced to wind up its affairs.

The monetary disturbances associated with the War of 1812 revived interest in a national bank. Such a bank, it was hoped, would pressure state banks into contracting their note issues and resuming specie payments. The Second Bank of the United States was established in 1816, again with a charter limited to twenty years. The Second Bank was similar to the First, but its capital was larger.

Although financial historians have often written favorably about the Second Bank, its career ended disastrously in the famous "Bank War." The Bank War pitted the Second Bank, led by its President, the aristocratic Philadelphian Nicholas Biddle, against an opposition led by the first President from west of the Alleghenies, Andrew Jackson. The exact reasons for Jackson's opposition to the Bank are still a matter of dispute.[2] Jackson was first elected in 1828. His outspoken criticism of the Bank began soon after, and led to an attempt to renew the Bank's charter before Jackson came up for his second election in 1832. The bill to renew the charter passed both houses of Congress, but was vetoed by Jackson. The veto message has been the subject of intense scrutiny and debate by historians. Jackson cited a number of reasons for vetoing the bill to recharter the Bank: foreigners held a considerable amount of stock (although they could not vote, a fact he failed to notice), a competition for the charter would produce more revenues for the Treasury, and so on. But the interesting point from our perspective is that Jackson stressed that the Bank was controlled by eastern moneyed interests, and had followed policies harmful to western farming interests. Jackson's reasoning on this issue has been faulted (Temin 1969). Nevertheless, it is clear that what Jackson perceived to be a conflict between eastern and western monetary interests inspired his opposition to the Bank.

Ironically, by the 1830s, opinion in the west had changed, and the Bank then enjoyed considerable support. Even in Tennessee, Jackson's mostly loyal home state, Congressman Davy Crockett, who represented poor farmers from western Tennessee (and who would later become part of American mythology as the "King of the Wild Frontier"), supported the Bank (Shackford 1986, passim).[3] Jackson, however, won an overwhelming reelection, sealing the fate of the Bank. Although there would be further battles, the war was lost. The charter of the Bank expired in 1836 and it wound up its affairs.[4] In the end Jackson's antagonism toward the Bank, rooted in his antagonism toward eastern moneyed interests, had produced a momentous change in the monetary institutions of the United States. The United States would not have any institution resembling a central bank until the Federal Reserve was established in 1913.

In 1837 the United States experienced a severe banking panic; numerous banks failed, and the banks were forced to suspend specie payments. In 1838 specie payments were resumed, and things began to look up. But a second panic in 1839 inaugurated a long recession marked by falling prices and a contraction in real output, although the degree of contraction in real output has been debated. To what extent did the Bank War contribute to the Crises of 1837 and 1839 and the subsequent recession? Peter Temin (1969) has argued that international forces, largely independent of the Bank War, explain the Jacksonian inflation and the Crises of 1837 and 1839. Marie Sushka (1976), however, has argued that the Bank War did have an impact by increasing uncertainty about the soundness of the monetary system. Undoubtedly, independent international shocks are part of the story, perhaps the major part. But it seems probable that the uncertainty about the future of monetary arrangements created by the Bank War made holders of bank liabilities more fearful about the soundness of the banking system than they otherwise would have been, at least in some measure, and contributed through this channel to the banking crises and the recession that followed.

Disunion

The Civil War was the result, of course, of the great national division over slavery. Nevertheless, financial factors did play a small role, influencing, perhaps, the timing of the War. Before the War the South had a relatively well developed banking system, and there is a good deal of evidence for capital market integration (Bodenhorn and Rockoff 1992). Indeed, Southerners were proud of their banking system, and their economic system based on "King Cotton." The crisis of 1857 was an eye-opener in both the South and the North. As Southerners saw it, the crisis was largely of Yankee making. It started in New York, with the failure of a branch of the Ohio Life Insurance and Trust Company, and spread through the rest of the country. In the end the South suffered relatively less than did the North. Many radical Southern secessionists seized on the evidence provided by the crisis of 1857 to push their case that the South would be better off as an independent country with its own economic and monetary policies. In the North the newly formed Republican Party tried, with some success, to pin the blame for the crisis on the Democrats. Thus the crisis had the ironic result of strengthening the two factions least willing to compromise on the issue of slavery (Huston 1987).

The war divided the nation into three monetary regions. In the East and Middle West a fiat money standard prevailed based on the greenback. In the South, another fiat standard held sway based on the Confederate dollar. The Pacific coast, however, remained on gold. The Southern monetary system, of course, gradually collapsed with the Confederacy, and came to an end in 1865. Returning to gold, and thus reuniting the two currencies of the United States took until 1879.

Reunion

After 1865 the South and Northeast were on the same (greenback) monetary system. There was no central bank. The supply of high-powered money was largely determined by the policies of Congress and the Secretaries of the Treasury. Republicans dominated. The goal of monetary policy was returning to the prewar price level and gold convertibility. These long-cherished goals were achieved on January 1, 1879 when the United States returned to the gold standard at the prewar parity. Throughout this period the policy of resumption faced determined regional opposition. Republicans in the Northeast favored resumption; Democrats and their allies in the Greenback Party based in the Middle West and the South opposed resumption and favored monetary expansion.

Southern and Western opposition to resumption

In 1866 Congress passed the Contraction Act, which called for the reduction in the number of greenbacks in circulation, with a view to early resumption of specie payments. When a recession ensued, considerable opposition to this policy developed. In the 1868 election the currency was a major issue. Western Democrats, following a now familiar refrain, demanded that Civil War bonds be paid in greenbacks unless the law specifically required payment in specie. Ulysses Grant, a financial conservative, however, was elected President. In March 1869 Congress voted to pay the Civil War debt in coin. Nevertheless, a more gradual approach toward resumption, referred to as "growing up to the currency," was adopted. Roughly speaking, the policy was to freeze the stock of high-powered money so that economic growth would produce a gradual decline in the price level.

Even this policy faced a severe political test. After the Panic of 1873, Congress voted for an increase in the stock of greenbacks. Grant vetoed the measure, triggering formation of the Greenback Party – "a combination of middle western farmers, small businessmen, and labor intellectuals" (Merk 1978: 445). In 1875 a lame duck Republican Congress adopted the Resumption Act which called for specie payments to be resumed on January 1, 1879.

Opposition to resumption coming from Greenbackers in the South and West, and Democrats with Greenback sympathies, was fierce. In 1876 the House voted 106–86 to repeal the Resumption Act, but repeal died in the Senate. In 1877 the House again voted for repeal and for measures that would have expanded the stock of money. But in the Senate in 1878 a compromise was worked out. The advocates of soft money were persuaded to support a limited expansion of the stock of silver money provided for in the Bland–Allison Act, and the policy of resumption was kept on track. Resumption, as I noted above, was achieved in 1879. But it had been a near thing.

The opponents of resumption could hardly have been expected to give up their cause simply because it produced uncertainty about the final outcome. Nevertheless, by repeatedly placing resumption in doubt, the soft money faction created uncertainty about future exchange rates, that affected nominal interest rates, and that probably created an additional hindrance to international capital flows (Calomiris 1994).

During this period, it should be noted, the West remained on the gold standard. Indeed, in 1873 the National Banking Act was amended to permit banks in California to issue currency redeemable in gold (yellowbacks). Thus from 1865 to 1879, when the greenback currency became convertible into gold, we have a monetary rarity: a strong political union, untouched by war, with two currencies, greenbacks and yellowbacks, circulating at a floating exchange rate. Interest rates on the Pacific coast were high, perhaps reflecting some of the exchange rate uncertainty. Rates, however, had been high before the war and would remain high after resumption. In any case, the "need" to reunite the currency, as contemporary observers saw it, strengthened the case for resumption.

Misunion?

Middle Western opposition to the gold standard continued to smolder after Resumption. In the late 1880s opposition burst into flame once more. The main problem was farmer unrest aggravated by low farm prices. Table 4.1 shows prices for the crops that were key in the regions where discontent was at a maximum. The real price of wheat had fallen from 100 at the time of resumption to 86 in 1890. Farmer Alliances were formed, and showed surprising strength in the 1890 congressional elections. Eight Middle Western and one Southern Populists were elected.

Congress took note of the growing pressure for inflation and passed the Sherman Silver Purchase Act in 1890 which required the Treasury to purchase 4.5 million ounces of silver per month, virtually the entire US output, paying with new legal tender currency redeemable in gold or silver at the discretion of the Treasury. The Silver Purchase Act was a compromise, designed to appease southern and western inflationists, and western silver interests, without going all the way to the free coinage of silver-backed currency. Fear of silver, however, produced a reduction in the Treasury's stock of gold, further increasing fears that the United States might abandon the gold standard.

Table 4.1 Agricultural prices and the NNP deflator, 1879–1900

	Net national product deflator[a]	*Real price of wheat*	*Real price of cotton*
1879	100	100	100
1880	110	93	105
1881	108	103	100
1882	112	104	105
1883	110	91	92
1884	105	85	97
1885	98	86	103
1886	96	80	94
1887	97	77	102
1888	99	87	100
1889	100	87	103
1890	98	86	113
1891	97	93	89
1892	93	80	83
1893	95	67	87
1894	89	59	78
1895	88	64	83
1896	85	70	92
1897	86	87	84
1898	88	94	68
1899	91	74	73
1900	95	69	100

Sources: NNP deflator: Friedman and Schwartz (1982: 122–3, Table 4.8, col. 4). Price of wheat and price of cotton: US Bureau of the Census (1975: 208–9, series E123 and E126).

Note
[a] 1879 = 100.

Although farm prices rose briefly in 1891, they tumbled again in 1892, and demands for monetary expansion were renewed. In 1892 the Northern Alliances entered the presidential race as the Populist Party. Their platform, the Omaha platform, was a wish list of radical reforms, monetary reforms prominent among them.

The stage was now set for the Great Depression of the 1890s, and the accompanying "Battle of the Standards" (gold vs. silver), the famous debate over monetary policy fought along regional lines. Before describing those events, however, I want to digress briefly and consider the extent to which those regions matched the criteria for optimal currency areas.

A digression on the optimal currency area criteria

Were the regions that opposed resumption in the 1870s, and that supported greenbacks and bimetallism in subsequent decades, separately optimal currency areas?

Optimal-currency-area theorists have described several factors that identify an area as a candidate for its own currency: (1) it must be a large area, (2) it must be specialized in the production of certain goods and subject to asymmetric shocks, (3) labor mobility between the candidate region and other regions must be limited,

(4) capital mobility between the candidate region and other regions must be limited, and (5) fiscal transfers between the candidate region and other regions must be limited. If the regional economies of the United States were relatively small, then the case for viewing them as candidates for separate currencies would be off to a bad start. It would be hard to make a case, for example, for a single state as an optimal currency area. The costs of currency conversion mount for a small open economy. But, in fact, the major census divisions of the United States were, by world standards, large economies. By 1900, for example, US national income was about twice that of Britain (Friedman and Schwartz 1982: 122, 130). Estimates of the distribution of personal incomes in the United States place the share of the Middle Atlantic region (economically the largest) at about 31 percent. So a back-of-the-envelope calculation might put the income of this region at 62 percent of Britain's.

These regions were subject, moreover, to asymmetric shocks. Regional agricultural specialization had begun in the colonial era. The famous "North Thesis" (North 1961) maintains that the specialization of the South in plantation agriculture, especially cotton, was the driving force behind American economic growth before the Civil War. After the Civil War the South remained a land specialized in the production of cash crops: sugar, tobacco, rice, and cotton. Indeed, because of the changes in the structure of Southern agriculture, the South produced more cotton after the Civil War, and devoted a larger share of its resources to the production of cotton, than it had before the war. The prices of cash crops rose and fell with the business cycle, but seemed to be especially hard hit in certain periods.

In terms of labor mobility the South was clearly a world apart until World War II. Gavin Wright (1996) in *Old South, New South*, has shown that while considerable integration was achieved across labor markets within the South (wages for unskilled white and black workers were almost the same) the Southern labor market remained a separate low-wage market. Racism limited mobility. Black Southerners, of course, suffered the most; but even white Southerners had to overcome stereotypes and ill will, especially after the Civil War. Once migration patterns were established, moreover, it was hard to change them in response to changing economic conditions, because earlier migrants provided information and support for later migrants. Mobility among other regions was much higher. But moving in response to regional shocks was, even into the 1930s, a process accomplished with considerable difficulties. The Joads were doing the right thing from an economic point of view – moving from a depressed region to an expanding region during the 1930s – but *The Grapes of Wrath* is an appropriate title.

The extent of capital mobility is more debatable. The standard view is that integration of regional capital markets was not achieved until the turn of the century because of a simple reluctance of capital to migrate, or because of institutional factors such as differences in banking and usury laws. Indeed, Bodenhorn's (1995) data shows that substantial interregional interest rate differentials persisted through the 1930s, although Bodenhorn attributes these differences to risk. One can say that after 1900, if not before, capital market integration served to ameliorate the effects of regional shocks.

In the United States today fiscal transfers tend to offset asymmetric shocks. Unemployment benefits, for example, will rise in regions suffering from high unemployment. In the nineteenth century, however, the federal government's revenues were simply too small a share of GDP to offset regional shocks through fiscal transfers. The largest federal transfer program by far was the Civil War pension program. And this program was somewhat responsive to economic conditions. The depression of the 1890s contributed in some measure to the expansion of benefits under the program that occurred at that time. But Southerners, immigrants, men who were too old or too young to have served, or who hired substitutes were not eligible. Women had to marry to become eligible. It was not until the adoption of programs such as unemployment compensation and agricultural price supports in the 1930s that one can point to fiscal transfers as a legitimate mechanism for overcoming asymmetric shocks.

The a priori case for believing that prices and wages in the separate regions were relatively sticky (thus strengthening the case for an independent monetary policy) appears to be relatively weak. The labor unions or oligopolistic industries that economists often point to as sources of stickiness were unimportant. There was considerable political agitation about the danger of the Trusts, but how much they contributed to price rigidity is debatable. In the South, even a significant portion of agricultural rental contracts was indexed: the famous sharecropping contracts.

Nevertheless, there were elements of institutional rigidity: taxes, mortgages, cash rentals, and so on. And beyond purely institutional sources of rigidity, there were the usual coordination problems. Adjusting to lower world prices for agricultural products meant a coordinated fall in wages, prices, and rents. Along most dimensions (labor and capital mobility, and fiscal transfers) the monetary union was strengthened during the 1930s. But along this dimension, the union was weakened.

Certain regions of the United States clearly exhibited many of the signs of good candidates for separate currencies, at least until the 1930s. But can one identify episodes in which substantial costs were imposed on these regions because they were part of a monetary union? Classic cases of optimal-currency-area dilemmas, a boom in one region combined with a recession in other regions, were probably rare. More common were differences among regions in the magnitude of cyclical fluctuations, and in the timing of contractions and recoveries.

The Great Depression of the 1890s

The Great Depression of the 1890s, like the Depression of the 1930s, involved two severe recessions in close order. The economy declined for 17 months from January 1893 to June 1894, and then, after a comparatively weak recovery, declined again for 18 months from December 1895 to June 1897. Unemployment figures are necessarily somewhat problematic, but the figures we do have show the rate of unemployment at double-digit levels from 1893 through 1898, with a peak of 18.4 percent in 1894 (US Bureau of the Census 1975: 135).

As we noted above, the early 1890s were characterized by concern over the maintenance of the gold standard stemming from the Sherman Silver Purchase Act, the decline in the stock of Treasury gold, and the rise of the Populists. In May 1893 a banking panic was touched off by commercial failures in New York. In June 1893, the administration revealed that it would press for the repeal of the Sherman Silver

Purchase Act, and this seemed to ease pressures in financial markets. In July, however, further commercial and bank failures led to a renewal of the panic. Bank runs and failures occurred in all regions. Starting in New York, banks throughout the country restricted the convertibility of notes and deposits into gold. The restriction on convertibility somewhat eased the situation. High interest rates drew gold into the United States and specie payments were resumed in September.

But the next three years were characterized by continued difficulties. Populists in the West and South continued to agitate for free and unlimited coinage of silver at a bimetallic ratio of 16:1. It was widely believed that adoption of bimetallism at that rate would have created substantial inflation and driven the United States off the gold standard. Uncertainty about the standard was reflected in higher interest rates. The Republicans favored continued commitment to the gold standard, although some Republicans, typically from the western states, called for an international conference aimed at restoring bimetallism, but at a bimetallic ratio that would permit continued circulation of both metals, and that would not produce inflation. The Democrats were badly split. The eastern wing of the party, led by former President Grover Cleveland, favored maintaining the commitment to gold; the western and southern wings favored bimetallism at 16:1. At the Democratic National Convention held in Chicago in 1896, the Westerners overthrew the Easterners. William Jennings Bryan, a Democratic Congressman from Nebraska with strong Populist sympathies, was nominated after a stirring speech, one of the most famous in American history, in which he declared that the Republicans would not be allowed to "Crucify Mankind upon a Cross of Gold."

Despite his oratorical skills, Bryan lost the election to William McKinley, who favored the Republican brand of international bimetallism. Bryan carried states only in the west and south. Ironically, new flows of gold soon began to reverse the deflation that had persisted since the end of the Civil War. Demands for inflation through bimetallism or fiat paper became superfluous. The United States formalized its commitment to the gold standard with the Gold Standard Act of 1900.

Why was the United States so badly split along regional lines over monetary policy? Historians, traditionally, have seen the issue as one of creditors (eastern bankers) against debtors (western farmers). One problem with this view, as was recognized by Bryan and others at the time, is that any help from inflation would likely be partial and temporary, because interest rates would rise to reflect expected inflation. Frieden's (1997) recent argument, that the support for 16:1 came primarily from exporters who looked to devaluation to improve earnings, seems more persuasive.

As we saw above, however, the regions at odds with each other were, in many ways, separable currency areas. It makes sense to look at regional stocks of money, or what in fact are available, regional deposits. Figure 4.1 shows deposits by region from 1875 through 1896. Deposits in each region were set to 100 in 1875 to make it easier to compare regional trends.[5] Granted, regional deposits reflected as well as caused changes in regional economic activity. Nevertheless, to the extent that these deposit movements reflected interregional transfers of reserves (balance of payments problems) or bank failures that might have been prevented by lender of last resort operations, they represent an independent influence on economic activity.

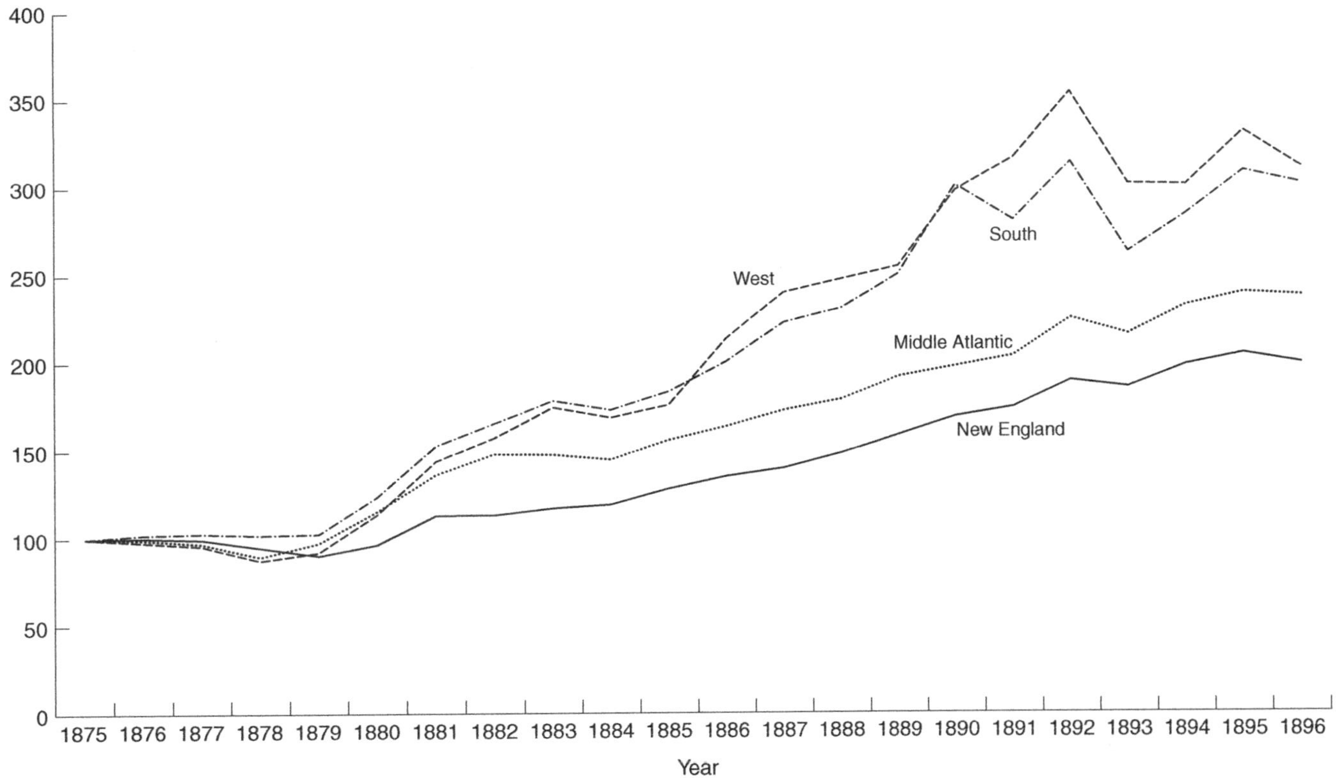

Figure 4.1 All bank deposits by region, 1875–96 (1875 = 100).

In any case, the picture is rather dramatic. The Great Depression of the 1890s left only a small imprint on deposits in New England or the Middle Atlantic region (dominated by New York and Pennsylvania). In New England deposits fell 2.4 percent from 1892 to 1893, but then more than regained their loss, rising 7.2 percent from 1893 to 1894. In the Middle Atlantic region, deposits fell 4.7 percent, and then rose 7.7 percent. On the other hand, the impact on deposits in the West and South, the centers of the Populist revolt, were dramatic. Deposits in the South fell 18.6 percent from 1892 to 1893 and regained only 8.2 percent between 1893 and 1894; in the West deposits fell 16.4 percent, and only recovered 0.4 percent. Deposits in both regions were lower in 1896 than they had been in 1892. Is it any wonder that politicians in the West and South were calling for measures to increase the stock of money (remonetization of silver, or more radically, agricultural price supports financed by issues of fiat money) and that politicians in New England and the Middle Atlantic States called for a stand pat policy?

Data for all banks (both national and non-national) are available during this period only for four regions. The Middle Western and Pacific regions were aggregated in the source for non-national banks. This is worrisome because the Pacific coast (which is dominated by California) was growing rapidly. Deposits in this region might have followed a somewhat different path than in other western states. In addition, the figures on non-national banks may be subject to reporting errors that vary in magnitude across regions and over time, despite the painstaking work undertaken by David Fand (1954) in putting these figures together. I have, however, computed National Bank deposits, which are likely to be more accurate, for five regions, separating the Middle West and the Far West.

These estimates are plotted in Figure 4.2. Again, the deposits in each region have been set to 100 in 1875. As expected, national bank deposits grew extremely rapidly on the Pacific coast, rising by a factor of 18 between 1875 and 1900. The most important point, however, is that the crisis of the 1893 is most evident in three regions: the Pacific coast and Territories, the West, and the South. Again, the Middle Atlantic region and New England record only small impacts from the crisis of 1893.

Who was right, the East or the West? I find it hard to believe that the falling stocks of deposits and bank credit in the South and West did not contribute in some measure to the economic distress those regions were suffering, and would not have been relieved by monetary expansion. Taking a longer-term view, Milton Friedman (1990a, and 1990b) has argued that adoption of bimetallism earlier in the postbellum period would have produced a more satisfactory behavior of the price level. He concludes, however, that by 1896 the time for adopting bimetallism had passed.

In any case, one thing seems clear. An unequivocal commitment to either gold or bimetallism would have avoided the uncertainty which itself was part of the problem. Milton Friedman and Anna J. Schwartz put it this way, in *A Monetary History*:

> In retrospect, it seems clear that either acceptance of a silver standard at an early stage, or an early commitment to gold would have been preferable to the uneasy compromise that was maintained, with the uncertainty about the final outcome and the consequent wide fluctuations to which the currency was subjected.
> (1963: 134)

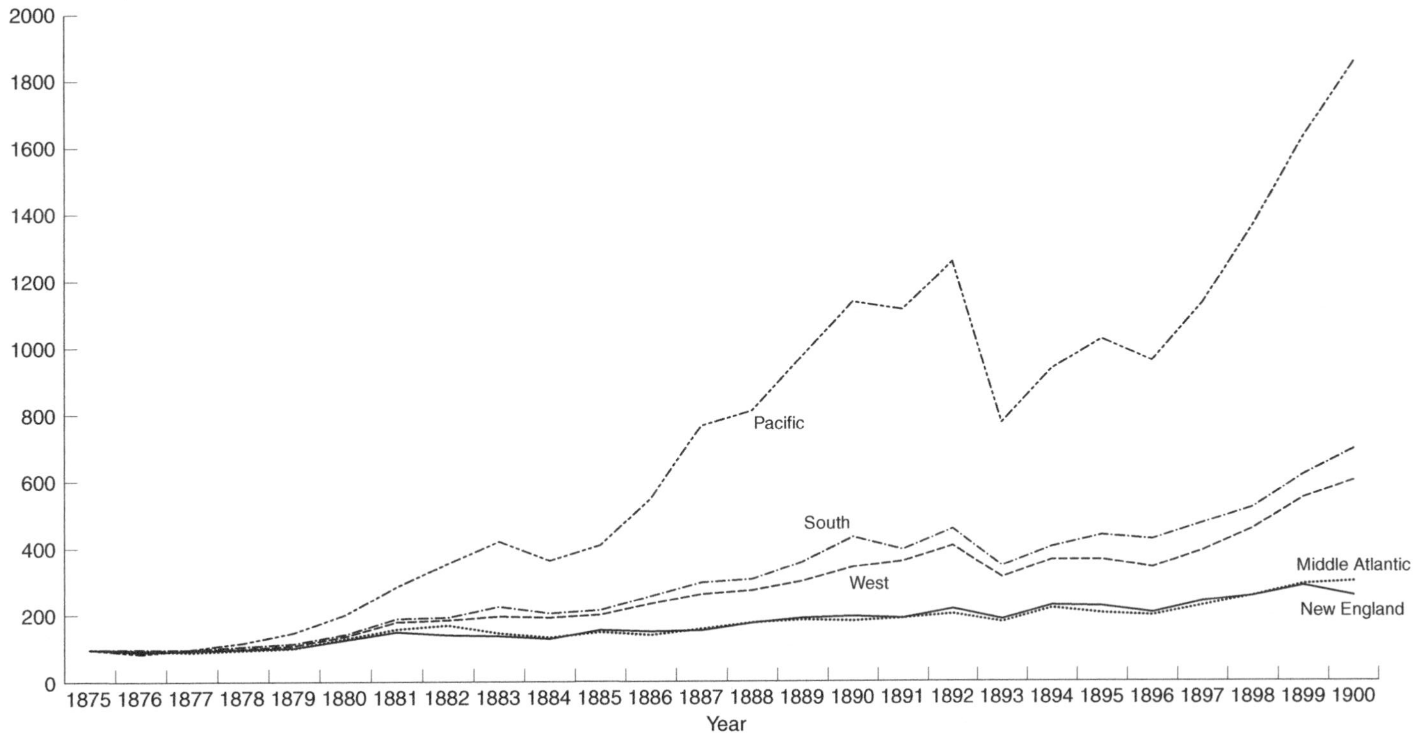

Figure 4.2 National bank deposits by region, 1875–1900 (1875 = 100).

Politicians, as Figures 4.1 and 4.2 show, were advocating the real interests of their own regions. Deposit growth in the East, although affected by the panic of 1893, was sufficiently close to trend to justify sticking with the current monetary policy; deposit growth in the South and West was depressed and justified a change in policy.

The optimal solution, were it politically feasible, might have been separate currencies, say for the East, the West, the South, and the Pacific coast. The West and the South would have adopted a silver standard in the 1890s, while the East and the Pacific coast, given its historical attachments, would have stayed on gold. Money stocks would not have fallen in the West and the South as much as they did. Their currencies, moreover, would have depreciated against gold, making it easier to dispose of wheat, cotton, and other agricultural products on domestic and world markets. The debate over monetary policy, and the resulting uncertainty, which affected banks in all regions, would not have happened.

The panic of 1903 (the "Trust" panic) and the panic of 1907

Figure 4.3 plots deposits by region for the period 1900 to 1914.[6] Deposits in each region have been set equal to 100 in 1900. The major events during this period were the panic of 1903 and the panic of 1907. Here the regional pattern is different from the 1890s.

New York financial markets came under severe stress in late 1902. Short-term interest rates shot up, the stock market crashed, and a number of financial houses went bankrupt. The associated cyclical contraction was relatively long (23 months), from September 1902 to August 1904. In the 1903 panic the biggest impact was on the Middle Atlantic (New York) region, although even in this region the panic shows up as a period of relatively slow growth in deposits, rather than as an actual decline. Deposits in the other regions, by way of contrast, were not affected much at all.

Although a severe jolt, the 1903 panic did not produce a banking panic or a severe economic contraction. The panic of 1907, however, produced a much broader and deeper reaction in the banking system. Pressure began to build in the New York money market in the summer and fall of 1907. A major shock occurred in October 1907 when a run on the Knickerbocker Trust Company forced it to suspend payments.[7] Other Trust companies were soon in difficulty as well. A banking panic gripped the nation, and the banks were forced to restrict the convertibility of bank notes and deposits into gold.

Nearly all regions of the country were affected. Only the plot of deposits for New England fails to show a dramatic imprint from the crisis. But as in 1903, the interesting feature of the data is the impact on the Middle Atlantic states, and the contrast between those states and the Middle West. Deposits in the Middle Atlantic states fell 2.38 percent between 1907 and 1908. Deposits in the South and on the Pacific coast fell by even larger amounts. But deposits in the Middle West fell by only 1.99 percent. The regional impact of the panic of 1907 was clearly very different from the impact of the panic of 1893.

As might be expected the political response to the crises in 1903 and 1907 was also very different than it was in the 1890s. During the 1890s, the Eastern establishment

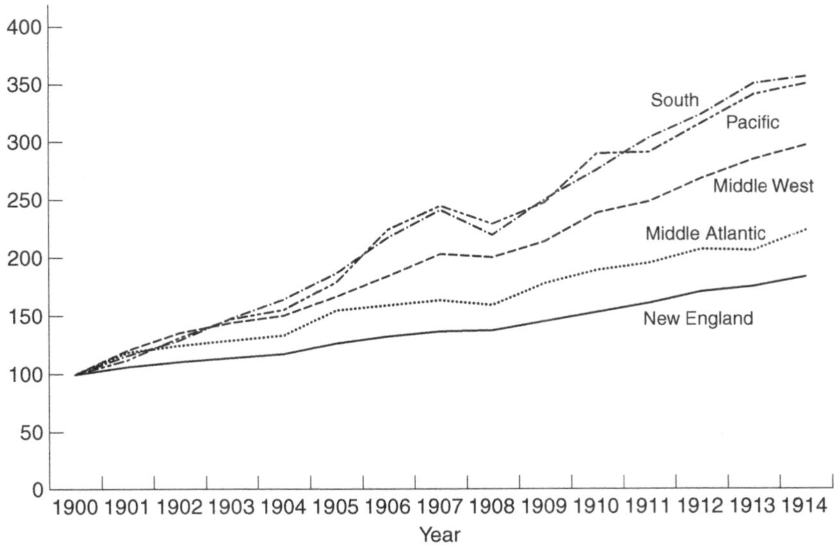

Figure 4.3 All bank deposits by region, 1900–14 (1900 = 100).

was convinced that monetary reform was a foolish idea pushed by dangerous Mid-western radicals such as William Jennings Bryan; now the East was convinced that monetary reform was a wise idea advocated by the best scientific minds. In the wake of the panic of 1907 the Aldrich–Vreeland Act (May 1908) was passed which created an emergency currency that could be issued during panics; and created the National Monetary Commission to investigate the monetary system, and recommend reforms. Senator Nelson W. Aldrich of Rhode Island, a long time Republican leader, and determined opponent of the Populists, headed the Commission. The main recommendation was the creation of a type of central bank. The United States would be divided into districts, and the banks in each district would keep their reserves in a district bank that was owned and controlled by the member banks. There would be a central board, controlled by the district banks, with the power to issue a gold-backed currency. Aldrich introduced a bill in Congress embodying this plan.

By the time that the bill came up for debate, however, the Democrats controlled the Congress and the Presidency. Goaded by the Populists among them, the Democrats insisted on changes in the bill. Indeed, Bryan, who carried Populist hopes for free silver in 1896, was then Secretary of State, and is said to have played an important role in the negotiations. The final result was legislation that differed from the Republican model in two ways, one that would remain important, and one that would not. First, the new institution was to be run by people appointed by the Federal Government, and not by the banks. Second, the right to issue currency would be the responsibility of the district banks, rather than the central board. The ability of the district banks to issue their own currencies would not prove to be a major feature of the system; it reflected a Populist hankering for a monetary system that would respond to the differing needs of differing regions.

The Great Depression of the 1930s

The Great Depression of the 1930s was the most severe in American economic history. Ever since the publication of Friedman and Schwartz's *A Monetary History of the United States* (1963), changes in the stock of money, and mistakes in monetary policy, have been granted an important role in the economic historian's account of the Depression. The extraordinary impact of the Depression can be seen in Figure 4.4, which plots all bank deposits by Federal Reserve district from 1922 to 1941. I have switched from broader regions to Federal Reserve districts, primarily because data for the Federal Reserve districts is readily available. Nevertheless, the Federal Reserve districts correspond, roughly, to economic regions, so little is lost in switching from broader regions to Federal Reserve districts. To make the figure easier to read, deposits in each region have been set to 100 in 1929.[8]

No region was immune to the crisis, but there were significant regional differences. Within the whole period I have highlighted two subperiods, 1929–31 and 1934–6, when there were marked regional differences in the rate of change of deposits, and when important mistakes were made in monetary policy.

The most famous, and probably the most important, error in American monetary history was the failure of the Federal Reserve to act as lender of last resort for the banking system during the contraction from 1929 to 1933. A great deal has been written about the reasons for the failure of the Federal Reserve to take appropriate actions during this period. The personal and institutional rivalries stressed by Milton Friedman and Anna J. Schwartz (1963: 520–6); the adherence to misleading doctrines about how policy actions worked (Calomiris and Wheelock 1998; Meltzer 1998); and the weight placed on adherence to the gold standard (Eichengreen 1992) undoubtedly were important in producing the lack of response to the crisis exhibited by the Federal Reserve. Regional loyalties had declined, in part because World War I had boosted nationalism over sectionalism.

Nevertheless, Figure 4.5, which focuses on 1929 to 1931, suggests that regional differences need to be woven into the traditional story.[9] The deviations among regions are striking. In June 1931, almost two years into the Great Depression, the stocks of deposits in the San Francisco, Boston, and Philadelphia districts, and in the weighty New York district, were still above the June 1929 levels.

Economists and policymakers from those regions, who tended to look toward events in their own region, whether consciously or not, would have been less likely to stress the need for drastic countermeasures. As evidence that the need for action was recognized by some observers, Friedman and Schwartz (1963: 409) cite representative Sabbath of Illinois writing to Federal Reserve Board chairman Eugene Meyer in January 1931: "Does the board maintain there is no emergency at this time? To my mind if ever there was an emergency it is now, and this I feel, no one can successfully deny." Can it be entirely irrelevant that at the time Sabbath was

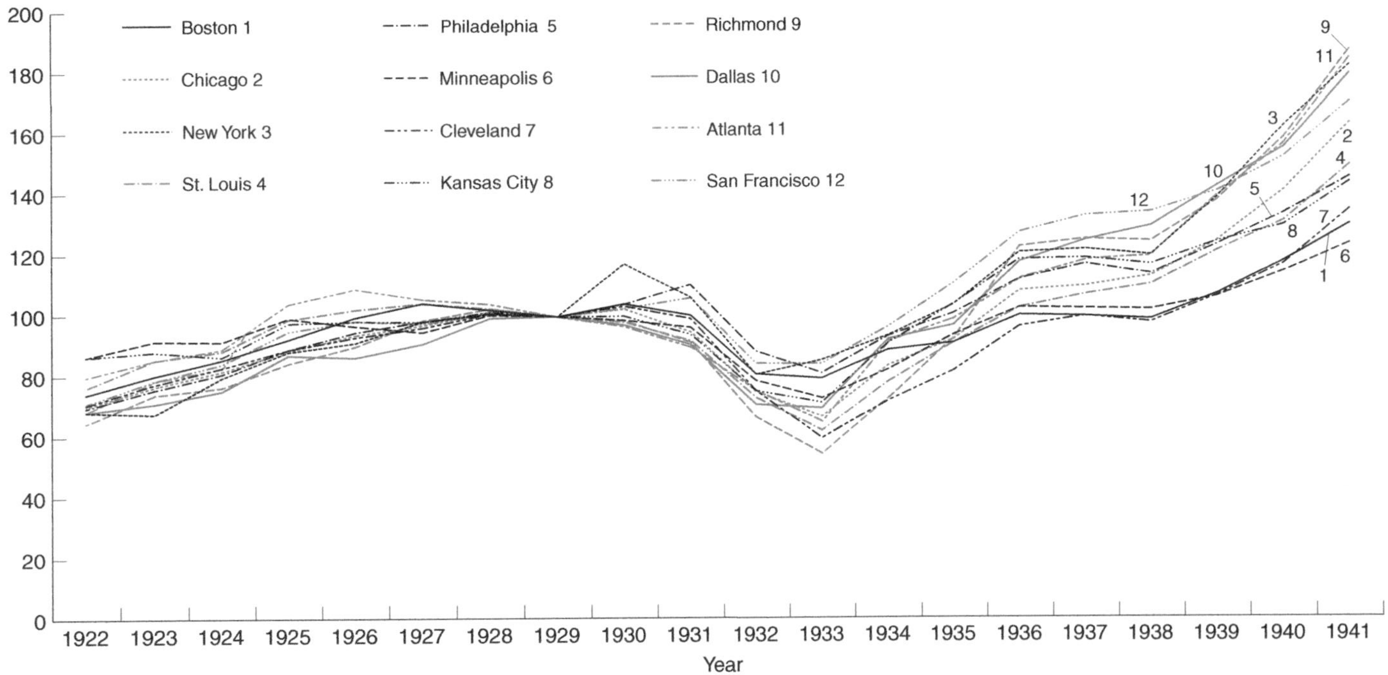

Figure 4.4 Deposits by Federal Reserve district, 1922–41 (1929 = 100).

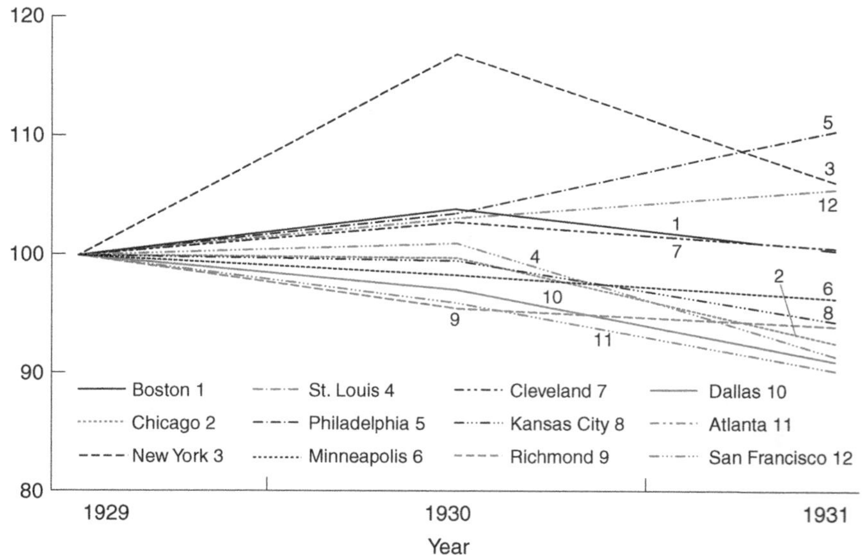

Figure 4.5 Deposits by Federal Reserve district: the first two years of the depression, 1929–31 (1929 = 100).

writing deposits had already fallen drastically in the Chicago district and the St. Louis district (which covers southern Illinois)?

Residence in a district hard hit by deposit losses, it must be admitted, was no guaranty of sensitivity to the crisis. James McDougal, President of the Federal Reserve Bank of Chicago, consistently opposed open market security purchases, in part because he thought it would be useless for the Federal Reserve to try to offset a natural market process: liquidating bad loans. Marriner Eccles, who became chairman of the Federal Reserve Board in 1935, might have been expected to be a consistent advocate of monetary expansion. He was a banker from the West (Utah), a region with a long tradition of monetary radicalism, and one that had been hard hit by the Depression as shown in Figure 4.4. He had been appointed, moreover, because of his sympathy for the New Deal. But his own study of the Depression, and his reading of the heretical under-consumptionist William T. Foster, had pushed him toward the view that monetary policy was a relatively impotent tool for controlling the economy. The real action was on the side of fiscal policy

Roy A. Young, President of the Boston Bank, however, at one point based his opposition to open market purchases on a regional argument: open market purchases would lead to a piling up of reserves in the money centers, with little effect on the regions of the country that really needed reserves. Thus, although policy positions in the 1930s do not divide as neatly along regional lines as they did in the 1890s, there is some evidence that differences in regional perspectives contributed, at least in a small measure, to the paralysis that gripped monetary policy making in the early 1930s.

The second major policy error during the Depression was the decision by the

Federal Reserve to raise bank reserve ratios in three steps – in August 1936, March 1937, and May 1937. Friedman and Schwartz (1963), and more recently Meltzer (1998), have explored many of the intellectual and personal currents that produced the decision. Nevertheless, the diversity in regional experiences shown in Figure 4.6 is suggestive. By June of 1935 the stocks of deposits in the New York, Richmond, and San Francisco districts, had all recovered their June 1929 levels. Rapid expansion in the ensuing year carried the stocks of deposits in these districts to levels between 20 and 30 percent above the levels of June 1929. Moreover, employment in these regions had also recovered well.[10] A Federal Reserve President in one of these districts, who based his conclusions solely on conditions in his own district, might well conclude that it was time to adopt a more restrictive monetary policy before things got out of hand and inflation threatened.

In the "heartland" districts, however, conditions were very different. In the Cleveland district deposits in June 1935 were little more than 80 percent of what they had been in June 1929, and although growth was rapid, deposits were still below the June 1929 level in 1936. Unemployment was still high. The president of a district bank in the heartland might well conclude that further monetary expansion was required. To put it differently, the Federal Reserve, at least to judge by deposit growth, faced an optimal-currency-area dilemma in 1936. Some regions needed stimulation; others needed restraint.

It is interesting to ask what would have happened had the United States been divided into separate currency areas – separate currencies for, say, the East, the South, the Middle West, and the Pacific – during the 1930s. Separate currencies,

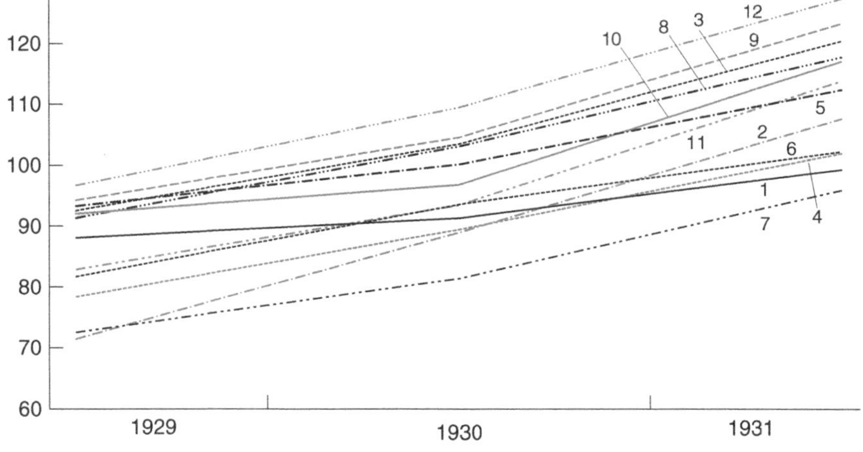

Figure 4.6 Deposits by Federal Reserve district before the doubling of reserve ratios, 1934–6 (1929 = 100).

course, were ruled out by political considerations. A currency is a symbol of sovereignty, like the flag, and it is as hard to imagine any country deliberately choosing to divide its currency. But thinking about separate currencies can throw light on the economics of the Depression. Even with separate currencies, monetary policies might well have been similar in the East, the South, and on the Pacific coast to what they actually were. The central bank of the East, for example, would not have acted as a lender of last resort in the early 1930s, but there would have been no need for it to do so. It would have slowed monetary expansion in the mid-1930s, but it would have been logical for it to do so.

The central bank in the Middle West, however, might have acted differently. With hundreds of banks failing in the region, with politicians calling for action, a central bank that had full responsibility for the region might well have acted as lender of last resort in the early 1930s. Moreover, a Middle Western central bank, under intense pressure from local interests, might well have followed a more inflationary policy. Silver interests were potent in the Middle West and might well have demanded additional purchases of silver financed through an increase in the monetary base. The mid-western currency might well have depreciated relative to other regional currencies. But this would have helped employment in the manufacturing sectors of the Middle West, which were among the hardest hit in the nation, because they suffered from increasing labor costs due to unionization, as well as from the decrease in demand for consumer durables.

To be sure, if someone like James McDougal, who advocated deflationary measures as President of the Chicago district bank during the 1930s, had been president of the Middle Western central bank that I am imagining, he might have succeeded in imposing deflationary policies despite political pressures to do otherwise. But not necessarily; the argument that open market purchases were actions taken by bankers in faraway places that influenced banks in faraway places would no longer apply. Long experience with the conduct of monetary policy might have made central bankers in the Mid West more adroit than central bank board members. In short, the monetary union, which in more stable times was a source of strength for the United States, appears to have been a liability during the 1930s.

Communion?

It is generally assumed that the United States became a smoothly functioning monetary union, at least for the purpose of comparison with the European Monetary Union, in the postwar era, for example: Feldstein (1997); Wyplosz (1997). The comparison may tend to exaggerate how well the US monetary union functions. There have been asymmetric real shocks, such as the oil price fluctuations that hit Texas particularly hard, or the changes in manufacturing that hit the "rust belt." Perhaps there were regional banking problems that exacerbated these disturbances that we have not paid sufficient attention to because we are accustomed to think in aggregate terms.

But it is true that several institutional changes took place during the Depression and World War II that weakened older divisions. One was the development of federally funded transfer programs, such as unemployment insurance, social security, and agricultural price supports, which cushioned regional shocks, and redistributed reserves lost through interregional payments deficits. Penelope Hartland (1949), using data from the Federal Reserve's Interdistrict Settlement Fund showed that the regions that had been hit by terms of trade shocks during the 1930s lost reserves to other regions through trade deficits, but that government transfers materially offset these losses. Between 1929 and 1933, for example, the Minneapolis Federal Reserve district lost $247 million in reserves on private transactions. This was offset, however, by a gain of $229 million on federal government transactions. On the other hand, the Boston Federal Reserve district gained $644 million in reserves on private transactions, while losing $575 million on federal government transactions (Hartland 1949: 397). Seymour Harris (1957: 174–92) noted the regional payments problems during the 1930s, and argued that separate currency areas would have ameliorated these problems. Harris also noted similar regional payment problems in the early post-World War II era.

A second institutional change was the breakdown of long-term isolation of the southern labor market. During the war a strong northern labor market and the absence of immigrants pulled workers, white as well as black, from the South, and established networks that provided information and support for later migrants. In addition, federal labor legislation in the form of minimum wages and regulation of hours and conditions of work, and federal incentives to mechanize agriculture, established during the 1930s added to the postwar flow of migrants from the South.[11]

A third factor that improved the functioning of the US monetary union after the war was the absence of major banking and financial crises emanating from regional shocks. Deposit insurance, and monetary policies that reacted quickly to economic downturns, tended to minimize the regional banking problems that characterized recessions in the prewar era.

Lessons from the troubled history of the US monetary union

Weighing the costs and benefits of monetary unification is a difficult task. On the one hand, monetary unification means reduced transaction costs, easier comparison of prices in different regions, long-term investment without fears of devaluation, and so on. On the other hand, unification means relinquishing the capacity to use exchange rate changes and monetary policy to prevent monetary problems from magnifying distress originating in other sectors. Frequently, the experience of the United States is cited as evidence that in fact the benefits of a monetary union greatly outweigh the costs. After all, the monetary union of the United States has survived (with a temporary break during the Civil War era) since the adoption of the Constitution in 1788. But the survival of the US monetary union is at best weak evidence that the net effects have been positive. There are many government policies, tariffs for example, which have survived for decades for political reasons, often the support of special interests, even though the claim that these policies contributed positively to the general welfare is dubious.

In truth, the US experience shows that fears about the loss of monetary autonomy are far from baseless. American monetary history provides numerous examples of regional shocks that were magnified by monetary reactions. Typically, a region-specific shock to financial or agricultural markets produced a loss of regional bank reserves through an internal drain, caused by fears about the solvency of the regional banking system, and an external drain, caused by a regional balance of payments deficit. The result would be a regional contraction of bank money and credit that would cause headaches even for businesses not affected by the initial shock. A political battle would often follow. The regions that had experienced the contraction would demand a reform of the whole monetary system. The resulting uncertainty about the future of existing monetary institutions would further aggravate the initial contraction in economic activity.

During these episodes the United States might well have been better off, from a purely economic point of view, had it been divided into separate currency areas. Regions hit by severe asymmetric shocks would have been able to devalue their currencies, which would have reduced interregional losses of reserves. Within the region, expansionary monetary policies would have shored up the banking system, preventing runs or severe contractions of credit. Other regions would have been free to follow more conservative monetary policies, eliminating political battles over monetary institutions. Separate currencies for separate regions were not ruled out by any logical inconsistency. During and after the Civil War (1861–79) the Pacific coast had its own currency, the yellowback. But separate currencies for separate regions were ruled out eventually by political considerations. In the course of the nineteenth century currencies came to be seen as symbols of sovereignty, and separate regional currencies became as unthinkable as separate armies.

Nevertheless, speculating about this counterfactual helps us to understand the US business cycle and may suggest some lessons for countries contemplating joining or remaining within a monetary union. For a country that is debating whether to join a monetary union the lesson is that the facile argument that the United States has had a monetary union, and therefore monetary unions must be good things, doesn't stand close scrutiny. Second thoughts are in order. For countries already firmly committed to a monetary union, the lesson is that it is extremely important to adopt the institutions that can accomplish the tasks performed by the institutions adopted by the United States in the 1930s – a system of inter-regional fiscal transfers and some form of deposit insurance, or regionally sensitive lender-of-last-resort facilities – so that asymmetric real shocks are not aggravated by banking crises.[12]

Although the Eastern financial centers, and industrial Middle West had been integrated by the turn of the century, it was not until the 1930s that all regions, including the South, could be said to be parts of a single optimal currency area (see Table 4.2). How long did it take the United States to become an Optimal Currency Area? A reasonable minimum might be one hundred and fifty years! Hopefully, it will not take the European Monetary Union quite so long.

Table 4.2 A chronology of the US monetary union

1788	The Constitution is ratified. States are prohibited from issuing paper money. The US monetary union is launched.
1791	The First Bank of the United States is chartered.
1811	The First Bank of the United States comes to an end.
1816	The Second Bank of the United States is chartered.
1832	President Andrew Jackson vetoes the bill to recharter the Second Bank, stressing the oppression of the West in his veto message.
1836	The Second Bank of the United States comes to an end.
1837	The nation is hit by a severe banking panic, inaugurating a period of hard times.
1857	The nation is hit by a severe banking panic. Southern firebrands and Northern Republicans both make political capital from the crisis.
1861	The Civil War begins. The United States is divided into three currency areas: Greenbacks in the Northeast, Confederate dollars in the South, and Gold in California.
1865	Lee surrenders. The Confederate dollar ceases to function.
1866	Congress passes the Contraction Act looking to a rapid return to the gold standard.
1873	The silver dollar is omitted from the list of official coins (The Crime of 1873). National Banks in California are permitted to issue notes backed by gold (yellow-backs).
1879	Resumption of specie payments. The yellowback and greenback are reunited.
1896	William Jennings Bryan, an advocate of free silver, is nominated by the Populists and Democrats; William McKinley, an advocate of international bimetallism, is nominated by the Republicans. Bryan carries only a few states in the West and South.
1900	The Gold Standard Act firmly commits the United States to the Gold Standard and symbolises the end of the "Battle of the Standards."
1907	A banking panic leads to the establishment of the National Monetary Commission.
1913	The Federal Reserve System is established. Republican proposals for a currency issued by a privately controlled central bank are defeated. Instead a federation of regional banks, each issuing their own currency, is created. William Jennings Bryan, now secretary of State, plays an active role in fashioning the legislation.
1929–31	Beginning of The Great Contraction. The Stock market crashes and a severe monetary contraction begins in the nation's heartland.
1936–7	The Federal Reserve raises required reserve ratios contributing to a sharp recession that prolongs the depression.

Appendix: sources of data

Deposits: 1875–1914

Exact figures on the stock of money by region are not available. The amount of coins within the United States, for example, can be estimated from figures on minting and imports and exports, but the amount within any one region cannot be estimated accurately. But figures on deposits, and in some periods bank notes, by place of issue (although not by where they are held) are available. Fand (1954: 72–6) estimated deposits in non-national banks in four regions: New England, Middle States, Southern States, and Western States for the years 1875–96. These regions do not correspond exactly to economic regions. Perhaps the main problem from this perspective is the combination of the Pacific coast with the other western states. It would be, however, extremely time consuming to build up separate estimates for the non-national banks for this region, so I have relied on the national bank data to provide a picture of the Pacific coast. To Fand's estimates of deposits in non-national banks, I added deposits of national banks. The source is a table by state that appeared regularly in the *Annual Report of the Comptroller of the Currency*. US Comptroller of the Currency (1920: 307–43).

1 New England: Connecticut, Maine, Massachusetts, New Hampshire, Rhode Island, and Vermont.
2 Middle Atlantic: Delaware, District of Columbia, Maryland, New Jersey, New York, and Pennsylvania.
3 South: Alabama, Arkansas, Florida, Georgia, Kentucky, Louisiana, Mississippi, North Carolina, South Carolina, Tennessee, Texas, Virginia, and West Virginia.
4 Middle West: Illinois, Indiana, Indian Territory, Iowa, Kansas, Michigan, Minnesota, Missouri, Nebraska, Ohio, Oklahoma, and Wisconsin.
5 Pacific coast, Western states, and Territories: Alaska, Arizona, California, Colorado, Dakota Territory, Hawaii, Idaho, Montana, Nevada, New Mexico, North Dakota, Oregon, Puerto Rico, South Dakota, Utah, Washington, and Wyoming.

Deposits: 1896–1914

For this period *All Bank Statistics* (US Board of Governors 1959) gives data for all types of deposits in all classes of banks by states. The data shown in the figure are a sum of demand and time deposits. The regions are defined above.

Deposits: 1914–41

For this period I have switched to Deposits by Federal Reserve District because the data are readily available; US Board of Governors of the Federal Reserve System (1943: 688–927).

Acknowledgements

I learned a great deal from the discussion of a preliminary draft by Ronald I. McKinnon, Anna J. Schwartz, and other participants in the Conference on Monetary Unions at the City University Business School, London, May 14, 1999, and from the participants in the meeting on the Development of the American Economy, the Summer Institute of the National Bureau of Economic Research, Cambridge MA, July 14, 1999. I have also learned a great about these issues from Michael Bordo, Robert Greenfield, Edwin Perkins, and Eugene White. Dongbo Pei provided superb research assistance. The remaining errors are mine.

Notes

1 Other important early contributions were McKinnon (1963), Kenen (1969), and Tower and Willet (1976). Kawai (1992) provides a clear summary.
2 See Perkins (1987) for the most recent analysis, and references to the earlier literature.
3 It should be noted that although Crockett's support for the Bank may have been based on general considerations, he owed money to the bank, a debt that was partially cancelled through the personal intervention of Nicholas Biddle.
4 The home office was able to continue for several years under a Pennsylvannia charter.
5 The appendix (pp. 99–100) describes how these numbers were computed.
6 All types of deposits in both national and non-national banks are summed.
7 The Trust companies were banks that had grown up as ways of getting around the strict asset regulations imposed by the Comptroller of the Currency and the New York banking authority.
8 All figures are for June dates, usually close to June 30.
9 The figures are for June 1929, June 1930, and June 1931; the cyclical peak was in August 1929.
10 It may seem surprising that the Richmond region followed the path of New York and San Francisco. In fact, however, as is now well understood, the South did relatively well during the depression.
11 Fiscal federalism and the improvements in the functioning of the labor market are discussed in Eichengreen (1998: chapters 2 and 3). Wright (1996) discusses the breakdown of barriers to labor migration. Libecap (1998) discusses the origins of agricultural price supports.
12 Capie (1998) has drawn a similar lesson from a variety of historical examples.

References

Bodenhorn, Howard and Hugh Rockoff (1992) "Regional interest Rates in Antebellum America," in Goldin, Claudia, ed., *Strategic Factors in American Economic History: A Volume to Honor Robert W. Fogel.* University of Chicago Press, Chicago.

—— and —— (1995) "A More Perfect Union: Regional interest Rates in the United States, 1880–1960," in Bordo, Michael D. and Richard Sylla, eds, *Anglo-American Financial Systems: institutions and Markets in the Twentieth Century.* Irwin Professional Publishing for New York University Salomon Center, New York.

Calomiris, Charles W. (1994) "Greenback Resumption and Silver Risk: the Economics and Politics of Monetary Regime Change in the United States," in Bordo, Michael D. and Forrest Capie, eds, *Monetary Regimes in Transition.* Cambridge University Press, Cambridge.

—— and David C. Wheelock (1998) "Was the Great Depression a Watershed for American Monetary Policy?," in Bordo, Michael D., Claudia Goldin, and Eugene N. White, eds, *The Defining Moment: the Great Depression and the American Economy in the Twentieth Century.* University of Chicago Press, for the NBER, Chicago.

Capie, Forrest (1998) "Monetary Unions in Historical Perspective: What Future for the Euro in the International Financial System," *Open Economies Review, 9* (Supplement 1).

Eichengreen, Barry J. (1992) *Golden Fetters: the Gold Standard and the Great Depression, 1919–1939.* Oxford University Press, New York.

—— (1998) *European Monetary Unification: Theory, Practice, and Analysis.* MIT Press, Cambridge, MA.

Fand, David I. (1954) *Estimates of Deposits and Vault Cash in the Non-National Banks in the Post Civil War Period in the United States: 1876–1896.* Ph.D. dissertation, University of Chicago.

Feldstein, Martin (1997) "The Political Economy of the European Monetary Union: Political Sources of an Economic Liability," *Journal of Economic Perspectives, 11.*

Frieden, Jeffrey A. (1997) "Monetary Populism in Nineteenth-Century America: An Open Economy interpretation," *Journal of Economic History, 57.*

Friedman, Milton (1990) "Bimetallism Revisited," *Journal of Economic Perspectives, 4.*

—— (1953) "The Case for Flexible Exchange Rates," in *Essays in Positive Economics.* University of Chicago Press, Chicago.

—— (1990) "The Crime of 1873," *Journal of Political Economy, 98.*

—— and Anna Jacobson Schwartz (1963) *A Monetary History of the United States.* Princeton University Press, for the NBER, Princeton, NJ.

—— and —— (1982) *Monetary Trends in the United States and the United Kingdom.* Chicago University Press, for the NBER, Chicago.

Greenfield, Robert and Hugh Rockoff (1996) "Yellowbacks Out West and Greebacks Back East: Social-Choice Dimensions of Monetary Reform," *Southern Economic Journal, 62.*

Harris, Seymour Edwin (1957) *International and Interregional Economics.* McGraw-Hill, New York.

Hartland, Penelope (1949) "Interregional Payments Compared with International Payments," *Quarterly Journal of Economics, 63.*

Huston, James L. (1987) *The Panic of 1857 and the Coming of the Civil War.* Louisiana State University Press, Baton Rouge, LA.

Kawai, Masahiro (1992) "Optimum Currency Areas," in Newman, Peter, Murray Milgate, and John Eatwell, eds, *The New Palgrave Dictionary of Money and Finance.* Macmillan, London.

Kenen, Peter B. (1969) "The Theory of Optimum Currency Areas: an Eclectic View," in Mundell, Robert A. and Alexander K. Swoboda, eds, *Monetary Problems of the International Economy.* University of Chicago Press, Chicago.

Libecap, Gary D. (1998) "The Great Depression and the Regulating State: Federal Government Regulation of Agriculture, 1884–1970," in Bordo, Michael D., Claudia Goldin, and Eugene N. White, eds, *The Defining Moment: the Great Depression and the American Economy in the Twentieth Century.* University of Chicago Press, for the NBER, Chicago.

McKinnon, Ronald I. (1963) "Optimum Currency Areas," *American Economic Review, 53.*

Meltzer, Allan (1998) "Chapter 6: In the Back Seat," Manuscript. Carnegie Mellon University, Pittsburgh, PA.

Merk, Frederick (1978) *History of the Westward Movement.* Alfred A. Knopf, New York.

Mundell, Robert A. (1961) "A Theory of Optimum Currency Areas," *American Economic Review* (September).

—— (1973) "Uncommon Arguments for Common Currencies," in Johnson, Harry and Alexander Swoboda, eds, *The Economics of Common Currencies.* George Allen & Unwin, London.

North, Douglass Cecil (1961) *The Economic Growth of the United States, 1790–1860.* Prentice-Hall, Englewood Cliffs, NJ.

Perkins, Edwin J. (1987) "Lost Opportunities for Compromise in the Bank War: A Reassessment of Jackson's Veto Message," *Business History Review, 61.*

Rolnick, Arthur J., Bruce D. Smith, and Warren E. Weber (1993) "In Order to Form a More Perfect Monetary Union," *Federal Reserve Bank of Minneapolis Quarterly Review, 17*(4).

Shackford, James Atkins (1986) *David Crockett: the Man and the Legend.* University of Nebraska Press, Lincoln, NE.

Schweitzer, Mary M. (1989) "State-Issued Currency and the Ratification of the US Constitution," *Journal of Economic History, 49*(2).

Sushka, Marie Elizabeth (1976) "The Antebellum Money Market and the Economic Impact of the Bank War," *Journal of Economic History, 36.*

Temin, Peter (1969) *The Jacksonian Economy*. Norton, New York.

Tower, Edward and Thomas D. Willett (1976) *The Theory of Optimum Currency Areas and Exchange-Rate Flexibility*. Special Studies in International Economics No. 11. Princeton International Finance Section, Princeton, NJ.

US Board of Governors of the Federal Reserve System (1943) *Banking and Monetary Statistics*. The National Capital Press, Washington, DC.

—— (1959) *All Bank Statistics, 1896–55.* Government Printing Office, Washington, DC.

US Bureau of the Census (1975) *Historical Statistics of the United States, Colonial Times to 1970*, Bicentennial Edition, Part I. Government Printing Office, Washington, DC.

US Comptroller of the Currency (1920) *Annual Report of the Comptroller of the Currency*. Government Printing Office, Washington, DC.

Willett, Thomas D. and Clas G. Wihlborg (1999) "The Relevance of the Optimum Currency Area Approach for Exchange Rate Policies in Emerging Market Economies," in Sweeney, Richard J., Clas G. Wihlborg, and Thomas D. Willett, eds, *Exchange-rate Policies for Emerging Market Economies*. Westview Press, Boulder, CO and Oxford.

Wright, Gavin (1996) *Old South, New South: Revolutions in the Southern Economy Since the Civil War*. Louisiana State University Press, Baton Rouge, LA.

Wyplosz, Charles (1997) "EMU: Why and How It Might Happen," *The Journal of Economic Perspectives, 11.*

Yeager, Leland Bennett (1959) "Exchange Rates Within a Common Market," *Social Research, 25.*

Comments on Chapter 4 – How long did it take the United States to become an optimal currency area?

Ronald McKinnon

In addition to its provocative title, Hugh Rockoff's paper provides a concise history of monetary union in the United States. From the demises of the First and Second Banks of the United States to the depressions of the 1890s and the 1930s, Rockoff neatly analyzes the political economy and monetary aspects of each episode. Reading the paper got me quickly up to speed on America's chequered monetary history.

However, Rockoff's overall historical narrative is also designed to test the hypothesis (and it is a little difficult to tell whether his hypothesis is tongue in cheek) that the US was *not* an optimal currency area for the first 150 years of its existence. That is, from 1788 to the mid-1930s, Rockoff hypothesizes that certain areas of the country such as the South, Midwest, and Far West could have done better economically if they had been on currency regimes separate from the industrial East. He provides useful data on differential (unsynchronized) cyclical fluctuations in bank deposits across these various regions. From these data and associated analysis, he suggests that, until the mid-1930s, having a single currency for all of the United States was not economically optimal. Thus, he concludes that the main, albeit very important, motivation for the US monetary union must have been political.

Rockoff recognizes the basic Friedman and Schwartz (1963) counter argument that much financial travail in the United States was because the country's common monetary standard itself was uncertain. In the nineteenth century, there was prolonged uncertainty over bimetallism. After the Civil War, the almost-successful agitation to abrogate the commitment to return to gold in favor of silver probably worsened the depressions of the early and mid 1890s. Populist agitation against whatever monetary standard existed was certainly aggravated. Similarly, the Federal Reserve's failure to use centralized open-market operations to prevent the onset of the great depression of the 1930s, in part because of (feared) gold drains, showed that the common American monetary standard was seriously deficient.

Apart from the inadequate common monetary standard, the structure of American banking and bank regulation through to the 1930s was also deficient. The proliferation of small unit banks, prohibitions on interstate branch banking, and the absence of a lender of last resort (until the Federal Reserve System was established in 1913) undoubtedly aggravated banking crises in general and regional downturns in particular.

Not much to disagree with so far. However, Rockoff wants to take the additional step of arguing, in the vein of Robert Mundell's 'A Theory of Optimum Currency

Areas' (1961), that greater monetary autonomy for the different regions of the United States would have been economically warranted even if a more stable monetary standard had existed in the (dominant) industrial East. Fluctuations in the agricultural terms of trade of the South and Midwest, and booms and busts in the Far West, often led to regional downturns with declines in their money stocks and runs on bank deposits.

Putting the matter in the argot of modern open-economy macroeconomics. Rockoff wonders whether such asymmetric shocks would have been less severe if there had been greater exchange-rate flexibility among regions. For example, in the face of a fall in the price of cotton, wouldn't it have been better if an independent southern monetary authority could have been more expansionary while allowing its currency to depreciate against that of the industrial East? Essentially, Rockoff is in the same camp as the large group of economists in thrall to the Mundell of 1961, the same group that in the 1990s opposed the advent of the euro on the grounds that a one-size-fits-all monetary policy was unlikely to be optimal for the diverse countries making up the EU.

Like most economists in the 1960s, Mundell still had a postwar Keynesian mindset in several related respects. First, he believed that governments could successfully fine-tune aggregate demand to offset private sector shocks on the supply or demand sides. Second, because factors of production, particularly labor, were only imperfectly mobile, he believed that this activism was best applied over a fairly small regional, or national, domain within which labor was fairly mobile and business fluctuations differed from those of its neighbors. (Rockoff goes out of his way to show that the southern labor market was separated from the rest of the country's.) Implementing a separate monetary policy would require each smallish region to maintain external exchange-rate flexibility. Third, Mundell's model of exchange rate determination – now commonly called the Mundell–Fleming model – was essentially static: people were assumed to have stationary expectations in the sense that markets – particularly the foreign exchanges – would not try to anticipate what the government might try to do, or how exchange and interest rates might move.

From this comforting postwar Keynesian perspective (to which the late Cambridge Nobel laureate, James Meade (1951), contributed), Mundell – and most other economists in the 1960s – presumed that a flexible exchange rate would be a smoothly adjusting variable for stabilizing the domestic economy. Whatever policy a central bank chose, a flexible exchange rate would depreciate smoothly if the bank pursued easy money, and appreciate smoothly if the bank pursued tight money.

Sadder but wiser after the 1971 breakdown of the Bretton Woods system of fixed dollar parities, we now know that untethered, or insecurely tethered, exchange rates can be volatile – better at disturbing the domestic macroeconomy than at absorbing shocks. And this volatility is greatly magnified if governments actively pull the levers of monetary and fiscal policy in the old Keynesian mode. Whence the modern forward-looking approach to exchange rate determination: today's exchange rate is largely determined by how markets guess country A's future monetary policy will evolve relative to that of country B – an easily and frequently changed guess that causes current exchange fluctuations.

In a not-much-later incarnation, Robert Mundell had already grasped much of this modern "forward-looking" perspective. At a 1970 Madrid conference on optimum currency areas, he presented two prescient papers on the advantages of common currencies. Perhaps in part because the conference proceedings were not published for several years, these papers have been overshadowed by his 1960s masterpieces.

The first of these papers, "Uncommon Arguments for Common Currencies" (Mundell 1973a), is of great intrinsic interest because very early it emphasized the forward-looking nature of the foreign exchange market. As such, it counters the idea that asymmetric shocks – i.e. those where an unexpected disturbance to national output affects one country differently from another – undermine the case for a common monetary standard. Instead, Mundell showed how having a common currency across countries can mitigate such shocks by better reserve pooling and more efficient forward contracting. Otherwise, leaving the exchange rate between the two countries flexible and thus uncertain would inhibit proper risk pooling in the international capital market.

Mundell's second Madrid paper, "A Plan for a European Currency" (1973b), makes clear his enthusiasm for monetary unification in Europe despite the seeming diversity of business cycle experiences in continental European countries. He recognized that a pan-European capital market couldn't possibly work satisfactorily in the presence of multiple currencies with uncertain exchange rates.

If the pre-euro European experience is any guide, the markets would naturally select one currency as the strong or "center" currency in the system. Before the advent of the euro, the German mark played the role of the safe-haven currency, and German bunds were regarded as "risk-free" bonds with the lowest interest rates. Then, around the periphery of Germany, countries with weaker currencies, i.e. those that were floating or insecurely fixed against the mark, ran with higher interest rates – sometimes much higher as in the cases of Greece, Italy, Portugal, and Spain. Only if European countries succeeded in integrating their monetary policies with that of Germany so that their exchange rates against the mark seemed secure – as with the Netherlands, Belgium, Austria, and eventually even France – could they run with interest rates only a percentage point or so higher than in Germany. And in the weak-currency countries, long-term private bond markets were virtually nonexistent.

In nineteenth-century America, the existence of fluctuating relative currency values would have greatly impeded, if not undermined altogether, the development of a nationwide capital market with proper asset diversification. In which currency would interstate debts have been denominated?

The industrialized East, the natural creditor in the system, would likely provide the strong currency. The currencies of the more agrarian and shock-prone regions of the South, Midwest, and Far West would look much riskier – particularly if their money managers engaged in Keynesian activism. These peripheral regions would then run with much higher interest rates for assets denominated in their own currencies – and would be forced to denominate their external debts in the East's currency. Interstate capital flows would become much riskier, and the problems of bank regulation, e.g. forcing banks to hedge their foreign exchange risks, would be more acute. Because of the bankruptcy threat to domestic debtors, a monetary manager on the periphery would be loathe to let its currency depreciate even in the face of an adverse terms of trade shock.

So, with separate regional currencies, the United States would have got the worst of both worlds: a poorly functioning capital market with imperfectly rigid exchange rates. Alexander Hamilton had it right back in 1790: better to strive for monetary unity from the beginning of an economic union as the continental Europeans, with the great success of their euro, have come to appreciate two centuries later.

References

Friedman, Milton and Anna Schwartz (1963) *A Monetary History of the United States*. Princeton University Press, for the NBER, Princeton, NJ.

Meade, James E. (1951) *The Balance of Payments*. Oxford University Press, Oxford.

Mundell, Robert A. (1961) "A Theory of Optimum Currency Areas," *American Economic Review, 51.*

——(1973a) "Uncommon Arguments for Common Currencies," in Johnson, H. G. and A. K. Swoboda, eds, *The Economics of Common Currencies*. Allen and Unwin, London.

——(1973b) "A Plan for a European Currency," in Johnson, H. G. and A. K. Swoboda, eds, *The Economics of Common Currencies*. Allen and Unwin, London.

Comments on Chapter 4 – How long did it take the United States to become an optimal currency area?

Anna J. Schwartz

Hugh has provided a useful survey of episodes from 1789 to post-World War II in which US monetary union imposed costs on certain regions hit by asymmetric shocks. In each instance, those regions relinquished "the capacity to use exchange rate changes and monetary policy" to ameliorate local distress originating elsewhere. Instead, they had to rely on interregional movements of labor and capital to relieve distress. Hugh concludes that the US did not become an optimal currency area until the 1940s. Turning from US experience to countries that are members of a monetary union, he stresses the importance of fiscal transfers for distressed regions as well as lender of last resort facilities or deposit insurance to prevent real shocks from evolving into banking crises.

I shall comment first on what the US record of monetary union teaches us about its costs and benefits, and then about applying what we've learned from the US record to European Monetary Union.

The US record of monetary union

I shall argue that the US was an optimal currency area from the start. Hugh lists five criteria by which to judge whether an area qualified as a candidate for its own currency. The US clearly qualified.

The first criterion is that it must be a large area. From 13 states at its beginning, the US was a large area that continued to grow until it encompassed 50 states.

The second criterion is that it must be specialized in the production of certain goods and subject to asymmetric shocks. The US was specialized in agricultural products at its start and then diversified into manufactures, and it was subject to asymmetric shocks from crop failures and hostile actions by other countries.

The third criterion is that labor mobility between the candidate region and other regions is limited. Labor mobility within the US was pronounced but limited outwards.

The fourth criterion is that capital mobility between the candidate region and other regions is limited. Capital mobility within the US was moderate but limited outwards.

The fifth and final criterion is that fiscal transfers between the candidate region and other regions are limited. Fiscal transfers within the US were moderate but limited outwards.

On the basis of these criteria, the US from the start was an optimal currency union. If it had not been optimal, it would not have endured. The assumption that the US monetary union could not have been an optimal currency area until fiscal federalism was achieved, which is the basis for Hugh's belief that optimality was not attained until 150 years after monetary unification, is faithful to the Mundell ideology but not to the internal and external reality.

The states were bound together by a sense of national purpose and a shared vision of their place in the world. The rest of the world from the start had no doubt that the US was an optimum currency area (even if it was never aware of the notion), with a common currency, the dollar. There was a nominal par value of the dollar per pound sterling. There were well-developed foreign exchanges for making foreign payments from 1790 on, including the payment of principal and interest on the foreign debt.

Hugh's argument, however, is that a monetary union is not *ipso facto* an optimal currency area. His evidence against optimality from the start is, first, his recital of the episodes in US economic history in which individual regions might have been better off with independent monetary policy and, second, the New Deal and postwar institutional changes.

Yet, as Hugh himself notes, the fact of regional disparities during US cyclical change is no different currently than in earlier episodes that he discusses. He cannot claim progress toward optimality on this basis. So can Hugh sustain the claim on the basis of the development of federally funded transfer programs, improvements in the functioning of the labor market, the creation of a federal safety net?

There is an underlying triumphalism in the account, as if the march toward optimality has been onward and upward. Yet each of the institutional changes Hugh mentions has not been wholly benign. Each has had negative side effects. Because fiscal transfers create winners and losers, they are politically divisive. The flaws in social security and agricultural price supports are well known but resistant to reform. Federal labor legislation has stifled employment. Postwar banking and financial crises have emanated from mispriced deposit insurance and misguided monetary policies.

It is doubtful, in my view, that US monetary union early or late ever achieved perfection. Regional disparities existed before the 1930s, when fiscal transfers for distressed regions were unimportant, and have existed since then, after the US adopted an extensive system of fiscal federalism. Perhaps monetary union because of fiscal transfers operates more smoothly, but I do not regard this development as the culmination of US monetary unification.

Applying US experience to EMU

Thinking about the US in 1789 and the EMU in 1999 suggests one big difference between the two monetary experiments. The early one had popular support; the later one does not. The goal of building a nation was not sought at the expense of obliterating the identity of the states of the Union. In 1999, the goal seems to be to obliterate national identity and to create a European identity.

The first question to ask about EMU is whether, on the basis of the five criteria that Hugh cites, it qualifies as an optimum currency area. It qualifies on the basis of size. There is less homogeneity in the composition of GDP among individual EMU countries than there was among the 13 states of the Union in 1789. EMU flunks the labor and possibly capital market mobility criteria, but does well on the fiscal transfers criterion. But if fiscal transfers within the EMU compensate for relative labor and capital immobility, as Hugh suggests, EMU overall still falls short of an ideal optimum currency area.

What is unknown at the present juncture is whether the introduction of a single currency in the EMU has brought transactions cost savings that outweigh possible increases in cyclical instability. There is temporal diversity of business cycle phases in individual EMU countries, so that a common monetary policy administered by the ECB will be inappropriate for some of the member nations.

The next question to ask about EMU is what role political union plays in the operation of a monetary union. Hugh refers to a paper by Rolnick, Smith, and Weber that regards monetary union as a prerequisite for political union. Feldstein, on the other hand, has argued that political union may have adverse effects on the monetary union. In the US case, political and monetary union coincided. The EMU will provide evidence on whether or not political union is essential to monetary union.

One argument that has been made for political unification is that it is needed to constrain fiscal laxness at the member country level that could destabilize the single currency. In the absence of political unification, a member country might incur large budget deficits that the central bank would in the end monetize. Power and authority over national budgets, on this argument, must be transferred to the federal level of the European Union. Fiscal autonomy must be sacrificed by the member countries along with monetary autonomy for monetary union to be successful. This view does not build on US experience, which leaves some budget authority to the states with the federal level dominant.

The pursuit of monetary union in Western Europe has not been an end in itself. Its architects have pursued it as a means of achieving a political end. The unification of European countries, with a common foreign and military policy and centralized economic and social policies, is a scheme to eliminate war among the constituent countries. There is a Rube Goldberg element of contrivance to the scheme.

There is no reason to believe that there will be perfect harmony in a federal Europe. It may lead to an increase in conflicts among the constituent countries rather than solidifying whatever the advantages of a single market and a single currency.

I conclude that what can be learned from US monetary union is in large measure not readily applicable to the European example.

5 The bank, the states, and the market: an Austro-Hungarian tale for Euroland, 1867–1914

Marc Flandreau

Something Old,
Something New,
Something Borrowed,
– And Something Blue . . .

The continent has finally embarked into monetary union. For years, the project has led to extensive debates among money doctors. In the Old World, some have recommended it as the only solution to avoid re-enacting Europe's tragic twentieth-century story, with its deadly cocktail of protection, lack of co-operation, and exchange rate instability. Many American doctors on the other hand have expressed their doubts. Europe, they emphasized, 'is not an optimum currency area' – a polite way to mean 'It Ain't Going to Work'. At any rate, all serious experts have unanimously concurred in their characteristically conservative style that 'something new is coming' (Dornbusch, Favero and Giavazzi 1998).

Economic historians tend to retain their doubts towards novelty. Indeed, research in this area has been especially active during the past twenty years. Numerous contributions have used the study of past monetary experiments as a way to shed light on current endeavours. Among the experiences which have received special attention, we find the Italian and German monetary unions of the nineteenth century, the US experience, as well at the Latin Union, and the Scandinavian Union. Other chapters in this volume provide references to these by now well known historical experiences.[1] This chapter, by contrast, focuses on one episode which so far has not received any attention. It is that of the Habsburg 'dual' monarchy, between 1867 and 1914. From an economic point of view, the 'dualist' system – or 'Cacania' as novelist Robert Musil called it to mock a complex legal-bureaucratic structure which is not without resemblance with today's eurocracy – was an agreement whose institutional design was shaped through a number of arrangements between its two constituent political entities, the Empire of Austria and the Kingdom of Hungary. These arrangements, known as 'Compromises', essentially provided for the free circulation of goods and capital within the union while at the same time leaving complete fiscal autonomy to each part. Moreover, while this feature was not initially a formal part of the first 'Compromise' of 1867, the dual monarchy retained a single central bank, inherited from Austria. Thus, while not a monetary union by name, the dual monarchy displayed several of the key characteristics of the current Euroland which combines a single market, a large 'subsidiarity' on fiscal matters, and a federal monetary system.[2]

During its 50 years of existence, the Habsburg economic union operated without major disruption, providing for an almost doubling of incomes per head. It took a global war with massive political consequences that were not limited to central Europe to destroy what had so far been a fairly stable construct. Ironically, it is only the *collapse* of the Habsburg monarchy, not its normal functioning over a course of 50 years, which has attracted the attention of researchers. But if some have claimed that the collapse of the Habsburg monarchy did have monetary relevance they were careful to restrict it to the post Soviet Confederation of Independent States.[3] Nothing one may say, Europeans should worry about. In fact, our memories of the operation of the Habsburg experiment seem to have been obscured by the trauma of its ending. But as this chapter intends to demonstrate, one has to go beyond the post war hyper-inflation and disintegration to find an economic system that bears more than casual resemblance with current European issues.

This article revolves around the following theme: because the Habsburg monetary union had no Stability Pact, governments could cover their deficits, either by borrowing in the international capital market, or possibly by deriving seigniorage from the common currency which was managed by the central bank. As a result, the dual monarchy brought together four players with potentially conflicting goals: the common central bank who waged a long war in order to increase its control over monetary policy; the two 'national' governments (Austria and Hungary) who in times sought to increase public spending in order to foster economic development in their part of the monarchy; and the 'market mechanism' which lent to governments and was thus concerned about minimizing the risks of investing in public securities. The combined actions of these four players determined the performance of the union as well as much of its dynamics. In particular, it will be argued that the market mechanism served as a disciplining device which contributed to the increase in the power of the common central bank. The desire to stabilize the gyrations of the exchange rate which had occurred in the 1880s at a time of fiscal profligacy led in the early 1890s to a comprehensive reform of the Austro-Hungarian monetary system which resulted in the emergence of the Austro-Hungarian central bank as a formidable institutional player.

The remainder of the paper is organized as follows. The first section provides a critical review of nineteenth century monetary unions. We argue that none of the existing experiences does offer a close enough parallel to the current European experience and suggest that the Austro-Hungarian experience may have, by contrast, much to tell. The second section surveys the evolution of fiscal and monetary rules within the Habsburg monetary union. The final section focuses on the record of market discipline and documents its operation.

Which lessons from nineteenth-century monetary unions?

At first sight, the second half of the nineteenth century provides an almost inextinguishable supply of experiences of monetary union. Concentrating on the European experience only, we find at least five major experiments. In chronological order: the Swiss unification in 1848 (Paillard 1909), the Italian unification of 1861 (Sanucci 1989), the Latin Union of 1865 between Belgium, France, Italy and Switzerland (Willis 1901; Flandreau 1993, 1995 and 2000; Einaudi 2000 and 2001), the Austro-German Münzverein of 1857 and the German unification of 1871 (Holtfrerich 1989 and 1993; James 1997) and finally the Scandinavian union of 1873 with Sweden, Norway, and Denmark (Bergman 1999; Henrikson and Koergard 1995; Jonung 2001). (See Hefeker (1995) for a synthesis on the making of monetary unions in the nineteenth century.) There was also a large supply of schemes – serious and not so serious – which were floated but never implemented. These include France's bid for a universal currency which was aired during the 1867 Paris conference (Flandreau 2001; Einaudi 2001), Bagehot's plan to merge the British currency with the American one (Bagehot 1869) and numerous blueprints volunteered by monetary cranks.[4] But despite the apparent wealth of episodes, none of the above mentioned provides an acceptable parallel to the current European experience. This is not because of the usual caveats which apply when one seeks to draw time comparisons between economic systems that change over time, but because of deep, structural differences between these historical experiences and that in which continental Europeans are currently engaged.

Nineteenth-century monetary unions, type I: international groupings

A substantial literature (Perlman 1993; Vanthoor 1996) has sought to draw lessons from nineteenth century monetary 'unions' for contemporary Europe. The conclusions from these works include the importance of political factors in bringing about these monetary unions, the need of a critical level of co-operation for them to survive and the importance of large economic shocks or political divergence in bringing the union down. However deep these insights are, the word 'union' to define the international arrangements of the nineteenth century (that is, the *Münzverein*, the LMU, the SCU) is a plain misnomer. These treaties, in effect, never sought to pool national monetary sovereignties under a common central bank. Each country retained its domestic note issue system (be it central banking or free banking), and merely agreed that gold or silver specie issued in one country be accepted within the 'union'. Thus these arrangements did not encompass banknotes or bills of exchange. Since in general the intrinsic value of the gold and silver coins was close to their nominal value, the risks associated with securing such a convention were small. In effect these arrangements merely legalized a phenomenon that was frequently driven by private agents: in regions close to the border, foreign coins often circulated alongside domestic ones, especially when they had identical weight and size (Willis 1901). As a result, there were calls for public action to put some order in this system, either by banning foreign coins, or by legalising their use. Through the Latin 'Union', for instance, governments merely agreed that these identical gold or silver coins which Italy, France, Belgium and Switzerland had issued in the past, and which already circulated abroad, would be accepted for payments in 'public treasuries'. The Latin Union was initially called '*Convention monétaire de 1865*', suggesting that contemporaries realized the difference between a currency 'treaty' and a true monetary union, which the Latin 'Union' was not.

Additional evidence of our claim is the fact that these pseudo unions did not eliminate internal exchange rate fluctuations. In the absence of a common central bank agreeing to clear international balances at a fixed price, importers had still to buy foreign exchange to settle their purchases or to arrange for sending specie abroad. Because sending specie entailed transportation costs, importers generally preferred to buy foreign exchange as long as the loss in exchange rate was smaller than the cost of shipping bullion. Thus bilateral exchange rates between member states could move within 'bullion points', in very much the same manner as it did between countries that were not part of the same monetary union but shared a common standard. Thus, these international groupings should be called 'common standard areas' rather than unions in a modern sense. Members of the *Münzverein* for instance, all shared the silver standard. Members of the Latin Union shared a bimetallic standard. Members of the Scandinavian Union shared a common gold standard.

It is true that because domestic specie was readily acceptable for foreign payments and did not need to be recoined when exported, one element of the bullion points was eliminated: in modern language this implied, other things being equal, a smaller 'target zone' for participants of such a currency unions, and thus presumably less monetary autonomy for each (Svensson 1994). But this element was not very large and with the transition to the gold standard, it became almost negligible. It was in any case dwarfed by the much larger transportation costs. During the 1880s for instance, owing to smaller transportation fees and better connections, the size of these bullion points was smaller between England and Germany (two LMU non-members) than between France and Italy (two LMU members).

A final proof that these groupings had little to do with true monetary unions becomes even more evident if we recall that nothing prevented any member of any of these 'unions' to engage in debt monetization. Under a regime of full monetary sovereignty, it is not possible to prevent any member from financing deficits through money printing. As a matter of fact, this was done by Italy in May 1866, just when the Latin 'Union' was ratified by the respective national parliaments. At this date, Italy decided to finance its war effort to free Lombardia-Veneto from the Austrian Empire through money creation. Convertibility was suspended, and Italian exchange rates moved beyond the 'union's' specie points: by this action Italy had *de facto* left the Latin currency area.

In effect, exchange depreciation – that is *de facto* departure from the union's parity – can be seen as the way through which, in a system where no rule was binding monetary policy, discipline was maintained: if one country inflated, it faced the possibility of exchange depreciation. Depreciation would lead to the suspension of participation to the arrangement. Moreover, such decisions had limited externalities on the monetary policies of other participating countries, at least if the departing country was relatively small.[5] Italy's depreciation of the 1860s for instance, did not cause exchange depreciation elsewhere in the Latin Union.[6] The only possible disruption which exchange depreciation could produce was to create transitory competitive advantages. But since none of these unions provided for a customs union, import duties could be used as an offsetting device: there were custom duties between the Habsburg Empire and German States participating to the *Münzverein.* Duties were fairly high among members of the SCU. And Latin Union members France and Italy waged a trade war in the 1880s.[7]

All this makes the nineteenth century 'unions' fairly different from the current situation which has often been presented as the natural extension of the single market. It shows why the nature of discipline in these unions was totally different from the one we have today. From that respect, the nineteenth-century European groupings do at most provide an imperfect parallel for the defunct ERM (Europe's former Exchange Rate Mechanism), which established parities, fluctuation bands a bit akin to the bullion points, and exit options.[8] But they cannot aid thinking about Euroland, where monetary sovereignty has been effectively surrendered to the European Central Bank and where a temporary float is no longer an option. Discipline cannot work in a decentralized fashion as it did in nineteenth-century groupings or under the ERM. And thus the great concerns and debates which the need to internalize fiscal and monetary discipline have attracted in Europe.

Nineteenth-century monetary unions, type II: nation-state building

By contrast to the 'international groupings' described above, Italy, Germany, and Switzerland's nineteenth-century experiences did lead to full monetary unification. A common specie standard was created and a common market was sealed. At the same time, a fully fledged central/federal level was created resulting in the limitation of the ability of authorities to borrow. Moreover, regional authorities had no longer access to seigniorage. Thus, unlike what happened in the international groupings, regions could not carry on their own monetary course. Hence at the same time when participating members lost the power to protect themselves against competitive devaluation through import duties, they also lost the very ability of implementing these monetary policies that could lead to regional exchange depreciation: these processes thus rested on political integration which mitigated the centrifugal regional forces. The robustness of the political construct even enabled these unions to set up their central bank only gradually, with monetary rules acting as a substitute in the more or less extended period before which full monetary centralisation was achieved. In practise in all these experiments, a long debate about the relative merits of free banking and central banking took place, reflecting the fact that former regional economic prerogatives were hard lived. But since regional banks of issue could no longer finance regional deficits, the debate had no public finance flavour, and could be carried on, among *laissez faire* supporters, in 'purely economic' terms.

And in the end all these countries evolved towards central banking: decisive steps were taken in 1876 in Germany (Holtfrerich [1989]), in 1894 in Italy (Sanucci 1989) and in 1907 in Switzerland.[9]

Despite the appeal which these experiments may have, we should be careful not to hasten too much in drawing implications for Euroland: today's Europeans have adopted a single currency without political unification, suggesting that the current experience is fairly different from the three 'national' precedents of the nineteenth century. In fact, the process through which Italy, Germany and Switzerland went, cannot be distinguished from the broader context of nineteenth-century nation-state building. The centre piece of these experiences was the creation (according to specific dynamics in each case) of a central or federal state with large spending, taxing and borrowing privileges. Of course, the degree of centralization was a matter of taste: Cavour opted for a French inspired, highly centralist, Italian state. Bismarck by contrast, had to deal with the fierce resistance of some opponents to Prussia – chiefly Bavaria – meaning that each former 'country' retained a measure of power and autonomy. But the 'Imperial' (Federal) state was run by a government designated by a Parliament: the German Reich was a nation.[10] Switzerland finally, although the most culturally heterogeneous country of the lot and the one in which, for that reason, local prerogatives were best protected, did adopt a federal government with authority over monetary and budgetary issues.[11] In all cases then, the centralization of political power thus meant a centralization of fiscal discipline.

It is obvious that these features of the 'true' monetary unions of the nineteenth century are at odds with the current European situation. Some may announce the making of the 'United States of Europe'. But the fact is that the critical level of basic agreement to create a supranational government with large economic powers seem to be lacking today, and that while we have been able to agree on currency unification, we seem much less able to agree on political union. Some advocate the creation of a larger federal budget as a way to foster regional stabilization in the wake of adverse economic shocks. But the painful debates which take place each time national contributions to the (tiny) EU budget are being renegotiated remind us of the challenges involved. In the last instance, deficits are borne not by a central budgetary authority but by regional budgets. Euroland is anything but a federal system where fiscal issues are concerned, and this is likely to remain so, as long as subsidiarity in budgetary matters shall continue to rule the waves. But then, in the absence of central institutions, the question of the way through which discipline is enforced comes back with a vengeance. How can we possibly combine federalism in the monetary area and sovereignty in the fiscal area? It could well be that the current experience is entirely new.

As explained in the introduction, it is paradoxically the one nineteenth-century arrangement which has never been called a monetary union which will retain our interest in this chapter. The reason is, as Table 5.1 makes it clear, that when it comes to institutional design, there are many more similarities between Euroland and the dual monarchy than between it and any of the nineteenth-century 'monetary unions'. Unlike the LMU, the SCU or the *Münzverein*, but very much like Euroland, the Habsburg monarchy did have a common central bank and a unified exchange

Table 5.1 Lessons from the past?

	Arrangement (creation)	*Common central bank/exchange rate*	*Common market/ trade policy*	*Fiscal federalism*
International groupings	LMU[a] (1865)	No	No	No
	SMU[b] (1873)	No[d]	No	No
	AGMU[c] (1857)	No	No	No
Nation building	Italy (1860)	Yes	Yes	Yes
	Germany (1871)	Yes	Yes	Yes
	Switzerland (1848)	Yes	Yes	Yes
Monetary unions	Austro-Hungarian monarchy (1867)	Yes	Yes	No (dualism)
	Euroland (1999)	Yes	Yes	No (subsidiarity)

Notes
[a] Latin Monetary Union.
[b] Scandinavian Union.
[c] Austro-German Monetary Union.
[d] Except for the transitory 1885–1905 clearing arrangement between central banks. The arrangement was suspended for fear of growing imbalances.

rate. Moreover it did have a single market – a customs union – like Europe: discipline could not be achieved through retaliatory protection, contrary to what had obtained within nineteenth-century pseudo monetary unions. On the other hand, unlike the Italian, German or Swiss experiences which had resulted in the making of national economic institutions, but again, very much like Euroland, the Habsburg monarchy, provided for fiscal sovereignty, thus leaving open the question of how fiscal discipline would be implemented. It is true that the Austro-Hungarian setting had not emerged, as has happened in Euroland, from a monetary 'marriage' between participating countries. Instead, the design of the dual monarchy was the product of a fiscal 'divorce' which occurred in 1867, and through which Hungary gained complete autonomy over its fiscal process. Yet if the starting points were quite different, the resulting institutional structures are strikingly similar. Thus for the same reason that we can say that Euroland was born in 1999 when participating countries adopted a common currency, we can say that the Austro-Hungarian monetary union, while never called that way, was born in 1867.

The Habsburg Monarchy as a monetary lesson

The defeat of the Austrians by Prussia in 1866 marked the end of the Habsburg attempts to rule over Central Europe. Austrians had to find a way to grant Hungary increased economic freedom while at the same time retaining the economic unity of the stumbling Empire. The result was the so-called 'Compromise of 1867' (*Ausgleich* in German, or *Kieghyezés* in Hungarian) a comprehensive agreement which carefully delineated political and economic rights and obligations.[12] The *Ausgleich* was signed for ten years. It was renewed every ten years until 1917 through negotiation rounds.

It recognized that the two parts of the monarchy were distinct political entities, and defined the domains where the two countries were fully sovereign, and those where sovereignty was shared. Among the latter we find the common market and trade policy, the common currency, a common army, a common diplomacy and foreign representatives. Among the former were the right for each part to have its own parliament, government, electoral system, laws and budgets. Thus the dual monarchy can be called a *de facto* monetary union.

Budgetary organization of the Habsburg Monarchy

The set up

Musil used to describe the constitution of 'Cacania' as more difficult to comprehend than the Mystery of the Holy Trinity. Trained as we are by the subtleties of the European Compromise (aka the Maastricht Treaty) the Austro-Hungarian budgetary set up may appear, if not of Biblical simplicity, at least manageable. It is summarized in Figure 5.1. Dualism meant full fiscal sovereignty. The Compromise thus defined a two-tier fiscal system with a 'confederal' level and a 'national' level. The 'common'

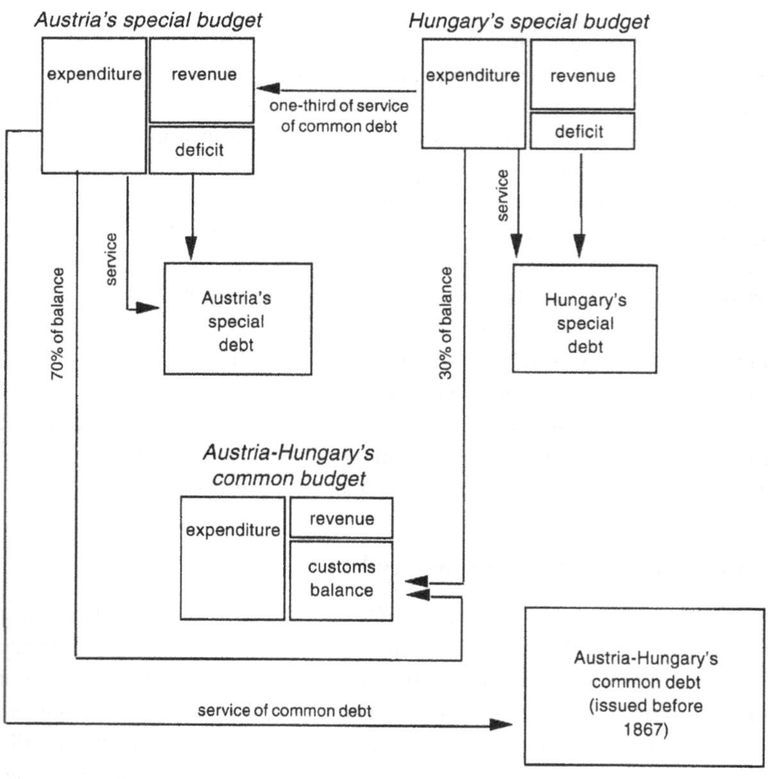

Figure 5.1 The Austro-Hungarian budgetary structure.

finances were placed under the joint supervision of the 'Delegations' made of representatives of each national parliament, implying that regional authorities controlled confederal ones, not the other way round.[13] Common finances had a 'government' appointed by the Emperor and King. But this government was a mere administration with no initiative, as the agreement of the Delegations was necessary before any decision could be taken, and the common government, once funding rules for the common debt were agreed upon, turned out to be a mechanism rather than an authority.[14] In the end the power of the confederate level was tightly limited by the prerogatives of the national governments.

On the expenditure side, the common budgets regrouped expenses of joint interest, mainly military spending (above 90 per cent of the total).[15] The interest service on the 'common debt' that had been issued before 1867 was supported, not by the common finances, but directly by Austria, with Hungary paying its counterpart an annuity corresponding to the share of the common debt (roughly one-third) which Hungarians had acknowledged as their own, as part of the Compromise. On the revenue side, the common budget was financed by the proceeds from customs.[16] Given the highly self-centred nature of Austro-Hungarian trade (most of Hungarian imports came from Austria and vice versa) these typically fell short of overall expenses and extra resources had to be found to make up the difference.[17] To limit the scope of the central government, common accounts were to be balanced, and no new debt issued, except if both parts agreed: any remaining common deficit had thus to be borne by Austria and Hungary's 'national' budgets, according to a pre-assigned rule of roughly two-thirds for Austria and one-third for Hungary. Of course, the precise sharing rule was the subject of intense negotiations between Austria and Hungary and were a prominent aspect of Compromise rounds.

At the 'country' level we find the 'special' budgets of Hungary and Austria. By contrast to the budgets of the Delegations, they were not bound to be in equilibrium. This reflected each country's sovereignty, and was thus an essential building block of Dualism. As contemporary observers remarked: 'Political dualism could not go without budgetary dualism, and, accordingly, the Compromise of 1867 clearly established the principle of separation between Austrian and Hungarian finances'.[18] In each part of the Empire, national parliaments had full authority over the fiscal process. To fund deficits, they could grant their respective governments the right to issue given types of bonds, for given amounts. Thus each country could accumulate, on top of the share of the common debt to whose service it did contribute, its own debt, known as the 'special' debt. Since new common loans were essentially ruled out and that the public debt outstanding in 1867 was subject to an amortization scheme, the size of the common debt with respect to the 'special' debts was bound to decrease.

The record

Such was the setting in which Austrian and Hungarian finances were managed. No stability pact, it will be observed, had been signed, and this was one difference with the current situation in Europe to which we shall come back later. This implied that both Austria and Hungary could go on borrowing on the capital market as much as they deemed fit. And indeed, the pressures for borrowing were large. Alexander Gerschenkron's theory of 'relative backwardness' has provided a well-known characterization of the policies which a number of Central-Eastern European states implemented in order to achieve 'big spurts' supposedly resulting in a quantum leap of economic development. These policies involved heavy public intervention in industrial investment through protection, subsidies, interest guarantees or direct undertakings.[19] They implied large spending and, since time was necessary to bring resources in line with revenues that would accrue from taxation once development had occurred, they required large borrowing. As a matter of fact, the Habsburg Empire had begun with these 'gerschenkronian' policies after 1848, but their implementation had often collided with diplomatic and military requirements. The re-orientation towards more peaceful policies that followed the final defeat against Prussia paved the way for an intensification of such endeavours.[20]

While the trauma that had followed the war and the need to reorganize its finances on a narrower basis induced the Austrian part of the monarchy to remain comparatively sober in the very first years of the dualist era (1867–73), Hungarians immediately engaged into aggressive investment policies (Eddie 1982). The creation and consolidation of a national economy meant heavy public borrowing most notably to improve transportation which, the Hungarians felt, had so far been neglected by the Habsburgs. Thus while Austria did not issue long-term loans until after 1875, Hungary immediately used its newly acquired fiscal autonomy to borrow in Vienna and abroad. The economic depression caused by the 1873 market crash, however, led Austria to join the band. The result was a rise in public borrowing in both parts of the monarchy.

Figure 5.2 describes the evolution of Austrian and Hungarian 'special' deficits as a share of government revenues.[21] It is clear that special budgets did exhibit strikingly similar patterns. Until the late 1880s, a tendency towards persistent deficits is visible. Moreover, we observe a number of 'hikes' corresponding to the construction or repurchase of railway lines by the two governments. Given that the extension of the railway network was sometimes the result of joint undertakings by both parts of the

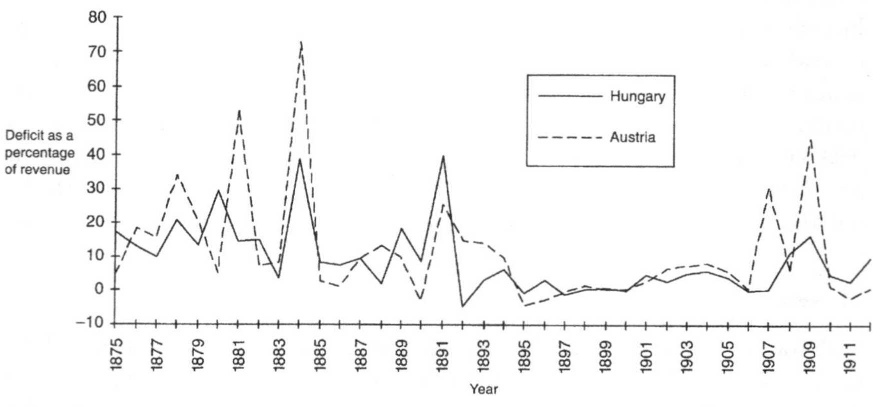

Figure 5.2 Deficits in Austria and Hungary, 1875–1912.

monarchy, it is only a half surprise that some of these hikes should occur at the same time, as in 1884. There was thus a Austro-Hungarian precedent to the Delors–Lafontaine scheme for public works in Europe. At the turn of the decade, however, both parts of the Empire began to make efforts to stem the recurrence of public deficits. In the Parliamentary debates we find intense discussion about tax increases. Several indirect duties, such as that on spirits, were raised (Eddie 1982). Railway building slowed down, as the large programmes designed in the 1880s came to completion. In Hungary, a last railway loan was issued in 1891 for the so-called 'Austro-Hungarian' line.[22]

The 1890s were years of relative sobriety in both parts of the monarchy, although Hungary was quicker than Austria in its effort to bring about equilibrium in public finances. But after the fiscal austerity of the 1890s, Hungary went back into deficit before the turn of the century and remained there during most of the period, except for the years 1907–8. These deficits, however, were moderate by historical standards. Austria, on the other hand, sustained its fiscal effort slightly longer, in effect until after 1900.[23] It is only after 1905 – that is, after the fall of the Körber government – that deficits resumed. While these were indeed large in some years, the claim by Eduard März (1984) that Austria was, in the pre-war years, a 'state living beyond its means' seems to be somewhat exaggerated. The mild deterioration of public finances was in part due to the growth of military spending which accelerated after the annexation of Bosnia-Herzegovina in 1908. As is visible from Figure 5.3 which compares the evolution of common expenses to that of common revenues, the balance to which Austria and Hungary had to contribute increased quite dramatically in these years. Common accounts thus provided a channel through which national accounts could be affected by external conflict, and had

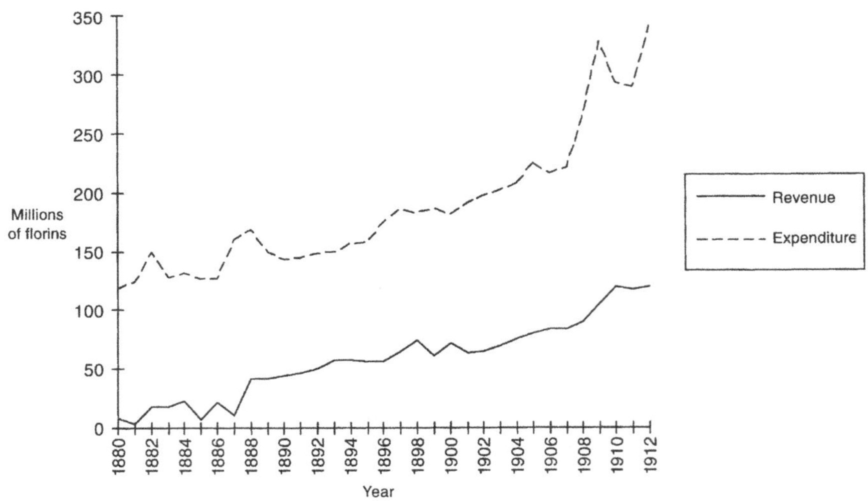

Figure 5.3 Common budgets in Austria and Hungary, 1880–1912.

Source: elaborated by the author from Crédit Lyonnais files.

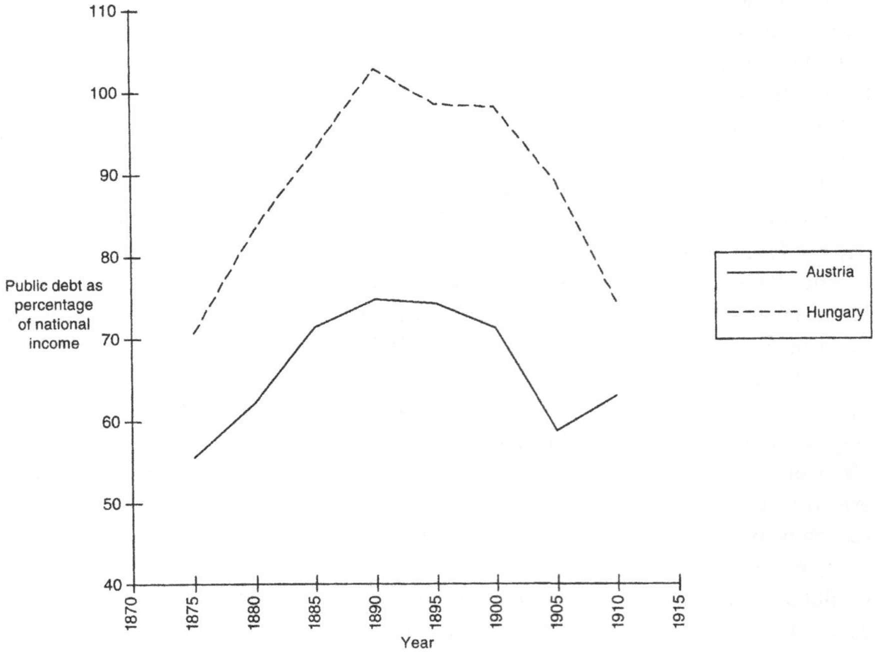

Figure 5.4 Quinquennial estimates of the burden of public debts in Austria and Hungary, 1875–1910. (Author's computations from Crédit Lyonnais archives (public debts) and interpolations on various estimates of Austro-Hungarian national incomes.)

some reasons to display a measure of correlation: this was certainly one reason why Franz-Josef repeatedly emphasized that peace was an essential ingredient for the stability of the Habsburg economic union.

Figure 5.4, to conclude, displays quinquennial estimates of the nominal public debts of Austria and Hungary (special debt and share of common debt added) in terms of national income.[24] We find that the evolution matches the general tendencies which we have identified so far. Both debt burdens series display a rapid accumulation until 1890. Hungary's initially higher stock of debt gives it a lead which it keeps during the 1880s. The two ratios slow down around 1890, and by 1895 the trend was reversed. The 1907–9 Austrian deficits are perceptible and cause the debt burden gap between the two parts of the monarchy to narrow. Both public debt ratios, however, became substantially smaller than those obtained during the 1880s, reinforcing the conclusion that, despite the comments of contemporaries such as Böhm-Bawerk, the deterioration of the Austrian fiscal balance after 1900 was fairly sustainable in both absolute and relative terms.[25] The same is *a fortiori* true for Hungary whose public indebtedness, in terms of national income, stayed on its declining trend.

These findings raise an interesting question: the respective fiscal performances in Austria and Hungary reveal trends which bear many similarities. The age of deficits and rising debts in the 1870s and 1880s was then followed by a period of budgetary equilibrium during the 1890s, before the two parts moved again into deficits, albeit this time in a somewhat different way. The common accounts were one channel through which fiscal shocks could be shared. But given their small share with respect to special budgets they certainly do not account for the overall tendencies observed over the 40-year period for which we have data. In the absence of a stability pact, this is a fairly interesting finding. Discussion of the monetary setting may presumably give us some clues.

Monetary rules in the Habsburg Monarchy

From the ÖNB to the ÖUB

In 1867, the dual monarchy inherited its monetary institutions from the Austrian Empire. The monetary standard, as for any country of the *Münzverein*, was silver. In effect the circulation was made of inconvertible paper money issued by both the government and the proto central bank, the Austrian National Bank. The Austrian National Bank (*Österreichische National Bank* or ÖNB) was a private institution created at the end of the Napoleonic wars in order to stabilize the Austrian currency. In the past however, the ÖNB had served as a banker for the Austrian State. Its resources were called upon every time the Empire was involved in military conflicts (Zückerkandl 1911). In 1862, the ÖNB had received its third privilege. The new charter had been designed to mop up the paper monies which the government had circulated at par with ÖNB banknotes to finance the war with Piedmont. Automatic credit lines to the government were ruled out but for an 80 million florin interest free advance. As Zeuceanu (1924: vi) observed, 'in the new statutes, there was more independence with respect to the State'. The 'agio' (discount of a paper currency against specie) on the florin declined and specie convertibility was in sight when the 1866 campaign (against Prussia and Italy, the same that had forced Italy out of the Latin Union) erupted. The Austrian government again obtained emergency credit by circulating government paper.

Such was the situation when the Compromise was signed. It was first decided that the government paper in circulation (reaching 400 million florins, about the same amount as the notes of the ÖNB) would remain legal tender with the joint guarantee of both parts of the monarchy. But new issues were ruled out. The Compromise stated that the two parts would share the same standard. In effect however the Austro-Hungarian currency was inconvertible.[26] The question of the bank of issue was not included in the Compromise itself. It was settled in September 1867 by a separate arrangement directly concluded between Hungary and Austria, by which the Hungarians promised not to allow any bank of issue to be created in their part of the Empire.[27] This placed them within the authoritative domain of the Austrian 'central' bank, since its notes had thus to be accepted in Hungary. Hence the introduction of dualism had not reached the realm of money: as before 1867 there was one currency for Austria-Hungary at large, one exchange rate, in effect one bank of issue, and everything monetary was run from Vienna. As argued above, the Compromise was only a fiscal divorce, and it left other institutions untouched – at least at the beginning.

Hungary had a long tradition of claims for sovereignty in all economic matters, and monetary questions did not escape this pattern (Lévy 1911: 137).[28] It was understood that the agreement concluded in September 1867 was preliminary at best, and the ÖNB decided to ask for a more formal and explicit charter for its operations in 'Transleithania', as the Hungarian part of the monarchy was known. It wanted the Hungarian Diet to acknowledge its monopoly of issue there. The Magyars were prepared to pass the bill in Parliament but had conditions. They wanted some overdraft facilities and insisted that the bank should open a *Direction* in Budapest (as opposed to the existing *subsidiary office*). The bank refused.[29]

The Hungarians remained dissatisfied and kept insisting. Their requests escalated after the 1873 crash of the Vienna stock exchange which resulted in economic stagnation throughout the monarchy, increasing the pressure for government action and raising the question of the support which the bank of issue could provide to more aggressive policies. Since the expiration of the privilege of the ÖNB at the end of 1876 conveniently happened to roughly coincide with the renegotiation of the Compromise in 1877, this provided room for a complete reshuffling of the monetary organization of the monarchy. Laborious discussions aimed at renewing the privilege of the bank began. On July 1, 1878, the ÖNB became the Austro-*Hungarian* Bank (*Österreichische-Ungarische Bank* or ÖUB – *Osztrak-Magyar Bank* in Hungarian). The new ÖUB inherited the balance sheet of the ÖNB, but it was reorganized to give Hungary greater control. The ÖNB became a bilingual institution with two main *directions* in Vienna and Budapest, and a central office in Vienna. The governor was to be appointed by the Emperor upon joint nomination of the Austrian and Hungarian finance ministers, and in general the Hungarian government could influence a number of appointments within the Bank.[30] The share of the Bank's profits which the state secured as a price for alienating the privilege of issue to a private company were divided between Austria and Hungary according to a pre-assigned rule. Finally, the duration of the privilege of the central bank was shortened to 10 years (it had typically been granted for 25 years at the beginning of the century), until the close of 1887. In other words, its renewal would again coincide with the negotiation of the third Compromise: interestingly, the question of the common monetary institutions and policies was moving into the realm of Austro-Hungarian negotiations rounds. There were becoming part of the general adjustment of interests between the two parts of the monarchy.

Partial fiscal dominance before 1892

The charter of the ÖUB was renewed in 1887 without substantial modifications. In the 1890s, however, the stabilization of the currency, which had floated so far, onto a gold basis produced drastic changes in the organization of the Austro-Hungarian monetary union. To understand why, we need to go back to some special features of the Austro-Hungarian monetary system. As we explained, in 1867, the monarchy had a silver standard, but in effect, an inconvertible paper currency. The depreciation of silver after the collapse of bimetallism in 1873 progressively reduced the gap between the value of the paper florin and that of the silver florin. After 1876 silver threatened to drag the florin in its fall, and in 1879 it was decided to sever the link between silver and the florin by suspending the free coinage of that metal for private parties (Eichengreen and Flandreau 1996).[31] However, the governments of Austria and Hungary retained the right to coin silver for their own account. Since each part of the monarchy had large obligations payable in either paper or silver, there existed both the possibility and the incentive to collect seigniorage. Moreover, since 1867, there still existed in circulation huge amounts of outstanding government notes (more than 50 per cent of the overall high powered money, according to Nemec 1924). The government papers created another source of instability. For instance they could be sterilized by fiscal authorities in times of abundance (e.g. when a loan was floated), and then injected again in the circulation when financial needs increased.

Thus because of the specific constitution of the monarchy's specie and paper systems, both governments had a soft budget constraint. Of course, this soft constraint was not without checks. On the one hand, each government's incentive to coin silver could not lead to issues beyond the point at which in Austria-Hungary the currency depreciated to become equivalent to a silver standard.[32] On the other hand, as mentioned earlier, the Compromise had made sure that no new issues of government paper could take place beyond the roughly 400 millions that circulated in 1867: once the government paper in the coffers had been entirely released, the budget constraint was again becoming tight. But it remains true that, as a result of this somewhat complex situation, the ÖUB was fairly powerless to stabilize the value of the florin. Its reserves, compared with the outstanding paper currency (bank notes plus government paper) were extremely small (around 20 per cent in 1890) compared to European standards. It was said that the possibility for the governments to inject state notes into circulation reduced the effectiveness of the discount rate as a monetary policy tool. And finally the governments' ability to coin silver posed a threat to the ÖUB's capacity to stabilize the florin in terms of gold currencies.

As a result, while no clear downward trend in the value of the florin was observed after 1875, the Austro-Hungarian currency experienced wide fluctuations on exchange markets (Figure 5.5). In the 1880s it was found that this was somewhat damaging for the credibility of the monarchy and plans to stabilize the currency were actively discussed in 1890 and 1891, causing further gyrations due to speculative activity (Yeager 1969). The reform began in 1892. The monetary laws of 1892 (Austria) and 1893 (Hungary) formalized the new basis of the Austro-Hungarian monetary union, and re-organized the existing relations between the ÖUB and each part of the monarchy. The gold content of a new gold crown was proclaimed and steps were taken to stabilize the florin in terms of the crown.[33] First, silver coinage for government account was discontinued. And second, it was decided that the two governments would repurchase their outstanding notes with gold which would then be remitted to the ÖUB.[34] While the currency was not yet stabilized, the soft budget constraint was coming to an end.

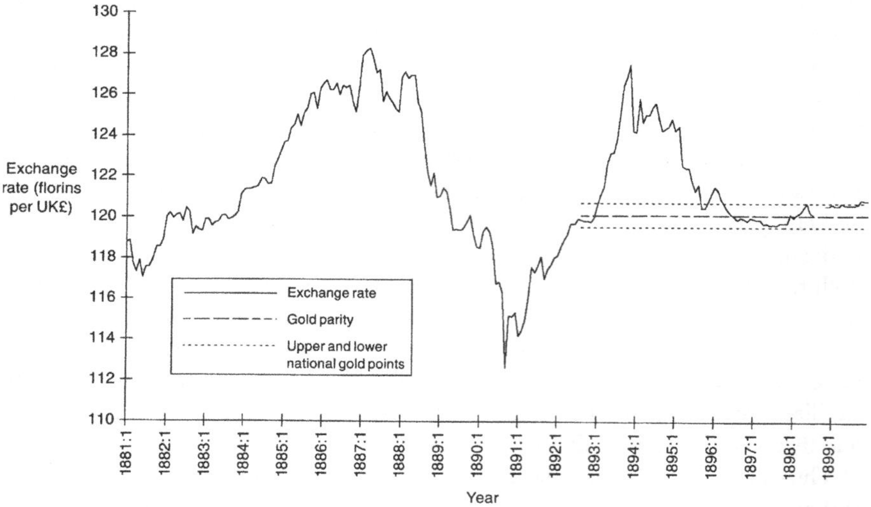

Figure 5.5 Exchange rate in Vienna, 1881–99.
Source: taken from *Währungen der Welt I.*

Monetary dominance after 1892

By abolishing the two mechanisms through which each part of the monarchy had retained a measure of monetary power, the reform of 1892 had in effect tightly restricted each government's ability to inflate the currency. This meant a shift in the balance of power between fiscal and monetary authorities which worried the two governments of his Majesty the Emperor and King. Hungarians in particular claimed they were dissatisfied and asked for compensation. According to external observers, 'the general opinion is that there ought to be substantial restrictions to [the] privilege [of the ÖUB]'.[35] The ÖUB, for her part, was concerned with exploiting the situation. It argued that in order to fulfill its goal of preservation of the external value of the currency, it had to limit as much as possible the advances made to both Treasuries and thus refused to compensate the two governments for the loss of monetary control they suffered as part of the process of monetary stabilization. This 'loss', it claimed, was really a gain of 'credibility' and did not call for compensation. Moreover, in order to make the arrangement more perfect, the ÖUB wanted a new charter to be extended until 1912, a typically longer period than that of Compromise rounds:[36] clearly, it wanted to free itself from the political pressures generated by the periodical Compromise rounds.

These arguments were presented in a pamphlet released by the ÖUB in the spring of 1894. Among the concessions which the Bank was prepared to grant in return, was the suggestion that it could give to both States a greater share of its dividends. It also proposed the creation of a '*curatorium*', analogous to the one that existed in Germany, that would consist of senior representatives of the Ministries of Finance vested with the responsibility to audit the bank's actions.[37] The proposals of the

ÖUB were at once rejected by the two governments. The resulting gridlock blocked the completion of the reform, as agreement between the three parties was necessary before introducing gold convertibility: but it was feared that if a comprehensive arrangement was not reached, subsequent disagreements could lead to a return to inconvertibility that could trigger a panic and damage reputation. The adoption of the gold standard was delayed and the florin kept floating.

While the fight about the new statutes continued, the bank found that it could display its *macht* and introduce the gold standard in practise while the two governments debated about theory. The measure would doubtless consolidate its power and legitimacy since the ÖUB would thereby establish itself as the true custodian of the external value of the national unit. By late 1895, the amount of gold which the two governments had transferred to the bank gave it an effective cover ratio that was above the ÖUB's statutory limit of 40 per cent. Feeling strong enough to undertake singlehandedly the stabilization of the currency, the OÜB implemented in early 1896, a 'shadow' gold standard, using its gold reserves to acquire foreign exchange and in turn foreign exchange to buy or sell Austro-Hungarian bills each time the exchange rate approached notional gold export or import points: the currency thus behaved 'as if' Austria was on a gold standard. The success of this scheme interventions is illustrated in Figure 5.5. Clearly, quite apart from political agreement between Austria and Hungary, the ÖUB demonstrated that – provided that full control be given to it over monetary questions – it could very well stabilize the currency.

After long and painful negotiations (in 1897 Austria and Hungary, failing to reach an agreement, had extended the privilege of the ÖUB from one year to the next) the charter was finally renewed through the law of September 21, 1899 for operation until 1910. Contrary to what had happened in 1887, the new statutes brought important changes. Hungary had stated that it would only accept the loss of monetary control if full parity within the bank was introduced. As a result, Hungary and Austria shared the exclusive privilege to designate half of the board, thus reducing the power of shareholders. Another change brought by the 1899 statutes was the increased influence of the two national 'commissaries'. The commissaries exercised each government's control over the common institution and they now had a right to request a special veto, motivated by '*raison d'état*'. This new clause amounted to including a measure of subsidiarity within the management of the common bank, and consequently, it has been variously assessed. Many later analysts interpreted this provision as a weakening of the 'independence' of the ÖUB, leading them to rank the Austro-Hungarian Bank 'behind the *Reichsbank*' (Hertz 1903; Németc 1924; Zeuceanu 1924: xiii).[38] Contemporary observers representative of the foreign investors' vantage point remained cooler, pointing out that this was after all the only form of 'state control'.[39] They saw the arrangement as a necessary counterweight to the enormous power which the ÖUB had acquired during the 1890s. According to them, the ÖUB could thus be called very independent, and in any case much more independent than in the past. Given that the monetary reform of 1892–6 had entirely severed the monetary power of fiscal authorities, it seemed reasonable that some checks be found to the exclusive rule of the central bank, especially since it 'belonged' to 'sovereign' states. Moreover, at no time until the war did the authority of the commissaries encompass decisions relative to the setting of the discount rate.[40] Thus monetary policy, as such, fully escaped the realm of politics and the exchange rate remained pegged to gold, through the ÖUB deliberate action and without interference from the government, until the war.

The market mechanism: Austro-Hungarian lessons for EMU

The growth of power of the ÖUB as a formidable macroeconomic actor was a fairly striking fact which did not escape the scrutiny of the most careful contemporaries. For one thing, Knapp's famous 'state theory of money' took the ÖUB as a case in point, arguing that the Austro-Hungarian was the prototype of modern central banking (Knapp 1905: 249–52, 377–94). This, he argued, was because the ÖUB, breaking with a practice inherited from the theory of money as a commodity (according to which strict specie convertibility was the only foundation of the value of paper currency which by itself was valueless), had demonstrated that the value of money could be institution-based. According to Knapp, it was the prestige enjoyed by the legal-bureaucratic system which the ÖUB impersonated that provided the backing for the stabilized florin. One may wonder why 'modernity' developed not at the heart of the gold standard system, but rather in an area which has traditionally been portrayed as one of its peripheries. Yet our discussion of the record of the Austro-Hungarian union point to one straightforward interpretation. Clearly, the new fiscal–monetary regime which emerged in the 1890s had opened an era of increased monetary power for the ÖUB which resulted in the period of balanced budgets or moderate deficits identified in the first section, and had paved the way for exchange rate stability. What remains to be understood, however, is the reasons which brought this 'change of regime' about. The following section will argue that the invisible hand responsible for this transformation was the discipline of the market.

Market discipline 1: early concerns over reputation

The theory of 'market discipline' features prominently among the arguments used by some modern opponents of the Stability Pact. The point is that efficient financial markets will charge badly behaved governments a higher risk premium and that this will provide them with incentives to improve their finances.[41] This form of discipline would be a much more efficient mechanism than the fiscal straightjacket which has been imposed to European governments through the Pact, as it would enable countries to run higher deficits in bad times and thus would provide more scope for stabilization. The Austro-Hungarian monetary union, it will be recalled, had no such pact: thus discipline if it existed, could only operate through the market mechanism. As Scott Eddie has put it 'Austria and Hungary were . . . subjected to the discipline of the capital market, and could run deficits only to the extent of the public willingness to lend to them' (Eddie 1982: 11).[42]

The capital market had two constituencies: the first was the underwriting syndicates responsible for issuing bonds, and thus mainly involved with the primary market. The syndicate *par excellence* was the Viennese Rothschild's – '*The* Syndicate' as the *Neue Freie Presse* called it.[43] It comprised leading Viennese and Berlin banks (such as *Bleichröder* and the *Disconto-Gesellschaft*). For its dealings with the Hungarian government, it involved some Hungarian institutions, such as the *Ungarische Creditbank.* The other side of the market comprised the long-term investors (domestic and foreign) in Austrian and Hungarian state securities that were traded in active and fully integrated 'secondary' markets, in Vienna and abroad. Of course, the price of public securities on secondary markets influenced the issuing conditions, and vice versa, and the governments of the dual monarchy had to worry about the yields of their securities, as this in turn influenced their ability to borrow – their position in negotiating with the Syndicate, or with its potential competitors, the conditions under which new loans would be issued.

The Habsburg monetary union displayed a continuing concern of borrowing governments vis-à-vis their reputation in the market place. These concerns were discernible from the outset, when the negotiations which resulted in the fiscal divorce of 1867 occurred. Among the challenges involved was the sharing of the outstanding 'common' debt between Austria and Hungary.[44] But the latter was a whole new fiscal authority with no reputation whatsoever. As emphasized by Gille (1967: 487) 'Hungary had to learn to manage its finances'. The Hungarians had initially claimed that this debt had served to finance Austria's imperial policies in central Europe: they were victims rather than contributors.[45] Yet it proved eventually possible to agree on a sharing rule. The Hungarians acknowledged that 'on the basis of equity [?] and for political considerations [?]' (Kövér 1988: 162)[46] they were liable to a fixed perpetual annuity 'not subject to further changes'.[47] This somewhat surprising move may be interpreted through reputational concerns vis-à-vis prospective investors. For a brand new country this was a way to 'buy', quite literally, a reputation by signalling to financial markets that Hungary had a notion of its financial responsibilities, at a time when it thought of tapping the capital market. Hence the Magyars' willingness to pay a debt which they insisted was not theirs, and the inclusion in the Compromise of an Hungarian contribution to Austria's service of the common debt.

A similar mechanism was again observed when the Austrian government, in order to smooth the profile of its interest service and reimbursements, but also to reduce the interest burden, undertook in 1868 – just after the signing of the Compromise – a forced conversion of the outstanding 'common' debt (a conversion with a 16 per cent witholding tax). To explain his action to the markets, the Austrian finance minister referred to Hungary's limited contribution to the service of the common debt, thus trying to split some of the blame.[48] In effect this led, after complex and drawn out discussions, to the exclusion of both Austrian and Hungarian securities from the London stock exchange in May 1870 unless compensation was given to British bondholders (Kövér 1988). Here again, the Hungarians worried about the resulting loss of reputation: in the early 1870s while the issue of a loan in London came under discussion, Hungary agreed to pay British bondholders the bill Austria had left there, thus making up for the capital loss which the foreign bond holders had suffered. Given the fairly moderate compensation required (England, by contrast to Belgium, Holland, Germany or France had not been in

1868 a large holder of Austro-Hungarian securities), it certainly appeared to Hungary that the advantages of being able to tap London vastly surpassed the costs of redemption.[49]

Market discipline 2: convergence of product quality

The completion of the fiscal divorce between Hungary and Austria clarified the situation. The responsibilities towards the common debt were by now more clearly defined. From that date on, new debts would be entirely 'national', thus enabling investors to discriminate between what was Hungarian and what was Austrian. But the incentives provided by the market continued to matter, perhaps with greater strength, generating a kind of quality competition between the two sides of the monarchy. In the first ten years of the monarchy, when Hungary alone was borrowing on the market, it did issue all kinds of debt instruments, often fairly heterogeneous. For instance various railway obligations of different types and maturities were floated on the market. But when Austria came to the market, a standardization of the securities issued by the two parts of the monarchy began to occur. For instance the Austrians were the first to create, in 1876, a 4 per cent perpetual gold rente, *steuerfrei* (i.e. free of tax). The Hungarians followed suit a few years later with a Hungarian equivalent. Similarly, when the Austrians created, by the Law of February 1881, the 5 per cent paper rente, again, *steuerfrei*, observers commented that this had been prompted by the succesful lead taken by Hungary in this segment of the market a few months earlier.[50] Not surprisingly, the 5 per cent paper rente and the 4 per cent gold rente were to become the two main components of the monarchy's outstanding debts.

The convergence observed among the debt instruments issued by the two parts of the monarchy in turn led to natural comparisons between the conditions at which each part of the monarchy borrowed. Analogous bonds led to straightfoward assessment regarding which part had the highest credit, thus creating price transparency. When in 1892 Austria and Hungary, taking advantage of the decline in long-term interest rates, undertook a conversion of the coupon from 5 per cent to 4 per cent, the Rothschild Syndicate met with officials, first in Vienna then in Budapest, and discussed the conditions that would apply to each part of the monarchy in reference to those granted to the other one.[51] Similarly the press reported the news concerning the performance of governments through pairwise comparisons between price changes for a given type of instrument: 4 per cent gold Hungarians were compared to 4 per cent gold Austrian, 5 per cent paper Hungarians to 5 per cent paper Austrians.[52] Thus conditions obtained by one part of the monarchy were a natural benchmark to judge those which the other part obtained. This situation, as recalled by Michel (1976), continued until the outbreak of the First World War.[53] It was certainly one motive which explained the reluctance of the Austrian minister of finance Böhm-Bawerk to go along with premier Körber's famous public works programme, causing its fall (Gerschenkron 1977). What would have happened had Austrian credit been assessed below that of Hungary?

Market discipline 3: monitoring through debt structure

The market mechanism also left its mark on the structure of the Austrian and Hungarian debts, and this, as we proceed to show, had an influence upon the evolution of the very rules presiding over the operation of the monetary union. Given that the Austro-Hungarian currency fluctuated widely, investors were less willing to hold Habsburg securities payable in paper florins than bonds with a gold clause. Accordingly, they charged a higher interest rate on the paper rentes, as opposed to gold-denominated obligations. Evidence of this is provided in Figure 5.6, which shows that during the 1880s the yield on gold bonds was lower than that on paper bonds for both Austria and Hungary. This of course suggests that a government worried with borrowing at the cheapest rate had an incentive to introduce gold clauses in their securities issues.

In effect, this is exactly what happened. As the governments in Vienna and Budapest kept borrowing to finance their deficits of the late 1870s and 1880s, they found the financial markets unwilling to provide cheap funding unless they were guaranteed a fixed income in terms of marks, francs or pounds, that is, gold currencies. This led them to increase the share of their gold denominated debts along with the increase of their debt burden. The switch towards more 'gold intensive' debts in the late 1870s and 1880s is illustrated in Table 5.2 which underlines the parallels between the share of gold obligations in total outstanding liabilities and public indebtedness.[54] The relation is perceptible across time and countries: while we see that both Austria and Hungary gradually increased the share of their gold obligations as their degree of indebtedness grew, more indebted Hungary had also, other things being equal, a larger share of its debt denominated in gold.

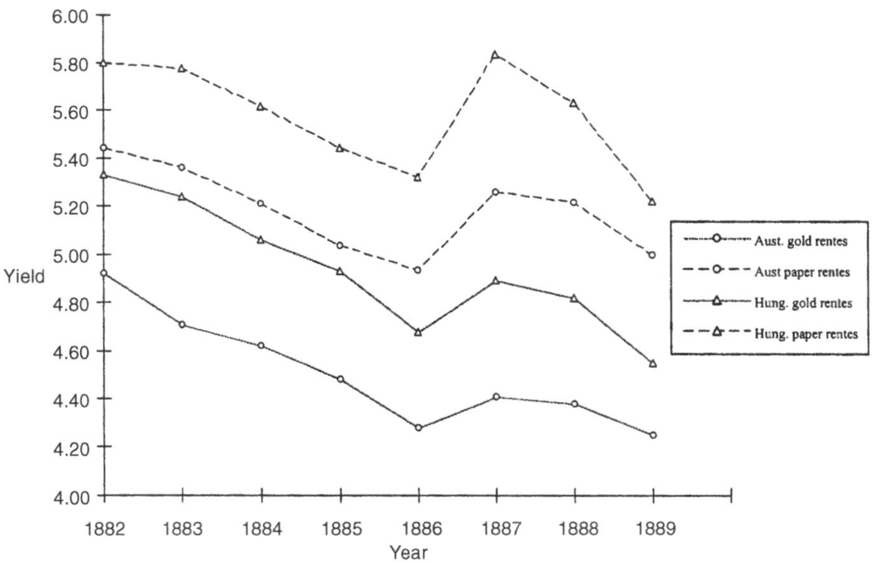

Figure 5.6 Yields on Austro-Hungarian securities: gold vs. paper, 1882–9.

Table 5.2 Debt burden and debt structure: Austria and Hungary

	Austria		*Hungary*	
	Debt burden	*Share of gold debt*	*Debt burden*	*Share of gold debt*
1880	63	11	78	25
1885	70	13	87	33
1890	75	17	99	32
1895	75	19	108	32

Source: Author's computations.

In turn, however, the growth of the gold-denominated fraction of the two debts imposed a 'discipline' on the two governments. A higher fraction of gold-denominated debt with a floating currency transferred the exchange risk from the lender to the borrower. But this in turn led gold-indebted governments to be more worried about exchange rate stability. This mechanism is well known by macro-economists who have suggested to interpret it as an optimal commitment technology: increasing the share of foreign currency (or in this instance, gold) denominated debt might be seen as a way to reduce a country's incentive to inflate its paper debt away. Debt monetization, by leading to exchange depreciation, will increase the burden of interest service on gold-denominated obligations (see e.g. Missale and Blanchard 1994). It is likely of course that the increase in the proportion of gold in the total outstanding obligations of Austria and Hungary was not designed out of such conscious and explicit reasoning. But the result was the same. The growth of the share of gold-denominated debts created serious motives for achieving greater monetary stability. Moreover, everything happened as if the market was able to customize the mechanism to fit each country's size: more indebted Hungary, being more concerned about reducing the interest service on its public debt because it was charged a higher interest rate than Austria, increased its share of gold debts way beyond the point reached by Austria, and had thus stronger reasons in the late 1880s to resist inflating away its obligations.

It is in this light that we must understand why the project of monetary stabilization gained momentum in 1888, precisely at a date when, because of renewed exchange rate instability, the spread between paper and gold obligations was biggest, reaching 100 basis points (Figure 5.6). One could not have it both ways. Either Hungary and Austria were prepared to pay the price of fluctuating exchange rates through higher borrowing paper rates for both State and private concerns, or they could try to reduce the burden of interest service by issuing gold-denominated securities. But this in turn increased the costs of currency instability, as depreciating currency translated into a short-term increase of the interest rate service and a resulting deterioration of public finances. The 'change in regime' which occured in the early 1890s can thus be interpreted as a solution to this problem. By empowering the central bank with a greater control of the monetary process, and, in particular, by severing the defective link between government budgets and monetary creation which had existed until the early 1890s, both parts of the monarchy would be able to secure lower interest rates for their paper obligations. Doing this led, as is shown by Figure 5.7, and before

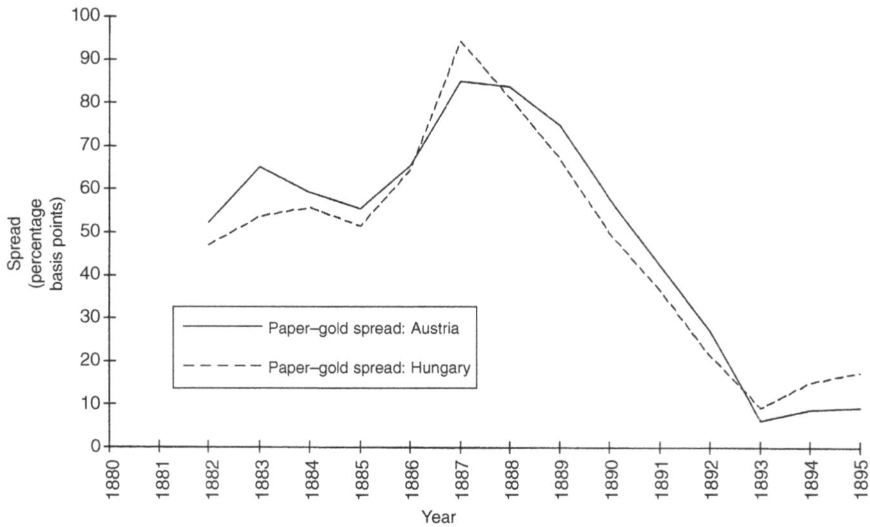

Figure 5.7 The spread between paper- and gold-denominated currencies in Austria and Hungary, 1880–95.

the currency was actually stabilized in 1896, to a sharp reduction of the paper–gold spread of both Hungarian and Austrian securities.

Clearly, the process was placing the Austro-Hungarian central bank at the centre stage of the Habsburg monetary union, providing an interpretation to the shift in power relations which we documented in the previous section. The credibility of the ÖUB was becoming a cornerstone of the Austro-Hungarian economic alliance. In front of the two national governments no longer with any control over monetary creation, the ÖUB was emerging as a super-actor to which both governments delegated the responsibility to foster currency stability. But this very process was operating a true revolution in Austro-Hungarian monetary and financial relations, as the value of its currency rested not on a gold backing, but on the credibility of the Habsburg compromise. Such was the origin of what Knapp had analysed as the acme of modernity.

Conclusions

The French scholar Pierre Vilar once argued that the history of money could be a way to improve our analytical understanding of monetary phenomena. This, he suggested, could be achieved through the use of a conceptual tool which he called 'theoretical equivalents' (Vilar 1974: 17). Monetary institutions do change over time: yet some fundamental issues survive owing to the very nature of money. According to Vilar, one such issue is the inflation tax: from the debasement of specie during the Middle Ages and until the nineteenth century to the use of the printing press to finance government deficits, one may see much change. Yet the essence of 'seigniorage' has remained the same. Because currency is a public good, it tends to be centrally managed. And because central authorities generally want to increase their resources, they tend to seek ways to exploit the money supply. Thus the modern printing press is the 'theoretical equivalent' of a debasement, and an independent central bank is the 'theoretical equivalent' of the mediaeval money courts which developed as a counterweight to the kings' attempts to collect seigniorage.

We hope that in the course of this article we have persuaded readers that the Austro-Hungarian precedent was a 'theoretical equivalent' for modern EMU. The reason for this is straightforward: unlike many other experiences of monetary unification which have relied either on a large decentralization of monetary and commercial authority (thus enabling individual participants to retaliate against inflationary policies implemented in some parts of the union) or on a process of political integration (thus ruling out misbehaviour in the first place), both Euroland and Austria-Hungary occupy the uncomfortable middle ground of full monetary and commercial unification, *cum* complete fiscal subsidiarity. And one implication of this 'equivalence' is the surprising replication of issues and dilemmas.

The main dilemma which both experiences have in common is that of designing a mechanism through which fiscal discipline can be enforced in order to prevent the development of disruptive forces. The Habsburg monetary union, for its part, chose to rely on the market mechanism. In that respect, it provides interesting lessons as it shows that the common central bank, rather than being predated by the two governments, gradually emerged as a strong player, indeed one of the main political actors of the monarchy. This was because, we argued, concerns over reputation loomed large. For instance, competition about reputation between both parts of the monarchy led them to standardize their debt instruments. This in turn improved the transparency of the price signals, so that investors could make direct comparisons between the credit standing of the two parts. Moreover, public distrust of the Austro-Hungarian currency (which could be inflated away) led the capital market to charge a higher interest rate on paper debts denominated in florins, as opposed to gold debts which were denominated in foreign currencies. Austria and Hungary thus reacted in increasing the share of their gold obligations as their borrowing needs intensified. But managing a gold debt was more costly when the currency floated than when it was stable, thus bringing incentives for currency stabilization. The steps required to stabilize the currency in turn involved increasing the power of the Austro-Hungarian central bank. This took place in the 1890s when full control over monetary issues was granted to the ÖUB. Market discipline had thus eventually caused the growth in ÖUB's prominence in the Habsburg *de facto* union.

We leave it to the reader to continue to unfold for himself the whole implications of the 'theoretical equivalence' between the Habsburg union and Euroland. For instance, the fiscal effort which took place in the 1890s in Austria and Hungary can be seen as a 'theoretical equivalent' to the convergence process that preceded the introduction of the euro. Similarly, the resulting increase in the power of the ÖUB can be seen as a 'theoretical equivalent' of the way through which the Maastricht convergence criteria have paved the road for the large power enjoyed by the ECB, perhaps one of the most formidable bureaucracies on earth. Or again, the market mechanism, with its ability to transform perceived changes in creditworthiness into yield premiums, can be seen as a the 'theoretical equivalent' of the Stability Pact. Of course, an important issue is to understand why the founders of the euro have taken the apparently more conservative route of explicit limits on fiscal profligacy, while Austro-Hungarian policy makers relied on the market. The recent trend in Europe, however, whereby the relevance of the stability pact is being questioned, suggests that we are gradually moving towards an Austro-Hungarian type of setting. This suggests that, once more, those who ignore the past are bound to live it a second time.

The pessimist, finally, may wish to know what could, in the European context, be the 'theoretical equivalent' of the way the ÖUB failed, after the First World War broke out and the common government began to exploit the money supply to finance massive military spending. For instance, according to Nemec,

> after the glorious period which goes from 1892 to 1914, the war is the dark spot in the history of the Austro-Hungarian Bank. For it became, from 1914 onwards, the abject agent of the governments in Vienna and Budapest and of their policies. It has so much been under their influence that it has made irrecoverable errors. The fall of these same governments and the appalling end of the monarchy have dragged the Bank to the abyss, and caused its sad downfall.
>
> (1924: 76)

To that pessimist we shall reply that he will have to think of what could be a modern theoretical equivalent of the First World War.

Acknowledgements

Many thanks to the Lyonnais archives and to Christine Paquentin at the OFCE reference library for outstanding help for sources and figures. The comments of several participants to the AMEX conference and to the European Summer Symposium in International Macroeconomics in Sintra, Portugal, are gratefully acknowledged. Special thanks to Luca Einaudi, Benedikt Koehler, John Komlos, Jacques Le Cacheux, Jacques Mélitz, Morris Perlman, and Gian-Maria Milesi Feretti. Errors remain mine.

Notes

1 See list of references, as well as the contributions of Mike Bordo and Lars Jonung (Chapter 3), and that of Hugh Rockoff (Chapter 4) in this volume.
2 We should remark that other aspects of the economic union between Austria-Hungary than those discussed here have been studied: Komlos (1983) focused on the custom union dimension of the Habsburg monarchy, while Eddie (1982) discussed the 'tax' union aspects.
3 The post Soviet lessons are presented by Garber and Spencer (1994), Dornbusch (1992) and Maurel (1998).
4 In the archives of the Paris Mint for instance there is a blueprint for a global currency sent by a retired French engineer in the midst of the late 1860s debates on European and

international monetary unification. The scheme, it might be expected, was supposedly revolutionary, but hardly understandable. Archives de la Monnaie de Paris, Série K.

5 Because the Latin union had provided for the intercirculation of subsidiary (debased) coins as well as of silver écus which became overvalued in the 1870s as a result of the demise of bimetallism, exchange depreciation also led to substantial exports of silver monies in other members of the union. This occurred in the late 1860s when France received a large amount of subsidiary Italian coins, and again in the 1870s when silver écus were received. The importance of these phenomena should not be underestimated: they were responsible, in the late 1860s, for the French Administration's reluctance to support Latin Union enlargement (Einaudi 2000). Yet the fact that countries had retained monetary sovereignty turned out to be a powerful weapon against such externalities, as it appeared in the 1870s (Flandreau 1993).

6 Note that, by contrast, France's decision to float at the outbreak of the Franco-Prussian war, led Belgium, where a number of financial institutions lived off French credit, to follow suit. But this had nothing to do with the Latin Union as such, but rather with the interdependencies between the Belgian and the French financial systems.

7 In effect trade integration within these unions was not larger than elsewhere, once allowance is made for other factors such as distance and size. Using a 'gravity model' it can be shown that neither within the Latin nor within the Scandinavian Union did countries exhibit any greater tendency to trade with each other than with any other European country (Flandreau 1998).

8 The reason why this parallel would still be imperfect is that the ERM was coupled with the single market, thus ruling out the use of trade barriers as a retaliatory device. This implies that under the ERM, there was an understanding that exchange rate depreciation should eventually be brought to a halt.

9 This conclusion is supported outside Europe by the experience of the United States (see Hugh Rockoff's (Chapter 4) contribution in this volume).

10 A nation can proceed without a common language as the Swiss experience reminds us. But given the more limited size of this country we have found that it was perhaps not wise to include it into the sample discussed here. Recall, however, that the Swiss experience has a lot of parallels with the Italian and German one. The creation of the common currency followed the political re-organization of 1848. Once the political situation was consolidated the creation of a common central bank could wait – in effect until 1907.

11 It must be said that Switzerland had a tradition of fiscal balance and monetary stability. As a result public debts were limited. The federal debt represented around 1890 about 3 per cent of GDP (see Flandreau *et al.* 1998). Cantonal debts, on the other hand, were backed by the income from railways which they had served to finance.

12 See Komlos (1983) for an introduction to this issue. The classic reference on Austro-Hungarian monetary vicissitudes is Pressburger (1966). Komlos (1987) and Köver (1991) contain economic discussions of Austro-Hungarian money and banking.

13 Each 'Delegation' consisted of 60 members of whom 20 were from the Upper House (*Herrenhaus, Förendihaz*) and 40 from the lower House (*Abgeordetenhaus, Kepviselohaz*). The delegations, summoned by the Emperor and King met in Vienna and Budapest alternately. They deliberated independently and communicated in writing only. If there was disagreement after three written communications, they had to meet together and settled the vote without discussion. From *Statesman's Yearbook*.

14 The common ministers were for War, Foreign Affairs and Finance.

15 The rest was spent on common foreign affairs.

16 As well as stamps on visas, military taxes, etc. but for inconsequential amounts.

17 According to Ferguson (1994), this situation would have acted as a check on the increase of military spending.

18 In Crédit Lyonnais, DEEF 73205, note générale, situation financière 1896.

19 The extent to which such policies were actually succesful is still the centre of much discussion. See for Austria-Hungary: Gerschenkron (1977), Eddie (1982), Komlos (1983), Schulze (1998).

20 The most comprehensive attempts to study the nature of public spending in the Habsburg Empire then in the Austrian part of the dual monarchy are Brandt (1978) and Wysocki (1975).

21 These were reconstructed from fiscal returns elaborated by the *Lyonnais* archives.

22 Archives du Crédit Lyonnais.

23 As is evident from Figure 5.2, the big canal and railway projects launched in Austria by the Körber administration in 1900–1 did not result in large deficits: this is hardly surprising given that we know that the plan was dropped (see Gerschenkron 1977, especially chapter 3). The figures involved in the original plan however (500 million florins or 1 billion crowns, spread over the course of 10 to 15 years) suggest that the effort was not that large even in its genuine form, when compared with the public spending of the 1870s and 1880s.

24 Estimates for national incomes in Austria and Hungary are notoriously difficult to obtain. I am grateful to Max Stefan Schulze for having discussed the matter with me.

25 Note that the inverted U-shaped pattern observed here is fully consistent with the international trends identified in Flandreau *et al.* (1998), and is explained in part by the post 1895 gold inflation which did much to relieve indebted countries from part of the burden of their public debts.

26 Since this occurred in the midst of the campaign for the adoption of a universal currency which climaxed in the 1867 Paris International Exhibition in Paris with the decision that a 25 franc gold coin should become the basis of the first truly global currency, the monarchy also considered the adoption of a new gold florin that would be such that 10 florins = 25 francs. A formal agreement was even signed between Austria's baron de Hock and France's Parieu, paving the way for the eventual admission of the monarchy within the Latin Union and to its move to gold. The Austro-French agreement is reprinted in Noël (1889).

27 Zuckerkandl argues that this arrangement was not formally communicated to the ÖNB until 1870.

28 During the 1848 uprising, for instance, the emergency Hungarian government had given the exclusive right of issue to the Hungarian Commercial Bank in which Kossuth, father of the future leader of the independence party, had played a key role. The defeat of the Hungarians forced them to acknowledge the privileges of the ÖNB.

29 In 1872 it nonetheless granted Hungary a credit line of 4.5 millions of florins, way below what the Hungarians wanted.

30 See Noël (1889), Conant (1895), Zuckerkandl (1911) for a thorough description of the precise rules.

31 See e.g. *Neue Freie Presse*, August 22, 1879, p. 6.

32 If so much silver was coined that the gulden depreciated to the level of its silver content, the advantage of coining silver would have gone to zero: thus the governments had an incentive not to overissue.

33 One kilogram of fine gold would yield 3280 cr (worth 1640 florins).

34 The circulation the state notes which at the close of 1892 amounted to 312 million florins. Of the 312 million florins of outstanding paper notes Austria committed itself to reimburse 70 per cent while Hungary had to pay 30 per cent.

35 Crédit Lyonnais, 'Réforme de la Valuta' DEEF 73211.

36 See Raffalovitch (1995: 15a) and Conant (1895: 233).

37 DEEF 73211, 'Réforme de la Valuta'.

38 On central bank independence under the gold standard, see Flandreau *et al.* (1998). Note that for contemporaries, the Reichsbank with its curatorium system and possible control by the government was perceived as the least independent bank among the three leading European institutions (Bank of England, Banque de France, *Reichsbank*).

39 Crédit Lyonnais, DEEF 73211.

40 See Michel (1976) who explains how commissaries in fact interved to prevent the application of heterogeneous interest rates in various regions, recalling that common institutions were bound to apply common conditions. In view of Forrest Capie's (1997)

emphasis on independence as independence in the setting of discount policy, the ÖUB can be said to have been very independent.

41 There is indeed evidence that such a mechanism existed in the pre-1914 era: in Flandreau *et al.* (1998) we formally tested this hypothesis for a comprehensive sample of European countries and found evidence that highly indebted countries experienced a measure of squeeze in the shape of exponential increases in risk premiums.

42 Eddie relates this situation to the fact that the 'economic alliance' between Hungary and Austria 'also included a provision expressly limiting the amount that could be borrowed from the Austrian National Bank, and set a ceiling to money creation'. We have not been able to find such a provision. Our understanding is that the limited access to financial help from the Austrian National Bank was a by-product of the statutes of this bank which since 1861 had limited government finance. The formalization of this arrangement as part of the economic alliance had to wait for the statutes of the common bank in 1878. And even then, it would be part of the statutes of the bank rather than part of the compromise.

43 See Michel (1976: 119–37). The masterminds of the Rothschild syndicate were Albert de Rothschild and Theodor von Taussig.

44 In many aspects the problems surrounding the negotiation of the 1867 Compromise can be seen as a small-scale version of the troubles that would develop after the First World War: an indemnity had to be paid to the victor (Prussia), currency was depreciating and the burden of foreign obligations was rising.

45 This principle was explicitly included in the Compromise law. As recalled by György Kövér, 'the Hungarian stance traditionally stated – and this was included in the law of the compromise, that the "debts . . . had been made without the lawful agreement of the country, and thus they did not concern Hungary" (1868. Art. 12 Par. 53.)' (1988: 162). Eddie concurs that 'the debt of the Empire, . . . could not be said to have commanded widespread support in Hungary' (1982: 10).

46 Our question marks.

47 Compromise Law of 1867, Art. 15. Par. 1. Kövér (1988: 163).

48 '"The different states of Austria, including Hungary, have to take their share of the old burdens" in order to "get rid of the label of refusing to pay"' (Kövér 1988: 164).

49 Kövér indicates that there was a capital of about £348,000 'converted under protest'. The compensation being 5 per cent of total capital, this meant a cost of about £17,400, not a very large sum indeed. In more flowery words, Hungarian economic historian Kövér, concluded that Hungary thus '"regained" its own credit and that of the Monarchy', (1988: 169).

50 Crédit Lyonnais, DEEF 73205, étude de 1896.

51 *The Economist*, January 7, 1893.

52 Ibid.

53 Chapter on public debts and syndicates.

54 Quinquennial estimates of debt burden (public debt divided by national income) are the same as in Figure 5.4. Share of gold obligations are pointwise averages constructed from data in the Crédit Lyonnais files.

Sources

Archival sources:
Crédit Lyonnais Archives, Paris.

Periodicals:
The Economist
L'Economiste Français
Neue Freie Presse

Data:
Figures on public debts and deficits were constructed using fiscal studies made by the Crédit Lyonnais. For a description of the type of work performed by Lyonnais economists and for an appraisal of their relevance, see Flandreau (1998).

Figures for interest rates were constructed on the basis of quarterly prices of Austrian and Hungarian bonds. The price for gold rentes was collected from the Paris stock exchange return, '*Cours Authentiques de la Bourse de Paris*'. The price for paper rentes was collected from the Vienna stock exchange return, '*Amtliches coursblatt der Wiener Börse*'. Since 5 per cent paper rentes were converted in early 1893 to 4 per cent obligations, a correction had to be made on the series. We used the price of the 4.2 per cent 'common paper rente', in effect, an Austrian obligation which was not converted in the 1890s and which, as efficient market hypothesis would predict, behaved in an almost identical fashion to the 5 per cent paper debt of Austria as long as no conversion was in sight. Thus in 1891–1892, we substituted the interest rate on the common debt for that on the Austrian bond, and the same series, augmented by the spread between Austrian and Hungarian paper obligations, for the Hungarian interest rate. While this procedure may induce some minor distortions in the exact process at work, it provides a very reasonable interpolation between the two known spreads of 1890 and 1893. Figures for the interest rate on the common debt also come from the '*Amtliches coursblatt der Wiener Börse*'.

References

Bagehot, W. (1869) *A Practical Plan to Assimilate British and American Money, as a Step Towards a Universal Money*. London.

Bergman, M. (1999) 'Do Monetary Unions Make Sense? Evidence from the Scandinavian Monetary Union 1973–1913', *Scandinavian Journal of Economics*, *101*(3).

Brandt, H.-H. (1978) *Der österreichische Neoabsolutismus: Staatzfinanzen und Politik 1848–1860*, 2 vols. Göttingen.

Capie, F. (1997) *Die Bedeutung der Unabhangigkeit der Notenbank fur die Glaubwurdigkeit der europaiischen Geldpolitik*. Vienna.

Conant, C. (1895/1915) *A History of Banks of Issue*, first and fifth editions. London.

de Mülinen, Comte (1875) *Les finances de l'Autriche*. Paris and Vienna.

Dornbusch, R. (1992) 'Monetary Problems of Post-Communism – Lessons from the End of the Austro-Hungarian Empire', *Weltwirtschaftliches Archiv*, *128*.

Dornbusch, R., C. Favero and F. Giavazzi (1998) 'Immediate Challenges for the European Central Bank', *Economic Policy: A European Forum*, *13*.

Eddie, S. (1982) 'Limits on the Fiscal Independence of Sovereign States in Customs Union: Tax Union Aspects of the Austro-Hungarian Monarchy, 1868–1911', *Hungarian Studies Review*.

Eichengreen, B. J. and M. Flandreau (1996) 'The Geography of the Gold Standard', in de Macedo, Braga, B. J. Eichengreen and J. Reis, eds, *Currency Convertibility: the Gold Standard and Beyond*. London.

Einaudi, L. (2000) 'From the Franc to the "Europe": the Attempted Transformation of the Latin Monetary Union into a European Monetary Union, 1865–1873', *Economic History Review*, *53*.

—— (2001) *Money and Politics. European Monetary Unification and the International Gold Standard*. Oxford.

Ferguson, N. (1994) 'Public Finance and National Security: the Domestic Origins of the First World War Revisited', *Past and Present, 142.*

Flandreau, M. (1993) 'On the Inflationary Bias of Common Currencies: the Latin Union Puzzle', *European Economic Review, 37.*

—— (1995) 'Was the Latin Union a Franc Zone?', in Reis, J., ed., *Historical Perspectives on International Monetary Arrangements.* London.

—— (1998) 'Caveat Emptor: Coping with Sovereign Risk without the Multilaterals 1870–1913', CEPR Discussion Paper N°2002, forthcoming, in Flandreau, M., C. L. Holtfrerich and H. James, eds, *International Financial History in the Twentieth Century: System and Anarchy.* Cambridge.

—— (2000) 'The Economics and Politics of Monetary Unions: a Reassessment of the Latin Monetary Union, 1865–1871', *Finacial History Review, 7.*

——, J. le Cacheux and F. Zumer (1998) 'Stability without a Pact? Lessons from the European Gold Standard 1880–1914', *Economic Policy, 26.*

Garber, P. and M. Spencer (1994) *The Dissolution of the Austro-Hungarian Empire: Lessons for Currency Reform.* Princeton Essays in International Finance no. 191. Princeton, NJ.

Gerschenkron, A. (1977) *An Economic Spurt that Failed: Four Lectures in Austrian History.* Princeton, NJ.

Gille, B. (1967) *Histoire de la Maison Rothschild,* vol. 2. Geneva.

Hefeker, C. (1995) 'Interest Groups, Coalitions, and Monetary Integration in the XIXth century', *Journal of European Economic History, 24*(3).

Henriksen, I. and N. Koergard (1995) 'The Scandinavian Currency Union 1875–1914', in Reis, J., ed., *International Monetary Systems in Historical Perspective.* London.

Hertz, F. (1903) *Die Osterreichisch-ungarische bank und der Ausgleich.* Vienna.

Holtfrerich, C.-L. (1989) 'The Monetary Unification Process in Nineteenth-Century Germany: Relevance and Lessons for Europe Today', in de Cecco, M. and A. Giovannini, eds, *A European Central Bank? Relevance and Lessons for Europe Today.* Cambridge.

James, H. (1997) 'Monetary and Fiscal Unification in Nineteenth-Century Germany: What Can Kohl Learn from Bismarck?'. Princeton Essays in International Finance, no. 202. Princeton, NJ.

Jonung, L. (2001) 'The Scandinavian Monetary Union', mimeo.

Knapp, G. F. (1905) *Staatliche Theorie des Geldes.* Leipzig.

Komlos, J. (1983) *The Austro-Hungarian Empire as a Custom Union: Economic Development in Austria-Hungary in the 19th Century.* Princeton, NJ.

Komlos, John (1987) 'Financial Innovation and the Demand for Money in Austria-Hungary, 1867–1913', *Journal of European Economic History, 16*(3).

Köver, György (1991) 'The Austro-Hungarian Banking System', in Cameron, R. and V. Bovykin, eds, *International Banking 1870–1914.* Oxford.

Lévy, R.-G. (1911) *Banques d'Emission et Trésors Publics.* Paris.

März, E. (1984) trans. Kessler, C., *Austrian Banking and Financial Policy: Creditanstalt at a Turning Point, 1913–1923.* New York.

Maurel, M. (1998) *Régionalisme et Désintégration en Europe Centrale et Orientale: une approche gravitationnelle.* Paris.

Michel, B. (1976) *Banques et Banquiers en Autriche au début du XIXème siècle.* Paris. [This is the published version of an unpublished Sorbonne dissertation (1970). The unpublished version is virtually identical but for footnotes and tables that have been excluded from the published version. For reference we used the original version held at the Bibliothèque de la Sorbonne.]

Missale, A. and O. Blanchard (1994) 'Debt Burden and Debt Maturity', *American Economic Review, 84.*

Nemec, C. (1924) *La Banque Austro-Hongroise et sa Liquidation.* Paris.

Noël, O. (1889) *Les banques d'émission en Europe*, 2 vols (only volume I was ever published), Paris.

Paillard, G. (1909) *La Suisse et l'union latine.* Paris.

Perlman, Morris (1993) 'In Search of Monetary Union', *Journal of European Economic History, XXII* (2).

Pressburger, S. (1966) *Osterreichische Notenbank 1816–1966.* Vienna.

Raffalovitch, A (1995) *Le Marché financier en 1894–95.* Paris.

Sanucci, V. (1989) 'The Establishment of a Central Bank: Italy in the Nineteenth Century', in de Cecco, M. and A. Giovannini, eds, *A European Central Bank? Relevance and Lessons for Europe Today.* Cambridge.

Schulze, M. S. (1997) 'Re-estimating Austrian GDP 1870–1913', LSE Working Paper in Economic History, No. 36/97.

Statesman's Yearbook. Statistical and Historical Annual of the States of the World. London.

Svensson, L. (1994) 'Why Exchange Rate Bands? Monetary Independence in Spite of Fixed Exchange Rates', *Journal of Monetary Economics, 33.*

Vanthoor, W. (1996) *European Monetary Union Since 1848, a Political and Historical Analysis.* Cheltenham.

Vilar, P. (1974) *Or et monnaie dans l'histoire.* Paris.

Willis, H. P. (1901) *A History of the Latin Monetary Union.* Chicago.

Wysocki, J. (1975) *Infrastruktur und wachsende Staatsausgaben: Das Fallbeispiel Österreichs, 1868–1913, Forschungen zur Sozial- und Wirtschaftsgeschichte,* Band 20. Stuttgart.

Yeager, L. B. (1969) 'Fluctuating Exchange Rates in the Nineteenth Century: the Experience of Austria and Russia', in Mundell, R. and A. Swoboda, eds, *Monetary Problems of the International Economy.* Chicago.

Zeuceanu, A. (1924) *La liquidation de la Banque d'Autriche Hongrie.* Vienna.

Zuckerkandl, R. (1911) 'The Austro-Hungarian Bank', in *Banking in Russia, Austria-Hungary, the Netherlands and Japan,* United States National Monetary Commission. Washington, DC.

Comments on Chapter 5 – The economics of Cacania, 1867–1914. Austro-Hungarian monetary lessons for Euroland

Luca Einaudi[1]

Marc Flandreau has correctly identified the Austro-Hungarian monetary arrangements as a relevant case of monetary unification, closer to our contemporary European Monetary Union than other nineteenth-century examples more frequently studied. The dual monarchy progressively transformed its monetary arrangements between 1867 and 1914 to build between Austria and Hungary a shared monetary arrangement but two separate fiscal policies with a separate governmental debt. Despite the initial differences in policy, eventually the two countries converged towards sound public finances and low interest rates. The absence of a formal stability pact and of mutual budgetary surveillance through yearly convergence or stability programmes did not ultimately handicap the achievement of financial equilibrium thanks to the operation of strong market discipline. The initial strong rise of deficits and debt which followed the compromise of 1867 was controlled by the market through the imposition of higher interest rates, structured in order to favour gold-denominated debt as opposed to paper currency debt. This mechanism induced the Austrian and the Hungarian governments to issue gold-denominated debt and then to stabilise the foreign value of the currency in terms of gold in the 1890s. In the process deficits and debts were strongly reduced.

Yet the description of a growing share of foreign debt as an optimal commitment mechanism to improve public finances management can not be generalised to all situations. Foreign debt certainly induces governments to emphasise exchange rate stability, but governments can use fixed exchange rates to reduce artificially the interest rate and the risk premium in order to be able to prolong unsustainable financial policies, concealed by market discipline rhetoric. The usual outcome of such a policy is an overvalued real exchange rate followed by a sudden and violent devaluation. The real weight of foreign debt is magnified by the collapse of the currency, worsening further internal and external finances. Market discipline is a double edged sword; it can be tampered with for a time and then deliver a fatal blow to those who tried to manipulate it.

Compared to the other major unions of the period, the 'Austro-Hungarian monetary union' (AHMU) seems to have been more successful, its operation did not create major disputes between member states and its institutional arrangement was more complete. In my opinion there are four major aspects which explain its success when compared to three supranational unions of the period, the Münzverein or

German Monetary Union (GMU, 1838–71), the Latin Monetary Union (LMU, 1865–1926) and the Scandinavian Monetary Union (SMU, 1873–1920). These reasons are:

- *The AHMU was the only real supranational monetary union of the period*, thanks to the ambiguous nature of the Austro-Hungarian empire, neither a nation nor a freely constructed alliance. The monetary unification of Switzerland (1850), of Italy (1862) and of Germany (1871) were simply the automatic consequences of nation building and did not involve continuous intergovernmental negotiations in order to operate. The SMU, LMU and GMU were in fact only supranational coinage unions (common standard areas in Flandreau's words), with more limited ambitions and powers. Each member of these latter unions issued national coinage in gold and silver under common rules, but maintained entire discretion for what concerned paper money and sometimes even for bronze coinage. The currency of a member state could depreciate without formally breaching the rules of the LMU. Therefore, as Flandreau points out, the exchange rate between France and Italy, both members of the LMU, fluctuated more than the Franco-British exchange rate.
- *The existence of a single and common bank of issue*, the Austro-Hungarian Bank (ÖUB), removed the threat of a separate overissue of paper money by the government of a single member state. Monetary financing of public debt, permitted by the absence of such a bank, had been the source of a large part of the internal conflicts of the LMU (Einaudi 1997: 327–61). In the GMU, excessive issue of paper money by small German states was often quoted as an urgent problem which could only be solved through adopting a rigid gold standard and a more unified monetary system. This happened with the creation of the German Imperial Mark in 1871 and with the formation of the Reichsbank in 1876. Even in the case of the Austrian National Bank, some time was necessary to transform it into a common bank of issue, but the existence of a common paper money made it unavoidable. Necessity became an opportunity and, as noted by Flandreau, Austria-Hungary developed at an early stage some central banking characters associated with paper currency management, independently from orthodox views of commodity money.
- *The cost of dissolving the AHMU was much higher than that of coinage unions.* The threat of dissolution is always a powerful instrument to discipline troublemakers in a monetary union: the more integrated monetary circulation is, the more expensive it is to disentangle it. Furthermore, for the threat to be credible, such costs must be asymmetric. The financial cost of dissolving AHMU was a strong disincentive which played against the Hungarian separatists of 1905–9. For the LMU the cost of dissolution after 1879 was limited to the expenses of repatriating migrated coins and to the losses on silver issues. That was sufficient to force the Italian and Belgian governments to accept French and Swiss monetary discipline on silver issues. For Hungary the price of separation was much larger; not only its monetary system had been completely integrated for centuries in the Austrian empire but a higher risk premium on its foreign debt

would also reappear together with larger interest payments. The operations of the ÖUB had moderated default risk and exchange rate fluctuation with the stabilisation of the currency in 1890–6, but all these achievements and the related credibility would be lost after political separation.

- *The AHMU was a simple two players game where monitoring was easy and negotiation direct.* The SMU had three members, the LMU five (six if we count the troublesome Pontifical State in 1866–70) and the GMU close to twenty-five. The LMU and the GMU clearly encountered problems with free riders, difficult to monitor at first. After 1870 the French government decided to block any new enlargement of the LMU to prevent any new cases of this type. In a large monetary union it was also more difficult to negotiate acceptable compromises between different national interests in terms of seignorage income and compensations. With more than two players, temporary alliances do play an important role in decision making. The relative simplicity of the AHMU may be the response to the question advanced by Flandreau in his concluding remarks. The EMU, with twelve members, and expecting many more, needed more formal explicit rules than AHMU, where the two players interacted directly.

Despite being a more articulate and modern monetary union, however, the AHMU collapsed under the same shock as the LMU and the SMU, the First World War. It is intriguing to notice that the political direction of the Austro-Hungarian process was the opposite of the one followed by the European Union. Whereas the Austro-Hungarian Empire had a single currency before 1867 (the Austrian florin), it kept a single currency with a dual name between 1867 and 1918 (the florin-forint and from 1892 the corona-korona), but by 1919 its territories were split between seven states and currencies. By 1998, the number of successor currencies had reached twelve (Austrian shilling, Hungarian forint, Czech krouna, Slovak koruna, Yugoslav new dinar, Slovene tolar, Croatian dinar, Bosnian convertible markaa, Italian lira, Polish zloty, Ukrainian hryvnia and Romanian lei). The AHMU was the only true monetary union of the period, but it was also too special to be an entirely credible precedent for EMU.

The repeated attempts of Austria and Austria-Hungary to join other existing supranational monetary unions from the 1850s to the 1890s confirms its dissatisfaction with the existing monetary arrangement, its fear of being marginalised and the strong connection between political alliances and monetary unions.

The Habsburg Empire was extremely concerned about the creation of the GMU in 1838, in which they did not participate, and the increase in Prussian influence in Germany. In 1854 the Austrians proposed the establishment of a common gold standard with the German states, in the expectation that the massive inflow of gold from California and Australia would lead to a depreciation of gold. This depreciation would help Austria to resume the convertibility of its bank notes that had been suspended with the 1848 revolution. The German states did not accept, fearing the weakening of their own coinage (Holtfrerich 1989: 216–40). In 1857, however, the Austrian finance minister Bruck obtained the creation of a *Münzverein*, or German–Austrian union of coinage. Austria resumed the silver convertibility of its bank notes in 1858 but dropped out again during the war with Italy and France in 1859.

The defeat against Prussia in 1866 did not automatically mean the exclusion of Austria from the Münzverein, since the peace treaty was leaving all options open. Vienna decided to leave the GMU only the year after, watching the development of the alternative LMU and expecting to be able to join it. A new French alliance was useful to gain access to the Parisian capital market, to import monetary credibility but also to prepare a possible revanche against Prussia. During the International Monetary Conference of Paris in 1867, the Austrian delegate, Baron de Hock, was one of the most ardent supporters of the French-sponsored attempt to transform the LMU into a universal system of coinage, based on the gold standard. Immediately after the Conference, de Hock negotiated with the French a monetary convention which prepared the accession of Austria-Hungary to the LMU. The convention was never ratified by the French government, despite a new formal application for membership in 1874. Austria-Hungary minted gold coins denominated both in florins and in francs from 1870 to 1892 (8 florins–20 francs and 4 florins–10 francs) and obtained their circulation at face value in the LMU. The French ministry of foreign affairs hoped to prevent Austria-Hungary from being attracted to the orbit of the German Empire thanks to strong monetary and financial links. The French finance ministry instead feared that formal membership of the LMU would be a threat, given the poor state of the dual empire's finances. Internal restraint in monetary issue could be weakened once seignorage became possible at the expense of other countries, since the LMU still had no central bank. The French Treasury rejected Austrian inconvertible paper money and accepted AHMU gold pieces only because it expected their circulation in France to be practically irrelevant even if politically significant (Einaudi 1998).

The monetary reform of 1892, which stabilised the currency of the AHMU, destroyed its connection with the LMU, introducing a new 'crown' unconnected to the franc. Politically, the move reflected Austria-Hungary's entrance into the orbit of the German Empire and the Triple Alliance.

Note

1 The views expressed in the article are those of the author and do not involve the institutions to which he is connected.

References

Einaudi, L. (1997) 'Monetary Unions and Free Riders: the Case of the Latin Monetary Union', *Rivista di storia economica, 3.*

Einaudi, L. (1998) 'Money and Politics: European Monetary Unification and the International Gold Standard (1865–1873)', unpublished PhD dissertation. Trinity College, University of Cambridge.

Holtfrerich, C. L. (1989) 'The Monetary Unification Process in Nineteenth-Century Germany: Relevance and Lessons for Europe Today', in De Cecco, M. and A. Giovannini, eds, *A European Central Bank?*. Cambridge.

6 The future of the euro

A public choice perspective

Roland Vaubel

Introduction and overview

Public choice analysis can be helpful in predicting the course of European monetary integration and policy. The median (or decisive) voter theorem, the theory of the political business cycle and the economic theory of bureaucracy are all applicable. The purpose of this paper is to explain and predict the behaviour of the European Central Bank (ECB) and the Council of Ministers on the basis of the available empirical evidence.

The next section relies on the median voter theorem to derive predictions for the inflation rate of the euro. It shows that inflation rates have to be explained by the voters' sensitivity to inflation rather than the independence of central bankers and that, in the initial years, the French members of the ECB Council held the median position in terms of past inflation, voters' sensitivity to inflation and predicted or simulated preferred inflation. In July 2002, the median position was taken over by the Finnish members of the ECB Council, implying a higher preferred rate of inflation for the euro.

The third section shows that, in May 2001, when the ECB began to lower its interest rate, a majority of the ECB Council supported the governments facing elections between May 2002 and May 2004. This period contains a cluster of election dates.

The fourth section argues that the euro's long-run effect on employment is ambiguous and cannot be predicted. However, European Monetary Union (EMU) is likely to have the largest negative, or smallest positive, effect on employment in Finland, Spain and Italy.

The fifth section presents evidence on whether an exchange rate policy for the euro is needed. It shows that, between the euro-zone and the US dollar, nominal exchange rate trends are increasingly in line with the required real exchange rate adjustments. In the more recent past, exchange rate flexibility has outperformed the Bretton Woods system in this respect.

The sixth section considers the possibility of enlarging the European Monetary Union by the current members of the European Union (EU) and by Eastern European countries. The evidence presented indicates that, of all fifteen EU members, Britain has been the least suitable EMU member in terms of real exchange rate adjustment and that British entry could induce the ECB to raise the cost of reserve requirements. Since the combined entry of Britain, Sweden and Denmark would affect the median position in the ECB Council and since the median country would have to agree to it, enlargement might require some form of compensation. Most of the Eastern European countries are shown to require very large real exchange rate adjustments. For them, the cost of joining EMU would be large. Only Hungary has the predicted exchange rate regime.

The last section derives the size and composition of EMU central bank staff from a labour demand equation estimated for twenty-one industrial countries. It shows that the European System of Central Banks (ESCB), notably the French, Belgian and Italian central banks, are highly overstaffed by international standards. Estimates of the required staff of the ESCB and the ECB are derived from international comparisons.

Inflation[1]

Monetary policy for the euro is determined by a simple majority of the Governing Council of the European Central Bank. Thus, the inflation rate of the euro will reflect the preference of the median ECB Council member (unless logrolling plays an important role.) To determine the median, the (relative) inflation preferences of the various ECB Council members have to be known.[2]

Quantitative analysis

The simplest and crudest method of predicting relative inflation preferences is to extrapolate past inflation rates. This method is justified if the following assumptions apply:

1 Central bankers are appointed or proposed by the government of their home country because they share the long-run inflation preference of that government.
2 The governments of the member states are elected because they share the long-run inflation preference of the median voter of their country.
3 The long-run inflation rate preferred by the median voter in each country has not changed.

Various stability tests (Collins and Giavazzi 1993; Hayo 1998a) show that, up to 1993, the third assumption cannot be rejected for any of the participating countries.[3] Even if inflation preferences have changed since 1993, the following analysis might be indicative of the relative positions of the national representatives. Alternatively, it could be interpreted not as a prediction but as an illustrative simulation of what would have happened if EMU had been introduced after the breakdown of the Bretton Woods system.

Table 6.1 reports the national compound average inflation rates since 1976. The initial year is 1976 because the Bretton Woods system finally collapsed in 1973 and because monetary policy affects inflation with a lag of about two years. Since monetary

Table 6.1 The inflation median in the Governing Council of the European Central Bank: consumer price index

Country	*ECB votes*	*1976–93*			*1976–98*			*1990–8*	*Votes in the European Council*
		Actual inflation per annum	*Annual real exchange rate appreciation vis-à-vis median*	*Median inflation adjusted for real exchange rate change*	*Actual inflation per annum*	*Annual real exchange rate appreciation vis-à-vis France*	*French inflation adjusted for real exchange rate change*	*Annual real exchange rate appreciation vis-à-vis France*	
Portugal	1	16.9	+0.4	7.1	13.7	+0.3	5.8	+1.5	5
Spain	2	10.8	+1.0	7.8	9.0	+0.6	6.1	−1.6	8
Italy	2	10.4	+0.7	7.4	8.8	+0.7	6.2	−1.5	10
Ireland	1	8.0	+1.0	7.8	6.6	+1.0	6.5	−0.5	3
Finland	2	6.8	−1.2	5.5	**5.4**	−0.6	4.8	−3.3	3
France	2	**6.7**	0	**6.7**	**5.4**	0	**5.4**	0	10
Belgium	1	4.5	−0.4	6.3	3.9	−0.3	5.1	+0.2	5
Luxembourg	1	4.4	−0.5	6.2	3.7	−0.5	4.9	+0.3	2
Austria	1	3.8	+0.9	7.7	3.4	+0.6	6.1	+0.5	4
Netherlands	2	3.2	−0.2	6.5	3.0	−0.2	5.2	+0.5	5
Germany	2	3.2	+0.2	6.9	2.9	+0.1	5.6	+0.7	10
Weighted average		7.0		6.9	5.8		5.6		

expansion may have been biased downwards by the need to meet the inflation criterion of the Maastricht Treaty (December 1991),[4] the base period used for prediction should probably not extend beyond 1993.

The first column indicates the current distribution of ECB votes. Each member of the Executive Board is assumed to share and represent the inflation preferences of the government which has proposed her.

Table 6.1 shows that, regardless of whether the base period ends in 1993 or 1998, the French inflation rate occupies the median position in the ECB Council of 1999. In 1976–93, it amounted to 6.7 per cent per annum which is somewhat less than the ECB-weighted average (7.0 per cent). The French ECB members also hold the median if, for the other participating countries, the French inflation rate is adjusted by their historical real exchange rate change vis-à-vis France or if Greece is added in 2001 (keeping in mind that the Dutch ECB President has the casting vote). But France lost its median position to Finland in July 2002 when Greece obtained a second seat at the expense of the Netherlands. Since Finnish inflation used to be higher than French inflation, this implies an increase in the expected inflation of the euro. The President's resignation in July 2003 does not alter the median.

The underlying assumption that the historical long-run inflation rates have actually been preferred by the national electorates, might as well be tested. The voters' sensitivity to inflation has been estimated by Hayo (1998a, b) for the twelve member states of 1993. It is indicated by the regression coefficient with which the current inflation rate affects the rank of price stability among four objectives.[5] Table 6.2, column 1, reports the sensitivity to inflation for nine of the eleven EMU countries. For Austria and Finland, survey data are not available before 1995 – the year in which they joined the European Union. Among the nine countries, once more, France holds the median position in the ECB Council. The same is true if, on the basis of past inflation (Table 6.1), the French sensitivity to inflation is assumed to be higher than the Finnish but lower than the Austrian.

Alternatively, the inflation aversion of monetary policy makers (the weight of the price stability target in the loss function) has been estimated from policy reaction functions by Lippi and Swank (1999, Ch. 8, notably Table 8.2). Their estimates for 1965–92 (Table 6.2, column 2) confirm the view that France occupies the median position in the ECB Council. The correlation between Hayo's estimate of the voters' sensitivity to inflation and the inflation aversion of policy makers as estimated by Lippi and Swank is positive and significant at the 1 per cent level ($r = 0.91$, $n = 9$).

To what extent does the voters' sensitivity to inflation explain the historical inflation experience? Table 6.3 reports a cross-section regression of actual inflation (1976–93) on Hayo's estimate of the voters' sensitivity to inflation. The best fit is provided by a constant elasticity specification. As expected, the regression coefficient is negative and significant at the 1 per cent level. The national sensitivity to inflation explains 85 per cent of the cross-sectional inflation variance. Table 6.2, column 3, reports the predicted inflation rates. Among nine countries, the inflation rate predicted for France (5.8 per cent) is the median in the ECB Council (without the Austrian and Finnish members). The same is true if, for Austria and Finland, the actual inflation rates are inserted. Equation 1 can be used to infer the Austrian and

Table 6.2 Sensitivity to inflation, central bank independence, DM pegging and inflation in EMU-11, 1976–93

Country (ECB members)	*Sensitivity to inflation*[a] *(S)* (1)	*Inflation aversion*[b] *(ß)* (2)	*Predicted inflation*[c] (3)	*Central bank independence (I)* (4)	*Predicted central bank independence* (5)	*Pegging to DM (f)* (6)	*Preferred inflation*[d] (7)	*Preferred inflation*[e] (8)	*Median preferred inflation adjusted for real exchange rate change*[e] (9)	*Spanish preferred inflation adjusted for real exchange rate change*[e] (10)	*Belgian preferred inflation adjusted for real exchange rante change*[e] (11)
Portugal (1)	0.33[f]	0.68	18.8	0.63	0.59	0	14.9	23.0	8.2	9.3	8.6
Spain (2)	1.35[f]	0.51	7.6	0.84	1.14	0.14	7.1	10.0	8.9	**10.0**	9.3
Italy (2)	1.28[g]	0.39	7.9	1.08	1.12	0.71	7.3	10.3	8.5	9.7	9.0
Ireland (1)	0.92[g]	0.11	9.7	UK: 1.93	UK: 1.31	0.71	8.7	12.5	8.9	10.0	9.3
Finland (2)	(1.60[h])	0.20	–	1.60	1.24	0	6.5	9.0	6.5	7.6	6.9
France (2)	**2.05**[g]	**0.79**	**5.80**	1.22	1.39	0.80	**5.69**	**7.78**	7.78	8.9	8.2
Belgium (1)	2.06[g]	1.56	5.78	1.25	1.40	1.00	5.67	7.76	7.3	8.5	**7.76**
Luxembourg (1)	2.84[g]	1.56	4.7	1.25	1.63	1.00	4.8	6.4	7.2	8.4	7.7
Austria (1)	(3.95[h])	4.55	–	1.98	1.90	0.68	4.0	5.3	8.8	9.9	9.2
Netherlands (2)	3.59[g]	1.23	4.0	1.69	1.82	1.00	4.2	5.6	7.6	8.7	8.0
Germany (2)	5.81[g]	3.51	3.0	2.72	2.28	0	3.3	4.2	8.0	9.1	8.4
Weighted average	2.44	1.28	6.83	1.49	1.46	0.51	6.25	8.2			

Notes
[a] Hayo (1998).
[b] Lippy and Swank (1999).
[c] From Table 6.3, equation 1.
[d] Predicted from Table 6.3, equation 6.
[e] Predicted from Table 6.3, equation 8.
[f] 1985–93.
[g] Significant at 5 per cent level.
[h] Estimated from Table 6.3, equation 1.

Table 6.3 Cross-section analysis of inflation in EMU-11 (ln), 1976–93

Equation	*Intercept*	*Sensitivity to inflation* $\ln S$	*Central bank independence* $\ln I$	*Independence without pegging* $\ln I^{(1-f)}$	*Pegging* $\ln e^f = f$	*Imports/ GDP* $\ln m$	R^2 R^2 *adj.*	*n*
1	2.221	−0.645					0.85	9
	(22.95[a])	(−6.37[a])					0.83	
2	2.139		−1.150				0.69	9
	(15.92[a])		(−3.94[a])				0.64	
3	2.158		−1.120				0.69	11
	(17.59[a])		(−4.44[a])				0.65	
4	2.230	−0.522	−0.297				0.88	11
	(27.18[a])	(−3.66[a])	(−1.07)				0.85	
5	2.225	−0.664		+0.063			0.87	11
	(25.14[a])	(−5.54[a])		(0.25)			0.83	
6	2.337	−0.527		−0.220	−0.300		0.90	11
	(19.76[a])	(−3.45[b])		(−0.69)	(−1.35)		0.85	
7	2.387	−0.606		−0.019	−0.214		0.81	15
	(18.16[a])	(−3.54[b])		(−0.05)	(−0.81)		0.76	
8	3.422	−0.593		−0.136	−0.009	−0.337	0.96	11
	(9.88[a])	(−5.80[a])		(−0.64)	(−0.05)	(−3.21[b])	0.94	
9	3.427	−0.591		−0.123	−0.026	−0.334	0.96	9
	(8.21[a])	(−4.45[a])		(−0.46)	(−0.13)	(−2.64[c])	0.92	
10	3.680	−0.698		+0.095	+0.105	−0.399	0.88	15
	(6.89[a])	(−4.77[a])		(0.33)	(0.41)	(−2.47[b])	0.83	

Notes
[a] Significant at 1 per cent level.
[b] Significant at 5 per cent level.
[c] Significant at 10 per cent level.

Finnish sensitivity to inflation from their historical inflation rates (see Table 6.2, column 1, in parentheses).

So far the analysis has assumed, for the sake of simplicity, that inflation depends only on the voters' sensitivity to inflation or that all other influences are randomly distributed. It has totally ignored the impressive body of evidence that inflation is also (negatively) affected by central bank independence (I). However, central bank independence may merely reflect the voters' sensitivity to inflation. Regressing central bank independence (an average of seven indices[6]) on the sensitivity to inflation,[7] we obtain the following estimate:

$$\ln I = \underset{(-0.08)}{-0.008} + \underset{(5.06^*)}{0.473} \ln S \qquad R^2 = 0.74 \quad n = 11 \tag{6.1}$$

As expected, the two variables are closely correlated. The sensitivity to inflation retains its significant regression coefficient ($t = 3.52^*$), if it is combined with a dummy for universal banking, the interest group variable used by Posen (1993a, b).[8] If the sensitivity to inflation is not in turn affected by the independence of the central bank, we can use the above equation to explain and predict central bank independence (Table 6.2, column 5). It turns out that in the UK and Finland the central bank is much more independent than we should expect from the sensitivity to inflation, and that in Luxembourg and Spain the opposite is the case.

While central bank independence can be explained by the sensitivity to inflation, the latter seems to be largely determined by the experience of hyperinflation in the past:

$$S_{i,t} = 1.57 + 0.069\,\pi_{i,t-n} \quad R^2 = 0.66 \tag{6.2}$$
$$\quad (4.55^*)\ (4.22^*) \qquad n = 11$$

where π_{t-n} is the (compound) annual average rate of inflation between 1900 and 1940 (Maddison 1991; Mitchell 1992).

Table 6.3 demonstrates that central bank independence has a less significant (negative) effect on inflation than the sensitivity to inflation does (equations 1 and 2)[9] and that, if both are used as regressors, the coefficient of central bank independence is no longer significant (equation 4).

However, the conventional approach of explaining inflation by central bank independence is conceptually flawed anyway. Central bank independence can hardly affect the long-term inflation rate if the government has fixed the exchange rate vis-à-vis a dominant currency. Thus, to explain inflation in a European cross-section analysis, central bank independence (or its unexplained component[10]) has to be weighted by the proportion of time during which the currency was not pegged to the D-Mark ($1 - f$). The proportion of time during which the currency was pegged (f) is reported in Table 6.2, column 6.

Table 6.3, equation 5, shows that central bank independence under a regime of flexible exchange rates does not have a significant effect on inflation if it is combined with the sensitivity to inflation. The coefficient of the independence variable does not even take the predicted sign.

However, equation 5 is still incomplete because it does not account for the effect of exchange-rate pegging (f) itself. Pegging may be regarded as a proxy for the competitive or disciplinary pressure from the Bundesbank which has now disappeared. Since the independence of the Bundesbank is normalised to e, $\ln e^f = f$ can be interpreted as the natural logarithm of the independence index of the Bundesbank exponentially weighted with the proportion of time during which the country pegged to the D-Mark. Thus, apart from the effect of the sensitivity to inflation, inflation is explained by a combination of central bank independence at home and in Germany, with $1-f$ and f serving as exponential weights. Table 6.3, equation 6, reveals that neither central bank independence at home nor pegging to the D-Mark has a significant effect on inflation if the sensitivity to inflation is included as a regressor.[11]

Central bank independence and pegging also fail to explain inflation if, in addition, the ratio of imports to GDP is included (equations 8–10). The theoretical justification for including this variable is that, with a higher import/GDP ratio, an unanticipated monetary expansion or devaluation has a faster effect on the price level because a larger share of the consumer basket is affected by the depreciation of the currency. As a result, voters are more likely to understand the monetary causes of inflation and object to an inflationary monetary policy (Johnson 1970: 105; Romer 1993). Equations 8–10 in Table 6.3 reveal that the import / GDP ratio does indeed reduce inflation significantly.[12] The members of the ECB Council are confronted with a less open currency area than the national central banks have been. In this respect, they are likely to tolerate a higher rate of inflation.

It is now possible to simulate the long-term inflation rates which the various members of the ECB Council would have preferred, if they had been as independent as the Bundesbank and if their currency had not been pegged to a currency like the D-Mark. The preferred long-term inflation rates are computed from equations 6 and 8, setting $f = 0$ and $\ln I^{1-f} = \ln e^1 = 1$. As columns 7 and 8 of Table 6.2 show, the French members keep their median position in the ECB Council regardless of the equation used if monetary union is assumed to imply that the participating states share a common inflation rate. If the historical real exchange rate change is extrapolated, the Spanish members of the ECB Council hold the median, and the simulated inflation rates rise (Table 6.2, columns 9 and 10). However, the simulated Spanish inflation rates (7.1 and 10.0 per cent, respectively) are still lower than the actual Spanish inflation rate in this period. The weighted average of the preferred inflation rates falls if equation 6 is used, and it rises if equation 8 is used. Thus, with regard to inflation preferences, the increase in central bank independence outweighs the loss of disciplinary pressure from the Bundesbank[13] but the fact that the import/ GDP ratio is smaller for the EMU than for the individual participating states shifts the balance towards higher preferred inflation.

Complications

In simulating the inflation rate of the euro, we have made a number of simplifying assumptions which have to be discussed.

First of all, is the European Central Bank as independent as the Bundesbank has been? On the one hand, the ECB is more independent because amendments of the EC Treaty require the assent of fifteen parliaments (each voting by simple majority) while the Bundesbank Law may be amended by a single parliament (also with a simple majority). On the other hand, the individual members of the ECB Governing Council enjoy less personal independence. The members of the German Central Bank Council have always been reappointed (after eight years) if they wished so and if their age permitted. This is not prescribed by the Bundesbank Law but is a tradition which has evolved over the years. By contrast, as Table 6.4 shows, nine of the twelve national Governors in the ECB Council depend on their government for reappointment (usually after five or six years) and, in May 2001, at least seven Governors were young enough to be reappointable.[14]

The members of the Executive Board, it is true, may not be reappointed but they may need career assistance from their government when their term is over and they return to their home country. As Table 6.4 demonstrates, the French and Spanish members of the Executive Board have not reached the retirement age when their term of office ends.

Moreover, the European Central Bank would enjoy less policy autonomy than

Table 6.4 Seigniorage gains and losses in EMU-11

Country	*ECB votes*	*Seigniorage wealth (billion euros)*[a]	*Share in seigniorage wealth (per cent)*	*Share in ECB capital (per cent)*[a]	*Total gains (billion euros)*	*Population (millions)*[a]	*Gains per capita (euros)*
Luxembourg	1	0.1	0.03	0.19	+0.49	0.4	+1,225
Finland	2	2.2	0.71	1.71	+3.08	5.1	+604
France	2	39.8	12.92	21.28	+25.75	57.9	+445
Portugal	1	4.3	1.40	2.41	+3.11	9.9	+314
Ireland	1	2.6	0.84	1.08	+0.74	3.6	+206
Italy	2	50.6	16.43	18.75	+7.15	57.2	+125
Belgium	1	10.8	3.51	3.67	+0.49	10.1	+49
Netherlands	2	17.6	5.71	5.51	–0.62	15.4	–40
Austria	1	10.5	3.41	3.04	–1.14	8.0	–143
Spain	2	46.2	15.00	11.02	–12.26	39.1	–314
Germany	2	123.3	40.03	31.35	–26.73	81.4	–328
Total	17	308.0	≈100.00	≈ 100.00	≈ 0	288.1	–

Note:
[a] Source: Sinn and Feist (1997), Table 1 (columns 3 and 5), Table 3 (column 8).

the Bundesbank has, if the Council of Ministers adopted an exchange rate target for the euro. In 1979, the Bundesbank obtained permission to abandon interventions in the exchange market whenever it might see a threat to price-level stability. It made use of this right in August 1993. The ECB does not seem to be entitled to take such a decision.

Even if the overall independence of the ECB were considered comparable to the former independence of the Bundesbank, the sources of central bank (in)dependence would have changed. Figure 6.1 shows how this affects the objective function of central bankers. Central bankers follow their own judgement, public opinion or the government (or a combination thereof). Popularity serves to maintain the central bank's policy autonomy and secure reappointment or career assistance. Autonomy is a means for attaining macroeconomic targets, political aims or the utility of personal power and prestige.

Relative to the Bundesbank, the policy autonomy of the European Central Bank is less threatened by amendments of its legal statute. Thus, it is less likely to seek the support of public opinion – the more so as a European public opinion does not exist. The main threat to the policy autonomy of the ECB is the possibility of an exchange rate target vis-à-vis the dollar. However, the introduction of a parity system requires a unanimous decision by the Council of Ministers (Art. 111 (1)). This means that the European Central Bank can focus on public opinion in one or a few participating countries which have a tradition of distrusting any pegging to the dollar (Germany, the UK etc.). Thus, the threat to policy autonomy and the cost of preserving it will be smaller for the European Central Bank than for the Bundesbank.

Since the members of the ECB Council enjoy more security of policy autonomy but less security of tenure, government objectives will matter more, and public opinion less, in European than in German monetary policy. To this extent, the

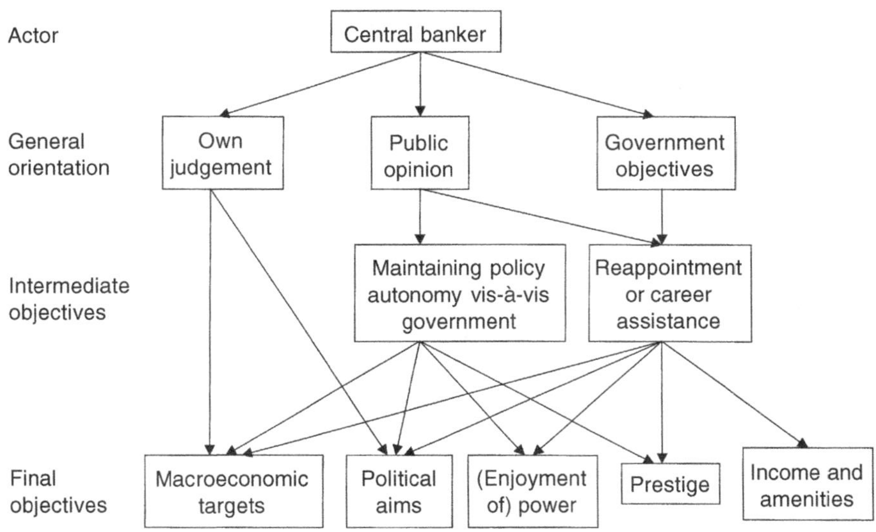

Figure 6.1 The central banker's calculus.

individual members of the ECB Council will pay more attention to the ideology of their government[15] and to the election cycle at home. Political business cycles are likely to raise the long-run average rate of inflation.[16]

As for government ideology, seven of the eleven participating states had socialist-led governments in 1998 but no more than six of the seventeen members of the ECB Council could be associated with socialist parties (Table 6.4). Among the governors, the reasons for this discrepancy differ from country to country. But why were five of the six executive directors conservatives even though the Executive Board had to be appointed unanimously?[17] Have the governments tried to offset a time inconsistency bias by appointing conservative central bankers as Rogoff (1985) has proposed?

There is an alternative explanation. If the European Council had been unable to agree on the members of the Executive Board, there would have been no monetary union.[18] The government which had most to lose (or least to gain) from EMU had a strong bargaining position. This was the German government, a conservative–liberal coalition government. It had most to lose because the German central bank had played a leading role under the previous regime, German inflation preferences are most deviant from the median (Table 6.2, column 1), Germany would be the main loser of seigniorage (Table 6.4), monetary union was rejected by an overwhelming majority of German voters, and a national election was imminent.

Future German governments will not have a strong bargaining position when new members of the Executive Board are selected. EMU will not break up if the Executive Board is incomplete or has ceased to exist. If there is no Executive Board, a simple majority of the national Governors will decide about monetary policy for the euro. With this fallback position, the government which (most nearly) shares the preferences of the median Governor will dominate the selection of new executive directors (if any).[19] The other governments will concur if they prefer to have an Executive Board for reputational reasons.

Tables 6.1 and 6.2 reveal that the French Governor occupied the median position among the eleven Governors in terms of inflation (1976–93 and 1976–98), voters' sensitivity to inflation and predicted or simulated preferred inflation regardless of whether equation 1, 6 or 8 is used.[20]

Germany's strong bargaining position in 1998 may also explain that, in November 1998, the ECB Council decided to postpone the redistribution of seigniorage for three years even though Italy, which occupies the ECB median in this respect, will benefit from the redistribution of seigniorage wealth (see Table 6.4 which is calculated from Sinn and Feist 1997).

To conclude the analysis of this section, a reminder seems to be in order. The predicted level of inflation is merely the mid-point of a confidence interval (which could easily be computed). Moreover, if inflation preferences in the median country had changed since 1993 or if they changed in the future under the influence of an independent ECB, inflation in the next 15–20 years could be much lower than predicted. However, the recent overture to the game is probably not a good guide to the future.

How soon will the ECB Council be tested? We turn from the long to the short run.

An electoral monetary policy cycle?[21]

In the short run, monetary policy for the euro may be affected by the national electoral cycles of the participating states. To the extent to which the election dates differ, electoral monetary policy cycles are less likely for the European Central Bank than they have been for the national central banks.[22] However, since the ECB Council pays less attention to public opinion and more to the demands of governments (see the previous section), there is an offsetting effect.

Electoral monetary policy cycles have been observed in many countries, including those which are generally considered to have independent central banks (e.g. Soh 1986, Table 5). This is to be expected when central bankers have partisan preferences. They may be independent but, nevertheless, loyal to the politicians who have appointed them and whose partisan preferences they share. The 'party loyalty hypothesis' has successfully been tested for both Germany and the United States (Vaubel 1993, 1997a, b; McGregor 1996). Of course, the hypothesis predicts a monetary acceleration before elections only if the government commands a partisan majority in the central bank council.

To apply the party loyalty hypothesis to the European Central Bank, it is necessary to examine the temporal distribution of the national election dates, the party composition of the incumbent governments and the partisan leanings of the ECB Council members. Usually, the partisan orientation, if any, of central bankers can be inferred from information about who appointed them. Table 6.5 gives the relevant information for May 2001 – the month in which the ECB began to lower its interest rate.[23] It shows that, at that time, a majority of the members of the ECB Council was likely to support the incumbent politicians at home.

Table 6.6 reveals a clustering of election dates from May 2002 onwards. It shows the size and composition of the coalitions in the ECB Council one year ahead of the elections, the weighted average of the regular election dates in their countries and the weighted standard deviation around this mean. The countries' supporting votes in the ECB Council serve as weights proxying their bargaining power. The winning ECB coalition which minimises the dispersion of election dates prevailed in May 2001 and consisted of central bankers whose governments stood or will stand for re-election between May 2002 and May 2004: the Netherlands, Ireland, Germany, Finland, Belgium, Austria, Spain and Greece.[24] The weighted average of the election dates and preferred peak is May 2003, i.e., the 53rd month of the monetary union. Of course, some of the later election dates may be advanced towards this date, thereby shifting the average to an earlier date.[25] In any case, the eight governments standing for re-election between May 2002 and May 2004 commanded a majority in the ECB Council in May 2001 when the ECB began to lower its interest rate. Of course, this is not to deny that other explanations are possible.

If, for some unforeseen reason, electoral monetary policy cycles do not materialise, the incumbent governments are likely to resort to expansionary fiscal policies. The German government once threatened to do so. According to the 'Pact for Stability and Growth', the imposition of sanctions requires a qualified majority decision of the Council of Ministers (excluding the government under consideration).

Table 6.5 Governments and the Central Bank Council in the EMU in May 2001

	A	*B*	*D*	*F*	*FI*	*GR*	*I*	*IR*	*L*	*NL*	*P*	*SP*
Government												
Partisan code	C+L	L+S+	S+	S	S+C_g +L+	S	S+C_g	C	C+L	S+L	S	C
Electoral term	4	4	4	5	4	4	5	5	5	4	4	4
Expected date of next election	03:10	03:06	02:09	02:06	03:03	04:04	01:06	02:06	04:05	02:05	03:10	04:03
Central Bank governors												
Partisan code	C	S	S	?	C_g	S	C	C	C	C	S	C
Age (in 2001)	62	55	59	59	55	54	65	n.a.	51	58	46	49
Date of last appointment	98:09	99:03	99:09	99:09	98:06	00:10	93:06	01:05	98:06	97:07	99:06	00:06
Term of office	5	5	8+	6	7	6	∞	7	6	7	5	1 × 6
Appointed by incumbents	yes	yes	yes	yes	yes	yes	yes	yes	yes	yes	yes	yes
Supporting incumbents	yes	yes	yes	?	yes	yes	?	yes	yes	no	yes	yes
Members of ECB Executive Board (appointed in June 1998)												
Partisan code	–	–	C	C	$C_{g?}$	–		–	–	S	–	C
Age (in 2001)			65	50	62	–	61			66		56
Term of office	–	–	8	4	5	–	7	–	–	8	–	6
Proposed by incumbents	–	–	no	yes	yes	–	yes	–	–	yes	–	yes
Supporting incumbents	–	–	no	?	?	–	yes	–	–	yes	–	yes

Sources: EMI (1997), ECB homepage and newspaper reports.

Table 6.6 Prospective election dates, ECB coalitions and political business cycles in the EMU, 2000–6

Election date	*Country*	*Month*	*Coalition in the ECB Council (one year ahead of election date)*	*Votes*	*Coalition prefers election month:*	*Standard deviation (months)*
2000:03	SP	15	SP(1)+I(1)+P(1)+NL(1)+D(1)+FI(1)+B(1)+A(1)	8/17	41	13.1
2001:06	I	30	I(1)+P(1)+NL(1)+D(1)+FI(1)+B(1)+A(1)+SP(2)	9/18	49	11.5
2002:02	P	38	P(1)+NL(1)+D(1)+FI(1)+B(1)+A(1)+SP(2)+GR(1)	9/18	53	9.9
2002:05	NL	41	NL(1)+IR(1)+D(1)+FI(1)+B(1)+A(1)+SP(2)+GR(1)	9/18	53	9.4
2002:05	IR	41	NL(1)+IR(1)+D(1)+FI(1)+B(1)+A(1)+SP(2)+GR(1)	9/18	53	9.4
2002:06	F	42	D(1)+FI(1)+B(1)+A(1)+SP(2)+GR(1)+L(1)+P(1)+NL(1)	10/18	64	14.1
2002:09	D	45	D(1)+FI(1)+B(1)+A(1)+SP(2)+GR(1)+L(1)+P(1)+NL(1)	10/18	64	14.1
2003:03	FI	51	FI(1)+B(1)+A(1)+SP(2)+GR(1)+L(1)+NL(1)+D(1)	9/18	67	14.8
2003:06	B	54	B(1)+A(1)+SP(2)+GR(1)+L(1)+NL(1)+D(1)+FI(1)+IR(1)	10/18	75	18.3
2003:10	A	58				
2004:03	SP	63				
2004:04	GR	64				
2004:06	L	66				
2006:02	P	86				
2006:05	NL	89				
2006:06	I	90				
2006:09	D	94				
2007:03	FI	99				
2007:05	IR	101				

Note: the Dutch member supporting his home government has the casting vote until May 2002.

Thus, it may be even easier to assemble a minority coalition blocking a verdict and sanctions in the Council of Ministers than to form a majority coalition in the ECB Council.[26] However, the incumbent governments are likely to prefer a monetary stimulus to a fiscal stimulus because the monetary stimulus would not implicate them directly.

Unemployment

Some authors have suggested that the euro will reduce unemployment. However, there are several effects which partly offset each other:

1. During the transition (in 1999–2001), additional manpower is required to adapt computer software, vending machines, price lists, etc.
2. Banks and other firms will reduce staff in their foreign-exchange departments. Instead of these services, other products will be demanded by consumers and industry. But these products are likely to be less labour intensive than the banking services which they replace. To that extent, the demand for labour will decrease.
3. As the cost of money changing, exchange rate information, exchange rate risk and exchange control risk disappear among the participating countries, competition and the demand for output and labour tend to increase. For most transactions, however, these costs seem to be very small (probably less than 1 per cent).[27]
4. The European Central Bank does not and cannot have the same reputation as the Bundesbank. Notably at times of pressure, the expected inflation rate will be higher for the euro than it would have been for the D-Mark and the currencies traditionally linked to it. If the ECB tries to establish a reputation, the actual inflation rate will have to be lower than the expected inflation rate, prices, wages and interest rates will be too high, and unemployment will be larger than otherwise. At the same time, the high level of unemployment undermines the credibility of the ECB.

This list is, of course, not exhaustive. Monetary union may also affect employment in indirect ways, for example, by inducing changes in wage setting behaviour or fiscal policy.[28] But there can be no doubt that EMU will affect unemployment in several, largely offsetting ways and that the net effect cannot be predicted – not even its sign.

It is easier to forecast how monetary union will affect the (relative) distribution of unemployment among the participating countries. In a monetary union, the relative prices and wages among the participating countries can no longer be adjusted through nominal exchange rate changes. Adjustment will be more costly and take more time. Past real exchange rate trends give some indication of future long-run adjustment needs. Table 6.1 reveals that, since 1976, Ireland, Italy, Spain and Austria have experienced the largest real appreciation vis-à-vis the median, while Finland and Luxembourg have suffered the largest real depreciation. More recently, after the opening of Eastern Europe (1990), the Benelux countries have switched from real depreciation to real appreciation, while Spain, Italy, Finland and Ireland have moved in the opposite direction. As their production is especially labour- and land-intensive, these four countries are severely affected by the supply shock from Eastern Europe. This is where monetary union is likely to have the largest negative, or the smallest positive, effect on employment. Spain, Italy and Finland do already have the highest unemployment rates in the European Union, and their labour markets are among the least flexible in the euro-zone.[29]

Exchange rate policy[30]

Exchange rate policy for the euro has been a matter of lively debate. German, French and Japanese ministers of finance have called for exchange rate targets between the euro, the U.S. dollar and the Japanese yen, while the President and the Vice-President of the European Central Bank, the Chairman of the Federal Reserve Board and a US Secretary of the Treasury have opposed the idea. (Central bankers tend to dislike exchange rate fixing because it constrains their room of manoeuvre, and, shortly before elections, incumbent politicians may need their support.) They have stressed the well-known instability of adjustable peg systems. But the theory of optimum currency areas is also relevant.

Ultimately, the theoretical criteria for optimum currency areas can be reduced to two: the openness of the economy and the need for real exchange rate adjustment (Vaubel 1978, 1988). The first indicates the benefits and the second the cost of freezing nominal exchange rates.

The euro-zone as a whole is much less open than the participating countries. Its external trade (the average of exports and imports) relative to GDP is only eleven per cent (compared with 20 per cent for Germany). The corresponding figures for the US and Japan are nine and eight per cent, respectively (Neumann 1998). As Table 6.7 shows, each area's trade with the other two is even much smaller: 2.5 per cent for the euro-zone, 2.6 per cent for the US and 3.3 per cent for Japan.[31] Thus, the benefits of exchange rate targets among the three currencies would be very limited.[32]

As for the costs of abandoning the exchange rate instrument, I have suggested

Table 6.7 Bilateral trade as a percentage of GDP, 1997

	EMU-11	*United States*	*Japan*
EMU-11	–	1.39	0.98
United States	1.83	–	2.32
Japan	0.67	1.21	–
Total	2.50	2.60	3.30

Source: IMF, *Direction of Trade Statistics Yearbook*, 1998.

Note:
The column head indicates the currency area for which the ratio is calculated. Bilateral trade is defined as the average of exports and imports.

that, ideally, nominal exchange rate adjustment should equal the required real exchange rate adjustment because this is the only way in which all currency areas could enjoy price level stability at the same time and because nominal exchange rate adjustment is the most efficient way of adjusting relative prices and wages between currency areas (Vaubel 1978). If E is the nominal exchange rate (say, euros per dollar), P_{EMU} and P_{US} the price level in the euro-zone and the United States, respectively, and Q the real exchange rate between the two currency areas, the following identity must hold:

$$E \equiv \frac{P_{EMU}}{P_{US}} \cdot Q \tag{6.3}$$

or, in rates of change,

$$\Delta e \equiv \pi_{EMU} - \pi_{US} + \Delta q \tag{6.4}$$

Clearly, if both currency areas are to enjoy price level stability ($\pi_{EMU} = 0$, $\pi_{US} = 0$), Δe has to equal Δq. I suggest, therefore, that the absolute difference between Δe and Δq is a useful criterion for appraising the performance of exchange rate regimes (apart from exchange rate volatility and the average inflation rate). To what extent has the nominal dollar exchange rate satisfied this criterion?

Figure 6.2 depicts the logarithm of the nominal and the real exchange rate between the D-Mark and the dollar, using consumer prices (IMF). Unfortunately, the observed real exchange rate changes are not independent of the nominal exchange rate changes. As the prices of goods and services adjust with a lag, short-run real exchange rate changes are mainly caused by nominal exchange rate changes. But in the longer run, once prices have adjusted, the real exchange rate is essentially independent of the nominal exchange rate.[33] Thus, the longer-run real exchange rate trends reflect the real causes of equilibrium real exchange rate change.[34]

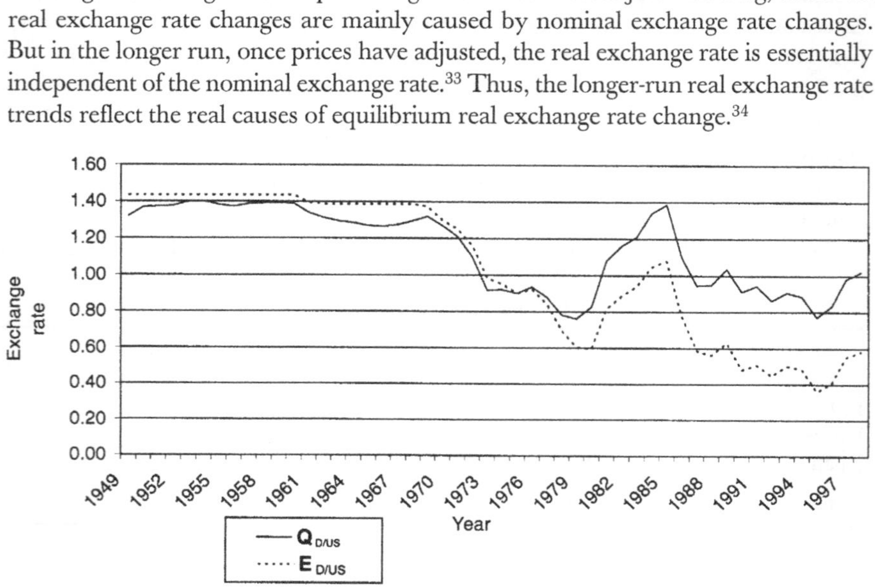

Figure 6.2 Nominal and real D-Mark/US$ exchange rates.

In Figure 6.2, we can identify four periods with significant stable real exchange rate trends (1949–59, 1959–69, 1973–80, 1987–96). Within each period, the exchange rate regime is constant. Table 6.8 reports the estimated real and nominal exchange rate trends and the differences between the two. As can be seen, the difference between the real and the nominal trend increased dramatically in the 1970s: the nominal depreciation of the dollar increased much more than the required real depreciation. However, in 1987–96, the difference between the real and the nominal exchange rate trend was quite small, indeed slightly smaller than before 1969 under the Bretton Woods system. Thus, flexible exchange rates can actually do better than the adjustable peg system as far as international adjustment is concerned. The Bundesbank and the Federal Reserve System seem to have learned to live with exchange rate flexibility, or the real shocks of the 1970s have been unusual (or both).

Figure 6.3 and Table 6.9 repeat the analysis for the real and nominal exchange rate between the euro-zone and the US dollar.[35] Once more, we observe a strong increase of the difference between the real and the nominal exchange rate trend in the 1970s but this increase is much smaller than the increase for the D-Mark. In 1987–96, the difference has dropped to a very low level – much lower than under the Bretton Woods system. However, this real exchange rate trend has been harder to predict – it is not significant at conventional levels ($t = 1.57$).

To sum up, long-term nominal exchange rate changes are increasingly doing what they are supposed to do. This is not to say that real exchange rate trends have been fully predictable. However, judging ex post and ignoring exchange rate volatility

Table 6.8 Real and nominal exchange rate trends, D-Mark per US$

	Real	*Nominal*	*Difference*
1949–59	+0.43[a]	0	+0.43
1959–69	– 0.96[a]	– 0.49[a]	– 0.47
1973–80	– 2.19[a]	– 9.63[a]	+7.44
1987–96	– 1.87[a]	– 2.27[a]	+0.40
1987–98	– 0.39	– 0.81	+0.42

Note:
[a] Significant at the 1 per cent level.

Table 6.9 Real and nominal exchange rate trends, EMU-11 per US$

	Real	*Nominal*	*Difference*
1954–59	+1.04	+2.72[a]	– 1.68
1959–69	– 1.38[a]	+0.35[a]	– 1.73
1973–80	– 2.63[a]	+0.26	– 2.89
1987–96	– 0.87	– 0.59	– 0.28
1987–98	+0.24	+0.50	– 0.26

Note:
[a] Significant at the 1 per cent level.

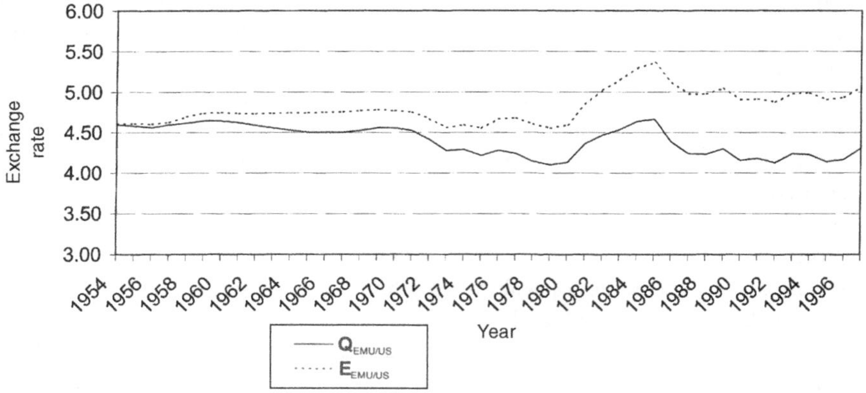

Figure 6.3 Effective exchange rates, EMU-11/US$.

and the average inflation rate, flexible exchange rates have recently performed better than any other exchange rate regime since the war. The evidence does not support the multiplying calls for a return to fixed exchange rate targets between Europe and America.

EMU enlargement

Enlargement by present EU members[30]

Britain, Denmark and Sweden are considering EMU membership. What are the benefits and costs? The costs of money changing, exchange rate information, exchange rate risk and exchange control risk, which would be eliminated, depend on the openness of their economies vis-à-vis the eleven EMU countries. As Table 6.10, column 2, shows, trade with the euro-zone (the average of exports and imports) amounts to 8–14 per cent of GDP for the potential entrants. The potential entrants are more open than France. As for the cost of joining, Table 6.10, column 7, reveals that, in 1976–98, long-run real exchange rate adjustment vis-à-vis France, the initial inflation median, has been small for Denmark but larger for Sweden (–1.0 per cent) and much larger for the UK (+1.6 per cent). In fact, the British real exchange rate change is the largest in the European Union.

Figure 6.4 and Table 6.11 show the real and nominal exchange rate trends between the U.K. and the euro-zone in the past. The differential between the nominal and the real exchange rate trend increased dramatically in the 1970s and dropped considerably thereafter (Table 6.10). But it never fell below the Bretton Woods level. The British differential in the 1990s was also larger than the corresponding differential for the dollar/D-Mark and the simulated dollar / euro exchange rates (cf. Tables 6.6 and 6.7). In other words, exchange rate flexibility for the pound has hardly been used to bring about the equilibrium real exchange rate adjustment vis-à-vis the EMU-11 countries.

Table 6.10 Enlargement of EMU by present EU members

		1997	1976–93			1976–98			1976–93				
Country	*Prospective ECB votes*	*Oppenness vis-à-vis EMU-11 [(exports + imports)/ 2 GDP]*	*Actual inflation per annum*	*Annual real exchange rate appreciation vis-à-vis France*	*French inflation adjusted for real exchange rate appreciation*	*Actual inflation per annum*	*Annual real exchange rate appreciation vis-à-vis France*	*French inflation adjusted for real exchange rate appreciation*	*Sensitivity to inflation*[a]	*Preferred inflation*[b] *(n = 15)*	*Preferred inflation*[c] *(n = 15)*	*Belgian preferred inflation adjusted for real exchange rate change*[c]	*Spanish preferred inflation adjusted for real exchange rate change*[c]
	(1)	*(2)*	*(3)*	*(4)*	*(5)*	*(6)*	*(7)*	*(8)*	*(9)*	*(10)*	*(11)*	*(12)*	*(13)*
Greece	2	8.5	18.1	+0.4	7.1	15.6	+0.6	6.0	(0.90[d])	11.4	19.9	12.1	14.3
Sweden	1	13.8	7.9	– 1.2	5.4	6.3	– 1.0	4.3	(1.27[d])	9.2	15.6	10.3	12.5
UK	2	10.3	7.70	+0.9	7.66	6.6	+1.6	7.1	1.82	7.4	12.2	12.6	14.9
Spain	2	12.1	10.8	+1.0	7.8	9.0	+0.6	6.1	(1.35[d])	8.9	15.0	12.7	15.0
France	2	9.8	6.7	0	6.7	5.4	0	5.4	2.05	6.90	11.19	11.6	13.9
Belgium	1	36.6	4.5	– 0.4	6.3	3.9	– 0.3	5.1	2.06	6.88	11.16	11.16	13.4
Denmark	1	12.9	6.3	+0.9	7.7	5.3	+0.4	5.8	3.40	5.1	7.9	12.6	14.9

Notes:

[a] Hayo (1998).

[b] Predicted from Table 6.3, equation 7.

[c] Predicted from Table 6.3, equation 10.

[d] Estimated from Table 6.3, equation 1.

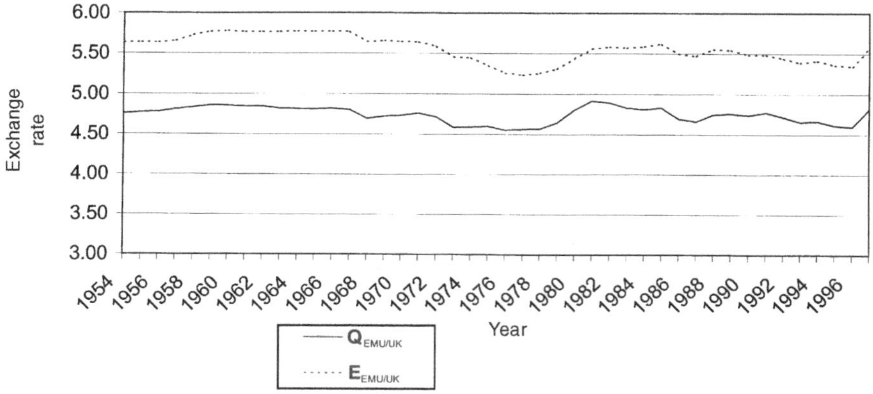

Figure 6.4 Effective exchange rates, EMU-11/UK£.

The relatively large discrepancy between nominal and real exchange rate trends under flexible exchange rates may seem to suggest that, in terms of real exchange-rate adjustment, the opportunity cost of joining EMU would be relatively small. However, since prices adjust with a lag of about two years, the real–nominal differential in 1993–7 must have been significantly affected by the ill-fated experiment of ERM membership in 1990–2. Without it, the pound might have done better.

The cost of British entry is, of course, not confined to the loss of the exchange rate instrument. Another cost is the weakening of competition among central banks. Competition among the suppliers of money tends to reduce inflation (Hayek 1976; Vaubel 1990), especially in open economies (p. 152). It is true that British inflation has been above the ECB median and average most of the time (Tables 6.1 and 6.10). But there have also been times when the Bank of England was a forceful competitor. In 1981–4 and in 2000–1, for example, British inflation was below the ECB median and average each year.

If Britain joined EMU, regulatory competition would suffer as well. Financial regulation of the City of London is known to be liberal – more liberal than regulation on the continent. Up to now, the regulation of banks has remained in the hands of the national institutions. But the President of the ECB has called for the

Table 6.11 Real and nominal exchange rate trends, EMU-11 per UK£

	Real	*Nominal*	*Difference*
1959–71	– 1.18[a]	– 1.20[a]	– 0.02
1973–8	– 0.62	– 4.94[a]	– 4.32
1981–9	– 2.53[a]	– 0.71	– 1.82
1993–6	– 2.32[a]	– 1.73[b]	– 0.59

Notes:
[a] Significant at the 1 per cent level.
[b] Significant at the 10 per cent level.

Table 6.12 National minimum reserve requirements prior to EMU (end of 1994), sight liabilities or money market cash reserve

Country	*Votes in ECB Council*	*Minimum reserve ratio (%)*	*Remuneration*	*Opportunity cost of reserve requirements (%)*
Italy	2	15	yes[a]	6.3
Austria	1	9	no	9
Germany	2	5	no	5
Spain	2	2	no	2
Portugal	1	2	no	2
Finland	2	2	no	2
France	2	1	no	1
Ireland	1	3	yes[b]	0.6
Netherlands	2	variable	yes	<1
Belgium	1	–	–	–
Luxembourg	1	–	–	–
Non-participating EU members (1999):				
Greece		9	yes	≈4.5
UK		0.35	no	0.35
Sweden		–	–	–
Denmark		–	–	–

Source: European Monetary Institute, Annual Report 1994.

Notes:
[a] At 5.5 per cent, market rate 9.5 per cent.
[b] At 80 per cent of market rate.

centralisation of banking regulation in the hands of the ECB.[36] According to Art. 105 (6) of the Treaty, any Council decision to 'confer upon the ECB specific tasks . . . relating to the prudential supervision of credit institutions and other financial institutions' would have to be taken unanimously. But the ECB Council decides about the level and remuneration of minimum reserves by simple majority (Art. 19.1 of the ECB Statute). If Britain joined EMU, reserve requirements could easily become more stringent.

In July 1998, the ECB Council decided to impose a minimum reserve ratio of 1.5–2.5 per cent and pay an 'adequate' remuneration on these reserves. Thus, the opportunity cost to the banks should be very small. However, as Table 6.12 shows, the ECB median of the national reserve ratios had been 2 per cent without remuneration.[37] In this case, therefore, the decision has not been biased towards Germany but towards Britain. This may be due to the competitive threat from the City of London. If so, British membership of EMU would probably encourage the ECB Council to raise the cost of reserve requirements. This would impair the City's competitiveness vis-à-vis New York, Tokyo, Zurich and other major financial centres outside EMU.

To join or not to join is evidently not just a question of monetary regime. Monetary union is apt to pave the way for the centralisation of budgetary policy, taxation, social regulation and wage bargaining (or for the levelling of differences and the cartelisation of policies in these fields). Moreover, there is a political dimension. After all, the euro is meant to be the stepping-stone for European Political Union and, ultimately, a European State.

Quite apart from the costs and benefits to the potential entrants and the Union as a whole, there are political obstacles to enlargement. As in Germany, many bankers and industrialists in Britain are attracted by the prospect of eliminating currency-related risks and transaction costs while the majority of voters is skeptical. But unlike the German government, the British government will hold a referendum. The British Prime Minister has declared that membership in the European Monetary System Mark II is out of the question and not a precondition for EMU entry whereas the European Commission and the ECB insist that Britain has to shadow the euro for at least two years if it wants to join EMU.

There is another political obstacle. According to the Treaty (Art. 121, 122), the admission of new members to the monetary union is a matter to be decided by the European Council and the decision requires a qualified majority (62 out of 87 votes). If the three potential entrants combined, they would command 27 votes. Since their joint entry would raise the expected inflation rate of the euro, it may be supported by only those euro-zone members which prefer a higher inflation rate than the current ECB median (Finland). However, as Tables 6.1 and 6.10 show, such a coalition (27 + 21 = 48 votes) would fall short of a qualified majority. To be winning, the coalition would have to include Finland, France and Belgium as well.[38] The latter, or some of them, may insist on a very strict interpretation of the convergence criteria[39] or ask for a price.

Eastern enlargement of EMU[40]

When Eastern European states are admitted to the European Union, they may sooner or later wish to join EMU as well. Most of them have already linked their currencies to the euro in one way or another. What are the costs and benefits? Which Eastern European states are the most likely candidates?

As before, the benefits are related to the degree of openness vis-à-vis the euro-zone. As Table 6.13 shows, trade with the euro-zone (the average of exports and imports) is large relative to GDP for many of these countries, notably Estonia, Slovenia, Hungary and the Czech Republic. This is because most of these economies are relatively small. The Eastern European states are to join the European Union in 2004. Most of them aim to become members of the European Monetary Union as soon as possible, i.e. two years after joining the European Union.

But Table 6.13 demonstrates that the costs of joining EMU will be very large. Except for Hungary and Slovenia, all countries exhibit a very high trend rate of real appreciation vis-à-vis the euro-zone – some even in the double-digit range (Lithuania, Ukraine, Estonia, Latvia).

Since the available data are limited to a short period,[41] the measured trends may still be affected by temporary problems of transition – notably the need for macroeconomic stabilisation. It is well known that disinflationary monetary policy and increasing budget deficits (relative to the other countries) tend to cause a temporary real appreciation of the currency. In 1993–8, fiscal consolidation in the

Table 6.13 Openness and real exchange rate trends of Eastern European states vis-à-vis EMU-11

Country	*Oppenness [(exports + imports)/2 GDP] 1997*	*Trends of real exchange rate appreciation (1993–8)*		*Inflation per annum (1993–8)*	*Current exchange rate regime (end of 2001)*[a]	*Predicted exchange rate regime*[a,b]
		Unadjusted	*Adjusted*			
	(1)	(2)	(3)	(4)		
Croatia	18.2	4.90[c]	4.16	16.5	MF (E)	F
Czech Republic	24.0	5.41[c]	5.19[c]	7.9	F	P/E/C, P/B/C
Estonia	33.7	17.86[c]	19.99[c]	19.3	CB/E	P/E/C, P/B/C
Hungary	27.1	1.10	1.10	16.9	P/B/C/M	CB/E, P/E/C, P/B/C
Latvia	13.7	16.75[c]	–	14.7	P/B	F
Lithuania	16.6	24.10[c]	20.87[c]	22.9	CB/$	F
Poland	13.5	5.64[c]	5.32[c]	17.6	F	F
Romania	12.7	6.34	1.27	61.8	P/C	F, P/B/C
Slovak Republic	23.1	4.60[c]	4.62[d]	6.9	MF	P/E/C, P/B/C
Slovenia	30.0	2.17[c]	1.73	9.8	MF	CB/E, P/E/C, P/B/C
Ukraine	5.3	19.89[c,e]	17.7[c,e]	115.0	MF ($)	F

Notes:

a The letters denote the following exchange rate regimes: CB: currency board linked to . . ., P: pegging to . . ., E: euro, B: basket of currencies, $: US-dollar, C: crawling, M: margins of fluctuation, F: floating with inflation or money supply target, MF: managed float.

b Cf. Table 6.13.

c Significant at the 1 per cent level.

d Significant at the 5 per cent level.

e 1993–7.

EMU countries may also have been a contributing cause. To allow for such transition effects, the logarithm of the EMU-related real exchange rates of these countries ($q_{i,t}$) has been regressed on $\mu_{i,t}$, a measure of the change of the money supply (relative to EMU), $\delta_{i,t}$, a measure of the reduction of the budget deficit (relative to EMU), t_i, national time trends, and C_i, a battery of country dummies, in a pooled time-series cross-section analysis.[42] The following estimate was obtained:

$$q_{i,t} = -10.98 + 0.024\,\mu_{i,t} + 0.41\,\delta_{i,t} - b_i t_i + c_i C_i \qquad R^2 \text{ adj.} = 0.9998$$
$$(-99.65^{*})\ (0.77) \qquad (1.32) \qquad\qquad R^2 = 0.9999$$

As an increase in q indicates a real depreciation (p. 162), the estimated regression coefficients of μ and δ take the expected signs. But they are not significant. The country dummies are not reported. The national real exchange rate trends are listed in column 3 of Table 6.13. Except for Romania, they are very similar to the unadjusted (or unconditional) trends, i.e. very large.

Table 6.13, column 4, shows that all Eastern European countries experienced high inflation rates in 1993–8. However, owing to the real appreciation vis-à-vis the euro-zone, the inflation rates of the Czech Republic, Estonia, Latvia, Lithuania and the Slovak Republic are compatible with an average euro inflation rate of less than eight per cent (Table 6.2, columns 8 or 11). These countries could be paired with the others so that the ECB median is not affected.

EMU membership is efficient only for those Eastern European countries which are very open, and do not need large real exchange rate changes, vis-à-vis the euro-zone. As Table 6.14 shows, only Slovenia and Hungary qualify on both counts (category A). But the admission of these two countries would probably raise the inflation median in the ECB Council. By contrast, the Ukraine, Poland, Latvia, Lithuania and Croatia fail on both counts (category D). They are better served by a

Table 6.14 Taxonomy of optimal exchange rate arrangements for the Eastern European states

		Openness	
		Very open (>20%)	*Medium (5–20%)*
Need for real exchange rate adjustment	Medium (0.5–2.0%)	A Slovenia Hungary (→ CB/E, P/E/C, P/B/C)	B Romania (→ F, P/B/C)
	Large (>2.0%)	C Estonia Czech Republic Slovak Republic (→ P/E/C, P/B/C)	D Ukraine Poland Latvia Lithuania Croatia (→ F)

Note
The letters denote exchange rate regimes. See the Notes to Table 6.13 on p. 169 for details.

policy of independent price level stabilisation, possibly with the help of a money supply rule. Estonia, the Czech and the Slovak Republic seem to be cases for a crawling peg system (category C). Romania is somewhere in between (category B).

A comparison of the predicted and the actual exchange rate regimes in the last columns of Table 6.13 reveals that only Hungary, Poland and Romania have chosen the predicted exchange rate regime.

Adjusting central bank staff[43]

In the future, the personnel of the ECB Executive Board is likely to grow both absolutely and in relation to the central banks of the participating countries. Table 6.15 shows the size of central bank staff in the euro-zone.[44] To what extent do the total and its composition have to change?

To answer this question, we shall compare actual staff size with the personnel predicted by a labour demand function. This function has been estimated for the central banks of 21 industrial countries or currency areas in 1993.[45] The following estimate has been obtained:

$$\begin{aligned} \ln L = 4.39 \; &+ \; 0.965 \ln N + 0.476 \ln \text{PBN} + 0.602 \ln \text{QC} + 0.665 \ln \text{DIS} \\ (4.50^{*}) \; &(10.84^{*}) \qquad\quad (1.81^{\circ}) \qquad\qquad (2.41^{+}) \qquad\qquad (0.67) \\ &+ 0.362 \ln I - 0.064 \ln E - 0.098 \ln Y \\ &\quad (0.45) \qquad\; (-0.24) \qquad\; (-0.32) \end{aligned}$$

$$R^2 = 0.91$$

where L is central bank staff, N is the number of inhabitants (as the best-fitting proxy for output demand[46]), PBN is a dummy which is equal to one if the central bank prints the bank notes itself and zero otherwise, QC indicates the extent to which the central bank actively controls the quality of the currency in circulation, DIS measures the extent to which the central bank discounts private bills of exchange and other commercial paper, I is the degree of central bank independence, E is a dummy for exchange rate pegging and Y is GNP (or GDP) per capita.

Thus, the demand for central bank staff is explained by the demand for central bank output, central bank technology and a proxy for the wage level. Labour supply to the central banks is assumed to be perfectly elastic in the relevant range. Since data on central bank equipment and land are not available, labour is the only factor of production. The data on PBN, QC and DIS have partly been supplied by a national central bank (which does not want to be quoted) and partly been collected with the help of a questionnaire. Variables and interactions allowing for other differences in the tasks of the various central bank (e.g. the responsibility for banking regulation) did not take plausible signs.[47] The log-linear functional form yielded the best fit.

In the above estimate, only the output proxies N and QC take fully significant regression coefficients. This may be due to the omission of other relevant variables, or it may indicate that the growth of bureaucracy is largely a matter of historical accident.

Table 6.15 Actual and predicted central bank staff prior to EMU

	1993/4			*End of 1998*			
	Actual	*Predicted*	*Percentage deviation from actual number*	*Actual*	*Predicted*	*Predicted minus actual*	*Percentage deviation from actual*
Austria	1,251	2,013	+61	1,152	2,057	+905	+79
Belgium/L'bourg	3,165	1,934	- 39	3,007	2,051	- 956	- 32
Finland	894[a]	643[a]	- 28	740	624	- 116	- 16
France	17,590[a]	10,162[a]	- 42	16,171[b]	9,000	- 7,171	- 44
Germany	17,632	13,912	- 21	15,891	14,059	- 1,832	- 12
Ireland	626[a]	736[a]	+18	638	701	+63	+10
Italy	9,542[a]	6,610[a]	- 31	8,956[b]	6,387	- 2,569	- 29
Netherlands	1,611	1,493	+7	1,597	1,521	- 76	- 5
Portugal	2,293[a]	1,809[a]	- 21	1,828	1,863	+35	+2
Spain	3,308	6,632	+100	3,100[b]	6,755	+3,655	+118
Total staff	57,912	45,944	- 21	53,080	45,018	- 8,062	- 15

Sources: Morgan Stanley Central Bank Directory (1994), Vaubel (1997a), European Central Bank.

Notes

[a] End of 1992.

[b] End of 1997.

As a first step, the estimate is used to predict the staff size of the various national central banks in 1993 and 1998.[48] Table 6.15 reveals that, in 1998 as in 1993, the national central banks of the eleven EMU countries have been highly overstaffed by international standards. The most outstanding examples are Banque de France, Banque Nationale de Belgique and Banca d'Italia. From 1993 to 1998, total central bank staff in the EMU countries decreased by 8 per cent but, in 1998, the required staff reduction was still 15 per cent. If the 'most efficient' central bank (Banco d'España) is taken as a guide, total staff in the EMU could even have been cut by 61 per cent.

With the advent of monetary union, the required staff size has to be calculated for the ESCB as a whole. If the ECB is considered to be as independent as the Bundesbank (i.e. $\ln I = 1$), if the euro is not pegged to a dominant currency (i.e. $\ln E = 0$) and if the ECB continues to refrain from discounting commercial paper ($\ln DIS = 0$),[49] the labour demand function predicts an ESCB staff of 47,052 for the beginning of 1999, i.e. a reduction by 6,520 persons or 12 per cent.

This estimate of required ESCB staff is somewhat larger than the sum of the national central bank staffs predicted for 1998 (45,018). The reason is that the increase in central bank independence and the termination of exchange rate pegging have raised the estimated staff size more than the abolition of discounting and some other minor changes have reduced it. If the staff component attributed to independence is not needed to defend the ECB's legal independence (which, as we have seen, is very secure), i.e. if it is simply a waste due to inadequate accountability, the required ESCB staff is, of course, much smaller. Thus, the above estimate is an upper limit.

Table 6.16 Actual and predicted central bank staff in EMU-11

Country	*Actual (1.1.99)*	*Federal Reserve model ($N_{ECB}/N_E = 6\%$)*			*Bundesbank model ($N_{ECB}/N_E = 16\%$)*			*Predicted national staff weights under the euro regime*
		Predicted	*Predicted minus actual*	*Percentage deviation from actual*	*Predicted*	*Predicted minus actual*	*Percentage deviation from actual*	
Austria	1,152	1,504	+352	+31	1,344	+192	+17	0.034
Belgium/Luxembourg	2,929[a]	2,079	- 850	- 29	1,858	- 1,071	- 37	0.047
Finland	740	619	- 121	- 16	553	- 187	- 25	0.014
France	16,171[b]	10,349	- 5,822	- 36	9,249	- 6,922	- 43	0.234
Germany	15,891	12,694	- 3,197	- 20	11,343	- 4,548	- 29	0.287
Ireland	638	708	+70	+11	632	- 6	- 1	0.016
Italy	8,956[b]	6,413	- 2,543	- 28	5,731	- 3,225	- 36	0.145
Netherlands	1,597	1,106	- 491	- 31	988	- 609	- 38	0.025
Portugal	1,828	1,327	- 501	- 27	1,186	- 642	- 35	0.030[c]
Spain	3,100[b]	7,430	+4,330	+140	6,640	+3,540	+114	0.168
Total	53,002	44,229	- 8,773	- 17	39,524	- 13,478	- 25	1.000
ECB	570	2,823	+2,253	+395	7,528	+6,958	+1,221	–
ESCB	53,572	47,052	6,520	- 12	47,052	6,520	- 12	–

Notes

[a] Excluding Commission de Surveillance du Secteur Financier de Luxembourg which has been separated from the central bank.

[b] End of 1997.

[c] With the transition to the euro, Portuguese banknotes will no longer be printed by the Portuguese central bank.

How is the adjustment to be spread over the ECB and the particular national central banks? The ideal 'weight' of the ECB can be determined in different ways.

The first is to take the Federal Reserve System as an example. In the US, the share of the Federal Reserve Board in total central bank staff has been 6 per cent (in 1994, the last year for which the Federal Reserve System has published these figures).[50] Table 6.16 shows that this implies an ECB staff of 2,823 if the component attributed to independence is not considered to be wasteful. The remaining staff is allocated to the national central banks using their predicted values as shares. The predicted values are computed by setting the logarithms of DIS, *I* and *E* equal to zero.

Another possible model is the Bundesbank. In Germany, the staff of the Direktorium accounts for 16 per cent of total Bundesbank staff. On the same assumptions, the German model would imply an ECB staff of 6,958.

If the staff component attributed to independence is regarded as pure waste, the U.S. model implies an ECB staff of 1,966 and the Bundesbank model a staff of 5,242. Depending on the assumed share of waste in the staff component attributed to independence, the appropriate ECB staff can easily be calculated.

Since the Governors of the national central banks have a majority in the Governing Council of the European Central Bank, the ESCB is more likely to adopt the US Federal Reserve System as a model. The necessary reduction of the national central bank staff could be facilitated by requiring the ECB to draw on the national central banks for a considerable fraction of its hirings.

Conclusion

The analysis of this article – like most empirical research – is merely suggestive. The point estimates tend to obscure that the future of the euro is highly uncertain. But they illustrate the mechanisms that will be at work.

There are other aspects of EMU central banking which might be explained or predicted by public-choice reasoning. Some explanations are straightforward. For example, it is not in the bureaucratic interest of a central bank council to publish its minutes shortly after the event. Nor was it to be expected that a majority of the ECB Governing Council would give priority to money supply targets. After all, only one of the eleven national central banks (the Bundesbank) had done so in the recent past. Experience so far suggests that the Governing Council is prepared to lower interest rates even when monetary expansion exceeds the reference rate and the euro is weak in the exchange markets.

It is easy to agree on an inflation target and leave open how it might be attained. If it is not attained, this might be attributed to factors other than monetary policy. After all, failure to attain the target will not be sanctioned.

Acknowledgements

Computational assistance from Ingrid Eitel, Bernhard Reichert and, most of all, Christian Teubner is gratefully acknowledged.

Notes

1 Data sources for this section: International Monetary Fund, International Financial Statistics; Eurostat; Hayo (1998 a, b); Lippi and Swank (1999); Maddison (1991); Masciandaro and Spinelli (1994); Mitchell (1992); Vaubel (1994).

2 See also the median-voter simulation of de Grauwe, Dewachter and Aksoy (1999). They derive desired values for the monetary instrument from hypothetical Keynesian loss functions, estimated trade-offs between the target variables (output, inflation and instrument smoothing) and historical output shock structures (1979–94). They report that, if both output shocks and preferences differ among the participating countries and if each member of the ECB Governing Council represents the interests of her home country, the transition to a common monetary policy creates the largest discrepancies between the decided and the desired value of the monetary instrument for Italy, Portugal, Ireland and Finland, i.e. the peripheral member states (Table 6.10).

3 In both studies, opinion poll data about the evaluation of economic or, more precisely, inflation performance are regressed on inflation. There is not a single country for which all four tests indicate a significant structural break (let alone, at the same moment in time). The results of Collins and Giavazzi for the period 1974–90 show that, at conventional levels, the aversion to inflation increased significantly in the UK and Denmark but not in the EMU countries (e.g. France, Italy, Belgium, the Netherlands and Ireland) and that it significantly decreased in Germany (in 1986). Hayo's three tests for 1976–93 (Table 2.14) show a significant increase of the sensitivity to inflation in the Netherlands and Luxembourg whose inflation rates are far below the ECB median anyway. However, according to Hayo's recursive regressions, there seems to have been some (insignificant) increase of the sensitivity to inflation in seven EMU countries – least of all in France.

4 As the International Monetary Fund, the European Commission and the European Central Bank have noted, fiscal consolidation in the euro-zone virtually came to an end in 1998 despite the temporary economic upswing.

5 The other objectives are public order, democracy and freedom of speech. The survey results are regularly reported by Eurobarometer (so-called Ingleheart index). The dependent variable is set at 1 if price stability is ranked first or second. Otherwise it is zero. The regression has been run over the period 1976–93 for each country except Greece (1980–93), Portugal and Spain (1985–93). I use Hayo's OLS estimates (β_{12} in Table 4 of Hayo 1998b) because his RALS and SURE estimates show these coefficients to be robust. In the unlikely event that exogenous changes in the rank of price stability negatively affected the actual rate of inflation within the same year (reverse causation), Hayo's regression coefficient would be biased downwards.

6 The average has been computed by Masciandaro and Spinelli (1993) from the indices of Banaian, Laney and Willett (1983), Bade and Parkin (1985), Alesina and Summers (1990), Burdekin and Willett (1990), Grilli, Masciandaro and Tabellini (1991), Cukierman (1991) and Eijffinger and Schaling (1992). To facilitate the calculation, this average of indices has been rebased so that its value for Germany is equal to *e*. See Table 6.2, column 4.

7 Since the Irish Punt, before being linked to the D-Mark in 1979, was pegged to the Pound Sterling, the Irish inflation rate has not been affected by the independence of the Bank of Ireland. In this sample and in equations 5–10 (Table 6.3), therefore, the Bank of Ireland is replaced by the Bank of England.

8 The dummy for universal banking takes a positive but insignificant coefficient. The same is true for Posens's measure of political instability. Posen's results are also questioned by de Haan and van't Hag (1995).

9 Hayo (1998b, Table 7) obtains the same result by computing rank correlation coefficients. His Spearman rank correlation coefficient is –0.91 for the sensitivity to inflation but only –0.72 for the best-fitting index of central bank independence. In line with the conventional approach, equations 2–4 in Table 6.3 explain Irish inflation by Irish central bank independence.

10 In this context, simultaneous equation estimation might be considered but it is not required for our purpose, which is forecasting.

11 The insignificant effect of *f* is not due to significant collinearity with the sensitivity to inflation: $r\,(f, \ln S) = 0.30$.

12 This result is also obtained by Campillo and Miron (1997) and Iversen (1999).

If we distinguish fixed and flexible exchange rate regimes as we have done in the case of central bank independence, the import/GDP ratio can be shown to have a larger effect under flexible exchange rates but the regression coefficients are merely significant at the 10 per cent level and R^2 adj. is virtually unchanged. Simulation with this equation would yield higher inflation rates than equations 6 or 8 do.

Some further control variables (the budget deficit/GDP ratio, the unemployment rate, union density) have been tried as suggested by Oatley (1999) but they did not have a significant effect on inflation or the regression coefficients of the other explanatory variables.

13 This result was also reached by Vaubel (1994) in a different analysis.

14 These were the Governors from Belgium, Finland, France, Greece, Luxembourg, the Netherlands and Portugal. The Italian Governor is appointed 'for life' (i.e. up to the retirement age). The Spanish Governor may not be reappointed.

15 Note that the prediction of the long-run rate of inflation has ignored ideological or partisan effects. This is innocuous if the partisan composition of governments in 1974–93 can be regarded as respresentative for the future.

16 According to Posen (1998), this effect is positive but not statistically significant at conventional levels.

17 They are political conservatives, not necessarily monetary conservatives. Another interesting feature is the assignment of functions to the individual members of the Executive Board. While the German government claimed the Directorates for Economics and Research, the French member obtained control over Administration, Personnel and Legal Services. While Germans believe in the power of ideas and craftsmanship, the French approach puts more emphasis on personal relationships (networks) and the strategic use of legal procedures.

18 It is hard to believe that the Governing Council could have operated without an ECB President and Executive Board. But even if so, the dissatisfied governments (Germany?) could have vetoed all later decisions, e.g. on the conversion rates, without which monetary union could not have started.

Berthold *et al.* (1998) even suggest that EMU was fragile as long as the national currencies continued to circulate.

19 If the Executive Board gradually shrinks, the median Governor, and the government agreeing with her, may temporarily lose the median position. The vetoing government has to discount this temporary loss.

20 If adjustment is made for the real exchange rate trend, the Belgian Governor is the median among the Governors (Table 6.2, column 11).

21 Data sources for this section: Vaubel (1994); EMI (1997); newspaper reports.

22 Williamson (1985) was probably the first to point this out.

23 The governments and central bankers are coded as social democratic or socialist (S), Christian democratic or conservative (C) or liberal (L). If parties of the same code are in government and in opposition the subscript g is used to distinguish them. In the case of coalition governments or cohabitation, the first letter indicates the party of the prime minister.

24 These incumbent governments would be supported by the central bank governors of Ireland, Germany, Finland, Belgium, Austria, Spain and Luxembourg and by the Executive Board members from Spain and the Netherlands, the latter having the casting vote. I assume that, in France, a more expansionary monetary policy would have benefitted the government rather than the President.

25 Early elections have been the rule rather than the exception in Belgium, Ireland and Spain, and they have been frequent in the Netherlands (Vaubel 1994).

26 The German government assembled such a blocking coalition in February 2002. The process of coalition building in the Council of Ministers could be analyzed on similar lines. But it is not obvious that the composition of these blocking coalitions would mainly depend on the sequence of election dates. Logrolling would be likely to occur.

27 For bank transfers between EU currencies, the deviation of the buying or selling rate from the mid rate has been about one-quarter of one per cent. The cost of forward cover is in the order of 0.05 per cent.The cost of exchange rate information is minute. Restrictions of capital movements have been generally prohibited since 1996 (Art. 72E of the Maastricht Treaty and Art. 56 of the Amsterdam Treaty). In the euro-zone, 'measures to protect the balance of payments' are outlawed as well (Art. 120 Amsterdam Treaty). If such measures were introduced by non-participating EU members, they could be suspended by the EMU members (i.e. a qualified majority of the Council).

28 Some authors believe that (inflation-averse) national trade unions will aim at larger real wage increases because, in the monetary union, the effects on the price level will largely be externalised and be smaller for each of them. Others emphasise that wage moderation and labour market deregulation are less likely in a monetary union because the beneficial effects on central bank credibility are now largely externalised. Still another group believes that real wages in the low-wage countries will catch up with the rest because monetary union facilitates international wage comparisons.

As for fiscal policy, some authors expect national governments to reduce their budget deficits, thereby increasing investment and employment. Others fear that the 'Pact for Stability and Growth' will not be effective and that EMU will lead to more government spending.

29 See Grubb and Wells (1993) and Dohse and Krieger-Boden (1998, Table 12).

We have assumed that international relative prices and wages have to be adjusted in the same direction. This is true in the case of demand shocks and most supply shocks. It is not true in the case of shocks to the supply of capital. But if the real depreciation of Finland, Italy and Spain had been due to an increasing supply of capital, their unemployment rates should have fallen in the 1990s.

30 Data sources for this section: IMF, International Financial Statistics, Direction of Trade Statistics Yearbook 1998.

31 A more precise indicator would include those countries which have irrevocably fixed their exchange rate vis-à-vis one, or a basket, of these currencies.

32 This could mean that the exchange rate between the dollar and Europe will become more variable (e.g. Cohen 1997, Neumann 1998). However, the contrary conclusion is reached by those who believe that the DM/dollar exchange rate has been used strategically (Martin 1997) or that the Bundesbank has reacted to shifts of demand between Germany and other ERM members (Bénassy-Quéré and Mojon 1998).

33 Recent panel studies indicate that such deviations have a 'half-life' of two years (e.g. Meier 1997; Bayoumi and MacDonald 1998).

34 Ideally, we would want to know all equilibrium real exchange rate changes that would have taken place in the absence of nominal exchange rate changes, regardless of whether they are permanent or transitory. However, empirical research has not been very successful in explaining real exchange rate variations (i.e. outperforming the random walk model), let alone in separating the effects of nominal und real factors. The main exogenous real factor seems to be the difference in productivity growth (e.g. MacDonald 1998: 28–30) which tends to follow a time trend. This could be the well-known 'Balassa effect'. Assuming reversion to trend after monetary shocks, i.e. long-run neutrality of money, the following analysis is confined to trend comparisons. It expressly ignores volatility and variance but it is likely to yield robust results. The decomposition of real exchange rate changes into a component due to monetary causes (not just money supply shocks!) and a component due to real causes is reserved for future research.

35 Using consumer price indices, the exchange rate indices for the eleven euro-zone countries have been weighted by private consumption. Owing to data gaps, the series do

not start before 1954. Thus, the first period (1954–59) is too short to yield a significant real exchange rate trend ($t = 1.85$).

36 For example, the interview with *Wirtschaftswoche* (27 May 1999). Before him, the International Monetary Fund (1998) as an international organisation, the EC-financed Centre for Economic Policy Research (CEPR 1999), and Thomaso Padoa-Schioppa (*Financial Times*, 25 February 1999), another member of the ECB Executive Board, have made the same proposal.

37 At the recommendation of the Commission, the Council of Ministers could have reduced the reserve ratio by imposing a ceiling in January 1999 (Art. 19.2 and 42 of the ECB Statute) but as Table 6.11 also shows, the required qualified majority would have been unattainable. In the future, unanimity and the assent of the European Parliament would be required (Art. 19.1 and 41).

38 The entry of Greece did not cause such problems because it did not affect the inflation median.

39 The experience of 1998 showed that the convergence criteria leave enough room for interpretation to justify almost any decision that is desired for political reasons. Without 'creative accounting' and once-and-for-all measures (which the Treaty excludes), France, Germany and Italy would have exceeded the 3 per cent limit of the deficit criterion (German Council of Economic Advisors, *Annual Report 1997/98*, para. 403f., Deutsches Institut für Wirtschaftsforschung, *Wochenbericht* 25/98, p. 450f.). Moreover, Austria, Germany, Italy and Spain have violated the debt criterion because their debt/GDP ratio exceeded 60 per cent in 1997 and had risen since 1991 when the Maastricht Treaty was concluded. Finally, during the two years prior to the decision about EMU membership, the currencies of Finland, Ireland, Italy and Portugal had not stayed within the margins in force in 1991.

40 Data sources for this section: IMF, International Financial Statistics; WIIW Handbook of Statistics; KSH Statistical Yearbook of Hungary; OECD, Economic Outlook, Main Economic Indicators, Short Term Economic Indicators for the Transition Economies; UN Monthly Bulletin of Statistics.

41 For some of these countries, the IMF International Financial Statistics do not contain the Consumer Price Index in 1992. Moreover, 1992 was still a year of considerable real exchange rate turbulence for the Baltic states. The data for 1998 are partly estimates. Bulgaria is not included because of large gaps in the data.

42

$$\mu_{i,t} = \ln \sum_i \left(\frac{M_{i,t}}{M_{i,t-1}} \Big/ \frac{M_{\mathrm{EMU},t}}{M_{\mathrm{EMU},t-1}} \right)$$

$$\delta_{i,t} = \ln \sum_i \left(\frac{1 - D_{i,t}/Y_{i,t}}{1 - D_{i,t-1}/Y_{i,t-1}} \Big/ \frac{1 - D_{\mathrm{EMU},t}/Y_{\mathrm{EMU},t}}{1 - D_{\mathrm{EMU},t-1}/Y_{\mathrm{EMU},t-1}} \right)$$

where M is the money supply (M1, Estonia: M2), D is the budget deficit and Y is GDP. The data for M_{EMU} and D_{EMU} have been taken from the February 1999 issue of the ECB Monthly Bulletin, i.e. they are aggregated at constant exchange rates (the conversion rates set in 1998). However, the results are almost the same if consumption-weighted rates of change are used.

43 Data sources for this section: Vaubel (1997a); European Central Bank; IMF, International Financial Statistics; OECD, Economic Outlook; Masciandaro and Spinelli (1994); National Central Banks (questionnaire).

44 The data for 1993 (or 1992) are taken from the Morgan Stanley Central Bank Directory which appeared in 1994. The current data have been supplied by the European Central Bank in May 1999. The ECB itself had 1,043 employees at the end of 2001 (European Central Bank, Annual Report for 2001).

45 The sample includes the following countries: Australia, Austria, Belgium/Luxembourg, Canada, Denmark, Finland, France, Germany, Greece, Ireland, Italy, Japan, Netherlands, New Zealand, Norway, Portugal, Spain, Sweden, Switzerland, UK and USA.

46 Other proxies like money supply, number of banks, area etc. have been tried in addition but they take completely insignificant regression coefficients (see also Vaubel 1997a). In a time-series analysis for Germany, I successfully used an index of central bank transactions but these data are not available on an international cross-section basis.

47 See also Vaubel (1997a). However, for a different sample which includes only very few EMU countries, the budgetary independence of the central bank was shown to have a significant positive effect on staff size.

48 In predicting staff size for 1998, average income per head in EMU-11 has been held constant at the 1993 level. Thus, changes in Y merely reflect changes in relative labour costs among the participating countries.

49 The decision not to have a discount facility can also be explained by the median voter theorem. De facto, it has been taken by the EMI Council. Nine of the sixteen Council members represented countries which did not operate a discount facility (Denmark, Finland, France, Ireland, Luxembourg, Portugal, Spain, Sweden and the United Kingdom; EMI, *Annual Report* 1994). De lege, the decision had to be, and has been, confirmed by the ECB Council where Finland (2), France (2), Ireland (1), Luxembourg (1), Portugal (1) and Spain (2) commanded a majority of 9 out of 17.

In predicting ESCB staff, ln PBN and ln QC are weighted averages of the national data. The weights are given by the predicted staffs of the national central banks, setting the logarithms of DIS, *I* and *E* equal to zero. Once more, average income per head in EMU-11 has been held constant at the 1993 level.

50 According to Wim Duisenberg, the Federal Reserve Board currently employs 1,700 persons of which 200 are in charge of banking supervision (interview with *Wirtschaftswoche*, 27 May 1999).

References

Bayoumi, Tamim and Ronald MacDonald (1998) 'Deviations of Exchange Rates from Purchasing Power Parity: A Story Featuring Two Monetary Unions', Discussion Paper 1932. Centre for Economic Policy Research, London.

Bénassy-Quéré, Agnès and Benoit Mojon (1998) 'EMU and Transatlantic Exchange-Rate Stability', in *The EMU's Exchange Rate Policy*. Zentrum für Europaeische Integrationsforschung, Bonn.

Berthold, Norbert, Rainer Fehn and Eric Thode (1998) 'Real Wage Rigidities, Fiscal Policies, and the Stability of EMU in the Transition Process', IMF Working Paper 99/83. Washington.

Campillo, Marta and Miron, Jeffrey A. (1997) 'Why Does Inflation Differ Across Countries?', in Romer, C. D. and D. H. Romer, eds, *Reducing Inflation: Motivation and Strategy*. Chicago.

Centre for Economic Policy Research (1999) 'The ECB: Safe at any speed?', *Monitoring the European Central Bank, 1*.

Cohen, Daniel (1997) 'How Will the Euro Behave?', in Masson, Paul R., T. S. Krueger and B. G. Turtleboom, eds, *EMU and the International Monetary System*. International Monetary Fund, Washington, DC.

Collins, Susan and Francesco Giavazzi (1993) 'Attitudes towards Inflation and the Viability of Fixed Exchange Rates: Evidence from the EMS', in Bordo, Michael and Barry Eichengreen, eds, *A Retrospective on the Bretton Woods System: Lessons for International Monetary Reform*. Chicago.

Dohse, Dirk and Christiane Krieger-Boden (1998) *Waehrungsunion und Arbeitsmarkt*. Tuebingen.

European Monetary Institute (1997) *Legal Convergence in the Member States of the European Union*. Frankfurt am Main, October.

de Grauwe, Paul, Hans Dewachter and Yunus Aksoy (1999) 'The European Central Bank: Decision Rules and Macroeconomic Performance', Discussion Paper 2067. Centre for Economic Policy Research, London.

Grubb, David and William Wells (1993) 'Employment Regulation and Patterns of Work in EC Countries', *OECD Economic Studies 21.*

de Haan, Jakob and Gert Jan van't Hag (1995) 'Variation in Central Bank Independence across Countries: Some Provisional Empirical Evidence', *Public Choice, 85.*

Hayek, Friedrich (1976) 'Denationalisation of Money', Hobart Paper Special 70. Institute of Economic Affairs, London.

Hayo, Bernd (1998a) *Empirische und Theoretische Studien zur Europaeischen Waehrungsunion,* Frankfurt am Main.

Hayo, Bernd (1998b) 'Inflation Culture, Central Bank Independence and Price Stability', *European Journal of Political Economy, 14.*

International Monetary Fund (1998) *International Capital Markets,* Sept.

Iversen, Torben (1999) 'The Political Economy of Inflation. Bargaining Structure or Central Bank Independence?' *Public Choice, 99.*

Johnson, Harry G. (1970) 'The Case for Flexible Exchange Rates', in Halm G. N., ed., *Approaches to Greater Flexibility of Exchange Rates.* Princeton, NJ.

Lippi, Francesco and Otto H. Swank (1999) 'Policy Targets, Economic Performance and Central Bank Independence', in Lippi, F., ed., *Central Bank Independence, Targets and Credibility.* Cheltenham and Northampton.

MacDonald, Ronald (1998) 'What Do We Really Know About Real Exchange Rates?', Working Paper 28. Oesterreichische Nationalbank.

Maddison, Angus (1991) *Dynamic Forces of Capitalist Development.* Oxford.

Martin, Philippe (1997) 'The Exchange Rate Policy of the Euro: A Matter of Size?', Discussion Paper 1646. Centre for Economic Policy Research, London.

Masciandaro, Donato and Franco Spinelli (1994) 'Central Banks' Independence: Institutional Determinants, Rankings and Central Bankers' Views', *Scottish Journal of Political Economy, 41.*

McGregor, Rob Roy (1996) 'FOMC Voting Behaviour and Electoral Cycles: Partisan Ideology and Partisan Loyalty', *Economics and Politics, 8.*

Meier, Carsten-Patrick (1997) 'Assessing Convergence to Purchasing Power Parity: a Panel Study for 10 OECD Countries', *Weltwirtschaftliches Archiv, 133.*

Mitchell, B. R. (1992) *International Historical Statistics. Europe 1750–1988.* New York.

Neumann, Manfred J. M. (1998) 'What Exchange Rate Policy in EMU?', in Zentrum für Europaeische Integrationsforschung (ed.), *The EMU's Exchange Rate Policy.* Bonn.

Oatley, Thomas (1999) 'Central Bank Independence and Inflation: Corporatism, Partisanship, and Alternative Indices of Central Bank Independence', *Public Choice, 98.*

Posen, Adam (1993a) 'Why Central Bank Independence Does not Cause Low Inflation: There Is No Institutional Fix for Politics', in O'Brien, R., ed., *Finance and the International Economy.* Oxford.

Posen, Adam (1993b) 'Central Banks and Politics', *Amex Bank Review, 20.*

Posen, Adam (1998) 'Central Bank Independence and Disinflationary Credibility: a Missing Link?', *Oxford Economic Papers, 50.*

Rogoff, Kenneth (1985) 'The Optimal Degree of Commitment to an Intermediate Monetary Target', *Quarterly Journal of Economics, 100.*

Romer, David (1993) 'Openness and Inflation: Theory and Evidence', *Quarterly Journal of Economics, 108.*

Sinn, Hans-Werner and Holger Feist (1997) 'Eurowinners and Eurolosers: the Distribution of Seigniorage Wealth in EMU', *European Journal of Political Economy, 13.*
Soh, Byung Hee (1986) 'Political Business Cycles in the Industrialized Democratic Countries', *Kyklos, 39.*
Vaubel, Roland (1978) 'Real Exchange Rate Changes in the European Community: a New Approach to the Determination of Optimum Currency Areas', *Journal of International Economics, 8.*
Vaubel, Roland (1988) 'Monetary Integration Theory', in Zis, George *et al.*, eds, *International Economics, Surveys in Economics*, London, New York.
Vaubel, Roland (1990) 'Currency Competition and Monetary Union', *Economic Journal, 100.*
Vaubel, Roland (1993) 'Eine Public-Choice Analyse der Deutschen Bundesbank und ihre Implikationen fuer die Euopaeische Waehrungsunion', in Duwendag, Dieter and Juergen Siebke, eds, *Europa vor dem Eintritt in die Wirtschafts- und Waehrungsunion.* Berlin.
Vaubel, Roland (1994) 'The Breakdown of the ERM and the Future of EMU', in Cobham, David, ed., *European Monetary Upheavals.* Manchester.
Vaubel, Roland (1997a) 'The Bureaucratic and Partisan Behaviour of Independent Central Banks: German and International Evidence', *European Journal of Political Economy, 13.*
Vaubel, Roland (1997b) 'Reply to Berger and Woitek', *European Journal of Political Economy, 13.*
Williamson, John (1985) 'International Agencies and the Peacock Critique', in Greenaway, D. and G. K. Shaw, eds, *Public Choice, Public Finance and Public Policy. Essays in Honour of Alan Peacock.* Oxford.

Comments on Chapter 6 – The future of the euro: a public choice perspective

Fabrizio Zampolli

Introduction

In the 1990s debate about European Monetary Union (EMU) revolved around the questions of whether the euro-zone constitutes an optimal currency area and of whether the institutional framework of EMU would ensure economic stability and foster further integration among its participating countries. Roland Vaubel's analysis, which is conducted using the tools of public choice theory (the median voter theorem, political business cycle theory, the economic theory of bureaucracy), seems to answer these questions in the negative, or at least warns against excessive optimism. His main findings can be summarised as follows:

- First, the historical record reveals that countries in the euro-zone have widely differing inflation preferences; since the European Central Bank (ECB) Governing Council decides monetary policy with a simple majority rule, it is the median voter's preferences which are decisive in shaping euro-zone monetary policy; the median voter's preferred inflation rate may turn out to be greater than the ECB's long-run inflation goal.
- Second, as a consequence of enlargement of EMU to include new member countries, the country occupying the median voter's position within the ECB Council may change. Since a qualified majority in the European Council should include the country that holds the median within the ECB Council, some form of compensation to this country is to be expected. In particular, France may not be interested in admitting Britain. As to the enlargement towards Eastern Europe, inclusion of the two best-qualified candidates, notably Slovenia and Hungary, would raise the median's preferred inflation rate.
- Third, political business cycle theory predicts that a boom is very likely to occur between 2002 and 2004 as a consequence of the concentration of a relatively large number of national elections over this period of time.
- Finally, judging from a cross-sectional estimation of central bank labour demand, a majority of the national central banks within the ESCB are largely overstaffed relative to international standards.[1]

As Vaubel himself stresses, these empirical predictions cannot but be 'merely suggestive', given the great uncertainty surrounding the future of EMU. Nevertheless, he interprets these predictions as illustrating the 'mechanisms at work'. Even with this note of warning, it is difficult not to raise some doubts about Vaubel's findings, for they depend crucially on largely questionable assumptions. In particular, his predictions of average inflation rates or of the 'relative positions of the national representatives' in the euro-zone and the consequences of union enlargement are essentially based on a simple extrapolation of past inflation rates; as such these predictions are an easy target for the Lucas critique. The likelihood of a political business cycle in the near future hinges on the assumption that the members of the ECB Governing Council are vulnerable to political pressure by the governments or parties that appointed them, and that the ECB system of checks and balances is not effective in diluting different principals' pressures. Finally, though there are good reasons to believe that some central banks are overstaffed as suggested by the economic theory of bureaucracy, the analysis is conducted using rather crude proxies for central bank output demand. It is possible that the numerical estimates of overstaffing may be exaggerated in some cases. The subsequent discussion is restricted to the assumptions upon which Vaubel's predictions are based.

Do inflation attitudes differ across member countries?

Vaubel's method for predicting relative attitudes towards inflation consists of a simple extrapolation of past inflation rates. This exercise reveals that inflation preferences among actual and prospective member countries differ widely. There is therefore the possibility that a 'strong-currency' country like Germany could be worse off being a member of EMU because the median voter within the ECB Governing Council is the representative of a country which has had a worse inflation record and may on average vote for a more inflationary policy than the hard-currency country would choose by itself. However, Lucas' critique is a reminder that simple extrapolations of past data can be misleading. Indeed, the birth of EMU probably constitutes as great a structural break with the past as was the collapse of the Bretton Woods system in the early 1970s. Today nobody knows for sure what the consequences will be, but past average inflation rates are not necessarily a good indicator for current and future (relative) inflation attitudes.[2]

There are a number of reasons.[3] First, inflation is feared most in countries that have suffered from high inflation in the past. For instance, countries with a recent history of price instability like Argentina, Chile and Israel are nowadays regarded as examples of successful stabilisation, contradicting the idea that high past inflation necessarily leads to high inflation in the future. Vaubel does show that there is a positive correlation between his measure of sensitivity to inflation and the annual average inflation rate between 1900 and 1940 (p. 152). Although hyperinflation is a more traumatic experience than moderate double-digit inflation, it remains to be explained why the relatively higher inflation that some countries experienced after the collapse of the Bretton Woods system did not change inflation attitudes in these countries. In fact weak-currency countries revealed their preferences for low inflation at some cost during the process of convergence to the euro. Despite significant tax rises and budget cuts the 'median voter' in these countries did not overturn this process.

Second, inflation is highly persistent. The policy mistakes of the 1970s, arguably due to a different understanding of the effects of activist monetary policy than that which prevails today, led to high and persistent inflation which would have been sub-optimal to reduce sharply given the high costs of disinflation. Hence the higher average inflation observed in some countries could simply reflect the initial mistakes and the subsequent responsible and prudent adoption of a gradual or opportunistic approach to disinflation.

Third, there is nowadays an overwhelming consensus among central bankers, elected officials and the private sector, as to what monetary policy can and cannot achieve. In fact central banks worldwide tend to set similar inflation targets and to behave in a very similar way, as shown by a large body of empirical research on policy reaction functions (see e.g. Bernanke *et al.* 1999).

Fourth, in terms of economic structure, historically high-inflation countries are arguably more similar to low-inflation countries today. Some factors like automatic wage indexation that can exacerbate the inertial effect of an initial jump in the inflation rate have been eliminated or drastically reduced everywhere. The social and distributive conflicts that were partly at the root of wage–price spirals in some countries in the 1970s are less common today. Furthermore, the need for seigniorage revenue in some weak-currency countries is lower than it used to be thanks to reforms that have raised both tax rates and the tax base.

Finally, the economic and political costs of defection from the euro-system are now much higher with a common currency. So now it is much more difficult for a single country to alter the system to produce more inflation.

In defence of his extrapolative exercise Roland Vaubel contends that inflation preferences have been stable at least up to 1993 (p. 156). One of the papers he cites in support of this claim (Hayo 1998) measures voters' sensitivity to inflation as the regression coefficient with which the current inflation rate affects the rank of price stability among four objectives (i.e. public order, freedom of speech, price stability, more democracy). Given that unemployment is not included in this ranking, it is difficult to interpret these results. In any case, while the regression coefficient is larger the higher the country's average inflation rate, the opposite is true for the intercept. Indeed the study shows that the share of the population which regards price stability as the greatest concern is larger in high-average inflation countries that in low-average inflation countries. This actually lends support to the idea that overall inflation aversion is actually higher in the former. The other study cited in support of Vaubel's claim (Collins and Giavazzi 1993) sets out to estimate the weights associated with inflation and unemployment in a Barro–Gordon-type loss function using consumers survey data. While there are serious reservations about the interpretations of these results (Fratianni 1993), the conclusion that the authors draw is that there is

> evidence of shifts in attitudes toward inflation and unemployment in Europe since the late 1970s. In particular, there appears to have been some convergence

> in attitudes, in the sense that initially high-inflation countries (such as France and Italy) have become less tolerant of inflation relative to unemployment while attitudes in traditionally low-inflation countries (such as Germany) have shifted in the opposite direction.
>
> (Collins and Giavazzi 1993: 567)

The above considerations do not imply that the future of the euro is without risk. The existing asymmetries, especially in the initial levels of public debt and unemployment rates, constitute a potential threat to the macroeconomic stability of the new currency area. But past inflation preferences do not seem a good guide for assessing how these asymmetries can translate into the risk of higher future inflation.

How likely is a political business cycle?

Vaubel's prediction that a boom is likely between 2002 and 2004 as a consequence of the timing of national elections is based on the 'party loyalty hypothesis'. According to this hypothesis the members of the executive board of a central bank are loyal to the parties or governments that appointed them despite their formal, legally independent status. On the one hand, the appointees may share the preferences of their appointing principals; on the other hand, even if they do not, appointees may need assistance to find another job at the end of their term in office and hence they are more likely to succumb to political pressures. Therefore we should expect to see a 'monetary acceleration' before the elections if a majority of the central bank board share the preferences of the incumbent government.

It has been argued that even if the board members are not completely insulated from political pressures, the system of institutional checks and balances should make it more difficult for each member to accommodate their political principals. The partially decentralised organisational structure of the ECB, which mimics that of the Bundesbank, should prove effective at mitigating political influences on euro-zone monetary policy. Because of the staggered timing of European and national elections, there should be a small chance at any given point in time that a majority within the ECB Council supports their national governments during the pre-electoral period.[4] Vaubel, however, asserts that 'it is very likely that the ten governments standing for re-election between May 2002 and June 2004 will command a majority in the ECB Council between May 2001 and June 2003'. In particular, Vaubel shows that there is a coalition within the ECB Council which minimises the dispersion of the election dates up to 2006 with a preferred election date in May 2003 (see Table 6.6). According to Vaubel this coalition will expand monetary growth to favour the re-election of their incumbent governments.

There are a number of problems with this conjecture. Even if the coalition that minimises the dispersion of elections materialises (see Table 6.6), one can ask whether the period over which the elections are due to take place is sufficiently short (the first elections are due in May 2002 while the last are in June 2004) and whether the dispersion around the mean date is sufficiently small to make a multi-national opportunistic monetary cycle practical. Engineering a monetary expansion which suits the needs of all governments in this coalition seems much more difficult than when monetary policy is in the hands of a single national central bank. Indeed the bulk of the effects of monetary policy on output and employment materialise with a time lag which varies across countries between one and two years depending on the transmission mechanism; there is also a lag between the effects on output and those on inflation. In addition, the period is sufficiently long that there could easily be an interim shock that induces some of the council members to take a different stance, thereby shifting the median position towards a less accommodative policy. In other words, it is difficult to create an expansion that benefits all governments in the coalition without destabilising the economy. Moreover, the likely necessity to keep monetary policy loose, even when new information about the state of the economy (e.g. an unanticipated rise in inflation) would suggest otherwise, will presumably not go unnoticed by the market and will result in higher inflation expectations. The reaction of the market could even end up being counterproductive for the re-election chances of the incumbent governments (setting aside the consequences for the prestige and reputation of the members of the ECB Council).[5] It is therefore more plausible to imagine that if there is a political monetary cycle, this will be of limited magnitude and its beneficial effects on the re-election chances of the incumbent governments will not be evenly distributed. But this makes the formation of a coalition within the ECB Council less likely in the first place.

In practice the empirical evidence on political cycles at the level of single countries is generally not favourable. Alesina and Roubini (1997) find no evidence of more expansionary monetary policy and of increases in output and employment in the United States during election years. In other industrialised countries they find evidence of electoral cycles on monetary policy instruments but not on output and employment. As stressed by Alesina and Roubini, these results are more consistent with the idea that monetary policy makers refrain from tightening monetary policy in election years than with the assumption that policy makers deliberately attempt to manipulate the economic cycle. Indeed, it is stressed that policy makers may not have sufficient control of the business cycle to engineer convenient expansions before elections and that rational voters may punish excessively opportunistic governments.

It is, however, possible that the most common empirical tests of the political business cycle have underestimated the importance of opportunistic monetary cycles by failing to control for the central banks' partisan preferences: we in fact expect to observe a monetary expansion only if the incumbent government commands a majority in the central bank board. Vaubel (1997) finds support for this hypothesis in the German data but Berger and Woitek (1997) find negative evidence using a wider range of methods.

Are national central banks overstaffed?

The finding that some national central banks are largely overstaffed is perhaps the most interesting and original result of Vaubel's analysis. The economic theory of bureaucracy explains what motivates a bureaucrat (e.g. power, prestige, etc.) to expand the size of his budget and staff beyond the net benefit maximising point in the absence of effective control by his sponsors. Even though it is reasonable to expect that this theory applies to central banks as well, Vaubel's estimates of the relative inefficiency of some ESCB central banks could be biased upwards. There are some factors that are unaccounted for in the analysis, which might make some central banks look less efficient than they actually are. Although these factors may not change the general picture, it would nonetheless be interesting to know how important they are. First, the data on staff numbers do not distinguish between employees directly involved in the operations of the bank and those employed in the provision of more general services (e.g. cleaning, catering, transport, etc.). It is conceivable, in the case of certain central banks, that some of the latter services may be outsourced, thereby reducing the total number of staff employed, other things being equal. Thus the data on staff numbers may not be sufficiently homogeneous for a comparison across banks.

Second, the regressors used in the analysis do not fully capture all the tasks performed by a central bank. A central bank may have a larger staff compared to an otherwise similar central bank because it simply performs tasks that are assigned to another public agency (e.g. the Treasury, etc.) in other countries. For example, some central banks may be responsible for the collection of certain statistical data, a task carried out by other agencies in other countries. Similarly, some central banks can carry out microeconomic research at the regional level, which other banks do not. As to research staff, some central banks employ more people on research topics less directly relevant to their decision-making process. Nonetheless this research can be regarded as a public good having the same or better quality than the research carried out, for instance, in government-funded universities. Does this constitute a waste? Similar considerations may apply to other bank activities the utility of which receives different valuation across countries.

Last but not least, some central banks are more successful than others in stabilising the economy and supervising the banking sector. It would then be interesting to know how the quality of central banks' output is related to staff levels.

Of course the data necessary to resolve the doubts raised above may be impossible or difficult to obtain. However, the above considerations suggest the need for caution in interpreting the estimates of central banks' relative inefficiency.

Notes

1 Vaubel also discusses the implications of EMU for long-run employment. My discussion will not focus on these implications because these are not derived from public choice theory and seem less original than the others.

2 Of course this does not mean that countries cannot have different preferences over inflation and unemployment. For example, right-wing countries may be more inflation averse than left-wing countries.

3 Some of the reasons and ideas presented below are discussed by Adam Posen (1998).

4 See for example the discussion in Lohmann (1998).

5 Alternatively, a monetary expansion can be timed to have most of its effects on output around the preferred mean election date of the coalition. Yet the effects may not be

sufficiently strong to favour the governments whose re-election dates are closer to the beginning of the period than to the mean. Besides, the re-election chances of the governments whose election dates are closer to the end of the period could be damaged by the ensuing rise in inflation.

References

Alesina, A. and N. Roubini with G.D. Cohen (1997) *Political Cycles and the Macroeconomy*. Cambridge, MA.

Berger, H. and U. Woitek (1997) 'How Opportunistic are Partisan German Central Bankers: Evidence on the Vaubel Hypothesis', *European Journal of Political Economy, 13.*

Bernanke, B. S., F. S. Mishkin, T. Laubach and A. Posen (1999) *Inflation Targeting: Lessons from the International Experience*. Princeton, NJ.

Collins, S. and F. Giavazzi (1993) 'Attitudes Toward Inflation and the Viability of Fixed Exchange Rates: Evidence from the EMS', in Bordo, M. and B. Eichengreen, eds, *A Retrospective on the Bretton Woods System: Lessons for International Monetary Reform*. Chicago.

Fratianni, M. (1993) 'Attitudes Toward Inflation and the Viability of Fixed Exchange Rates: A Comment', in Bordo, M. and B. Eichengreen, eds, *A Retrospective on the Bretton Woods System: Lessons for International Monetary Reform*. Chicago.

Hayo, B. (1998) 'Inflation Culture, Central Bank Independence and Price Stability', *European Journal of Political Economy, 14.*

Lohmann, S. (1998) 'Institutional Checks and Balances and the Political Control of the Money Supply', *Oxford Economic Papers, 50.*

Posen, A. (1998) 'Why EMU is Irrelevant for the German Economy?', CFS Working Paper 98/11.

Vaubel, R. (1997) 'The Bureaucratic and Partisan Behaviour of Independent Central Banks: German and International Evidence', *European Journal of Political Economy, 13.*

Comments on Chapter 6 – The future of the euro: a public choice perspective

Mark Salmon

Professor Vaubel has produced a wide ranging and stimulating discussion of European Monetary Union from a 'political economy' point of view. Given that it has now been over a year since the euro came into existence it is interesting to recall how the debate has changed from the time when it seemed that the entire emphasis lay on the convergence criteria. Overnight, once those eligible to enter EMU were determined, virtually no comment at all has been passed on the need to continue policies that promote the convergence process and reduce asymmetries within the euro area. Maybe there is a fundamental lack of political will to face this structural issue yet it would seem inescapable that the future of the euro will be determined, over time, by the ability of the single monetary policy to accommodate divergence within the euro area. The second issue which also was equally apparent before the birth of the euro and remains outstanding is the management of the euro's external value. The *laissez faire* approach that has been adopted enables the free market to push the exchange rate where it will and any subsequent sustained fundamental divergence from equilibrium will surely only make the problem of designing the common monetary policy even more difficult. While the extensive devaluation of the euro in its first year may have been willingly accepted by German and French exporters and politicians alike, the market wind can blow in other directions with equal force at other times. With these thoughts in mind let us consider the arguments put forward by Roland Vaubel.

Professor Vaubel's public choice perspective leads him to argue, unlike much of the accepted academic literature, that the realised level of inflation in an economy is not so much due to the credibility of monetary policy[1] but a question of the inflation preferences displayed by a heterogeneous ECB council whose members represent distinct national preferences for inflation. He seems to ignore from the outset that Council members are required to adopt a *European* perspective and forget their national origins. The simple majority voting mechanism and the median voter will then, he argues, determine the resulting inflation rate we can expect within the euro area in the future.

I have a number of difficulties with this approach which would have perhaps been relieved if some more convincing theoretical argument for his position had been put forward. Given the considerable academic support and practical success of the independent central bank approach to anti-inflationary policy it would seem difficult to justify his rejection of what has become a standard view of monetary policy throughout the world. Professor Vaubel's argument seems to rest on cross-section regression results with seven degrees of freedom! Moreover the argument he makes for the insignificance of the effect of central bank independence and pegging to the D-Mark on inflation in equation 6 of Table 6.3 when the sensitivity measure is included is, I believe quite simply, wrong. Having already established that multicollinearity is present, since he shows the central bank independence measure he uses is highly correlated with the sensitivity to inflation index, it is simply not possible to then conclude that one or the other is the correct measure of the common signal in the data. Moreover the econometric basis of the sensitivity measure is itself difficult to judge since it appears to be determined (Hayo 1998) through the use of ordinary least squares in a qualitative dependent variable regression which is well known to lead to biased inference.

A further problem I have with the approach adopted is that any argument that uses *historical* records of inflation to infer inflation *preferences* in the future is clearly difficult to justify and implement rigorously. In particular apart from assuming a fundamental constancy it implies there were *no failures of policy* such as politically motivated expansions nor *any inability of policy* to control inflationary forces in the event of exogenous shocks. For instance the data period used extends over the oil price shocks of the 1970s and I would find it difficult to believe that European preferences for inflation were accurately reflected by realised inflation over this period. This argument obviously applies quite generally to other policy failures. There are difficult questions determining the extent to which policy moderated the underlying inflation rate and how this can be reconciled with the Lucas Critique. If the argument is that policy both accurately reflected preferences, and was effective in implementing these preferences then these primitive hypotheses need to be rigorously examined. Instead *ad hoc* cross-sectional regression results[2] that yield relatively high values of R^2 which are almost certainly due to the very small number of degrees of freedom become the basic tool of the argument. Such correlation certainly does not imply causation. The Lucas Critique might also argue that the introduction of monetary union would potentially represent a regime shift and hence historical records would be irrelevant in predicting inflation under the new euro regime. While France is established as the median it is far from clear under such a regime change that it would remain in that position.

An alternative to the form of analysis used by Professor Vaubel to investigate the future path of inflationary pressures under EMU is that of Canzoneri *et al.* (1998) and Alberola-Ila and Tyrvanin (1998). We then move from political economy considerations to assessing productivity differentials in the euro area within the context of the Balassa–Samuelson model of real exchange rate determination. This latter work builds on a substantial existing body of empirical evidence drawn from long panels of time series and cross-section data looking at the validity of the productivity hypothesis. The basic idea here is that sectoral asymmetries within the euro area, shown through productivity differentials that exist between traded and non-traded goods sectors of the individual economies, will lead to inflation differentials between the members of the EMU. Canzoneri *et al.* demonstrate, after rigorous econometric analysis and panel unit root tests, that there are persistent implied inflation differentials with respect to Germany of up to 2.4 per cent. This highlights the issue I raised in the introduction of how the existing divergence within the EMU area can be accommodated and managed within the constraints of a single monetary policy alone. It is not clear to me that the political economy perspective provided in Professor Vaubel's analysis has yet offered any resolution to this question. It also has clear implications for the question of the management of the external value of the euro.

Consider the current situation within the euro area and the case of the Irish economy in particular. Growth in Ireland is currently running at 8.7 per cent with unemployment below 5 per cent, and its budget surplus is the largest within Europe. Inflation on the other hand has doubled to 4.6 per cent in the last year – the highest rate in the EU. This, to my mind, is the real policy issue facing euro policy makers since, although Ireland's economy is small within the EU context, it highlights non-convergence. Interest rates set to promote growth in France and Germany are simply inappropriate for Ireland which is in danger of running out of control unless the economy can be slowed. The implications for other periphery economies such as Spain, Italy, Portugal and Finland seem clear. The effective real exchange rate movement will erode its competitiveness while wages and prices rise and foreign investment will slow; compare this with the current situation and policy needs in France. Ireland also has a relatively open economy, importing some 75 per cent of what it consumes mostly from the US and the UK which are obviously outside the euro area and since it trades more in US dollars and sterling than any other euro member it suffers proportionately more from the euro's weakness over the last year. On top of this situation a final political cohesion issue appears. The Irish government has recently announced more than one billion dollars worth of tax cuts. It is going to be very difficult to see how any median voter designed single monetary policy can accommodate the divergent needs to slow down the Irish economy while at the same time stimulating growth in Germany and France. Non-convergence and the continued lack of a coordinated political response both generally and particularly in fiscal policy remains central to the future of the euro to my mind.

Roland Vaubel's analysis of the *effective* independence of the ECB is interesting and potentially important in practice – time will tell. The pressures within the ECB council will necessarily depend on the ensuing divergence within the euro area which we have just discussed.

Electoral policy cycles are a real issue, not so much I believe as Professor Vaubel emphasises in monetary policy but through divergent fiscal policy. There seems to be some evidence that central bank independence within the UK has led to political manipulation of *fiscal* policy and this remains a real threat within the constraints imposed by the Stability Pact. One aspect that has been raised by Demertzis *et al.* (1999) is that given the apparent conservatism of euro-wide monetary policy there may be domestic pressure within the euro area to elect more expansionary or left-wing governments to stimulate fiscal policy. The coordination of monetary and fiscal policy then seems central and the real possibility of a permanent left wing political bias induced through the movement to independent central banks seems worthy of greater analysis. This may indeed nullify any median voter type of analysis for monetary policy. It also raises the critical issue of transparency in policy making and will affect the timing of new entrants. Once again I find it interesting that Professor Vaubel's analysis immediately denies the basic rationale for the independence of monetary policy by accepting that political manipulation of monetary policy is feasible.

The next step in Professor Vaubel's paper is to consider the question of the effect of the euro on unemployment. I find it difficult as, I believe, does he to make much headway here except to remark that I suspect that the innovations that are being made in the 'new economy' industries, and the different rates at which these changes are occurring throughout the euro area, will dominate traditional analysis based on historical trends; again the potential for real divergence seems critical. It is not clear to me that the traditionally high unemployment economies of the euro area are those undergoing the greatest productivity gains and transformations in this respect.

The loss of the exchange rate instrument and the absence of an explicit exchange rate policy for the euro will become a major restriction on the ability of euro economies to accommodate growing divergence to my mind. The time scale by which these processes will work themselves out remains to be determined but again depends on the lack of political cohesion which I believe Professor Vaubel's analysis could have addressed. However, contrary to his argument, the free market has not always delivered the required equilibrium exchange rate adjustment as the experience with the dollar over 1980–5 is widely accepted to show. While it is clear that the euro area is a less open economy as a whole, the different constituent economies will progressively suffer different real exchange rate pressures and some means beyond simply allowing market pressures to force domestic adjustment may be politically necessary. Unemployment is a very local political issue! Again to my mind the establishment of some exchange rate policy is a critical issue for the stability of the euro area in the medium term. At least some attempt must be made to minimise excessive deviations from long run equilibrium positions. One related issue on which the author and I would clearly seem to agree is that it is not in either the UK's or the euro area's interest for sterling to join at present; the degree of divergence is simply too great for a single monetary policy to bear and the additional strain may be critical. Far greater emphasis should be put both within the euro area and within the UK towards a continuation of policies aimed at achieving greater convergence if sterling's entry is to have any hope of success.

Finally Professor Vaubel provides an stimulating analysis of the optimal size and employment levels within the ECB – I wonder how function specific his results must be, given that the remit of the ECB is substantially broader than most existing Central Banks.

Altogether I complement Roland Vaubel for his stimulating and thought provoking analysis of these issues from a public choice perspective. It is refreshing to see familiar questions addressed from a different point of view even though I cannot agree with all his conclusions. The continuing divergence within the euro area seems to me to be the most pressing policy issue influencing the future stability of the euro and yet it seems to be one which is relatively ignored by euro area policy makers and indeed the ECB.

Notes

1 Hence the issue of the independence of the Central Bank or the pegging of the exchange rate to a reliable anchor.
2 For instance weighting by the percentage of time the currency was pegged to the D-Mark as a measure of the credibility effect of pegging.

References

Alberola-Ila, E. and T. Tyrvainen (1998) 'Is There Scope for Inflation Differentials in the EMU?' mimeo, Bank of Spain.

Canzoneri, M., R. Cumby, B. Diba and G. Eudey (1998) 'Trends in European Productivity: Implications for Real Exchange Rates, Real Interest Rates and Inflation Differentials', mimeo, Georgetown University.

Demertzis M., A. Hughes Hallett and N. Viegi (1999) 'An Independent Central Bank Faced with Elected Governments', CEPR Discussion Paper no. 2219.

Index

Abbreviations: Tab = Table; Fig = Figure

A Monetary History (Friedman, M. and Schwarz, A. J.) 88
A Plan for a European Currency (Mundell, R.) 106
Ausgleich 117; *see also* Austro-Hungarian monetary union
Austro-Hungarian Bank: creation 124; establishment of power 126–7, 143
Austro-Hungarian monetary union 5, 111–12
  attempts to join other monetary unions 144–5
  budgetary organisation , 117(Fig 5.1), 118–19
  collapse 134–5, 144
  common budgets 121, 121(Fig 5.3)
  comparison with EMU 116–17
  comparison with other nineteenth-century monetary unions 142–4
  Compromise of 1867 117, 123
  creation of banks 123–4
  debt burden structure 117(Tab 5.1)
  deficits 120–1, 120(Fig 5.2)
  exchange rates 1881–99 126(Fig 5.5)
  investment policies 119–20
  market discipline
    convergence of debt instruments 129–30, 142
    currency spread: gold vs. paper 133(Fig 5.7)
    monitoring through debt structure 130–3, 142
    reputation 128–9
    yields on securities: gold vs. paper 131(Fig 5.6)
  post-1892 126–7
  pre-1892 124–6
  public debt 121–2, 122(Fig 5.4)
  theoretical equivalence with EMU 133–5
  see also monetary unions
Austrian National Bank 123–4
  see also Austro-Hungarian monetary union

'Bank War' (United States) 79–80
  see also United States monetary union
banks *see* Bundesbank; central banks; European Central Bank (ECB)
Bhagwati, J., exchange rate control 37
bonds 32–4
Bordo, M.
  acknowledgement 100
  overview of paper 1–3
Bornefalk, A., acknowledgement 63
bullion points 114
  see also nineteenth-century monetary unions
Bundesbank 152, 155, 160, 174

Cacania *see* Austro-Hungarian monetary union
Capie, F. H., introduction to text 1–6
capital mobility 37–8
  United States 77, 84
central banks
  bankers
    objective functions 155, 155(Fig 6.1)
    party loyalty 157, 185–6
  effect of independence on inflation 151–3
  staff size, adjustments 171, 173–4, 182, 186–7
    actual/predicted by nation in EMU-11 173(Tab 6.16)
    actual/predicted by nation prior to EMU 172(Tab 6.15)
  United States, creation 91–2

see also European Central Bank (ECB); inflation rates
CFA Franc Zone 54
see also monetary unions
Cohen, B., acknowledgement 63
common currencies *see* monetary unions
conferences
City University, London, May 1999 1, 100
International Monetary Conference, Paris, 1867 145
Congdon, T., comments on 'The future of EMU' 70–2
currency areas, index of unsuitability (Bayoumi and Eichengreen) 9–10
currency boards 3
creation 16, 54
Ireland/Britain 55–6
currency crises 7, 21, 31
Flood-Garber models 12–14
output-inflation trade-off 30–1
currency unions 3, 16
inflation rates 26

East Caribbean Currency Area 3, 54
see also currency unions; monetary unions
Eastern European states, admission to EMU
costs and benefits 168–71
exchange rate trends 169(Tab 6.13)
optimal exchange rate arrangements 170(Tab 6.14)
Einaudi, L.
acknowledgement 135
comments on 'Austro-Hungarian monetary union' 142–5
Eitel, I., acknowledgement 174
electoral monetary policy cycles 157–60, 185–6, 191–2
see also European Central Bank (ECB); European monetary union (EMU)
European Central Bank (ECB)
centralisation of banking regulation 166, 174
creation 42
determination of monetary policy 147
Executive Board
re-election 153, 158(Tab 6.5)
selection 156
Governing Council
national inflation rates 1976–93 148(Tab 6.1)
party loyalty 157–60, 158(Tab 6.5), 185–6
prospective national election dates 159(Tab 6.6)
re-election 153, 158(Tab 6.5)
independence 153–5
minimum reserve ratios 166–7
power 134
shortcomings 42–3
surrender of monetary sovereignty to 115
see also central banks; inflation rates
European Exchange Rate Mechanism (ERM) 29, 43, 115
European monetary union (EMU) 63, 111
applicability of US experience 109–10
comparison with C19th monetary unions 113–17
creation 42, 74
debt of member countries 75
electoral monetary policy cycles 157–60, 185–6, 191–2
enlargement 182
Eastern European countries 168–71
effective exchange rates EMU-11/UK£ 166(Fig 6.4)
EMU-11 vs. UK£, real and nominal exchange rate trends 166(Tab 6.11)
present EU members 164–8, 165(Tab 6.10)
exchange rate policy 161–4, 192
flexibility 59–61, 74
future crises 61
labour markets 43–4
national vs. multinational arguments 58–9, 70
openness of economy 161
opposition to 73
optimal currency area 62–3
optimum inflation rates 75, 146, 182
political unity in Europe 61–2, 73
seigniorage 71, 154(Tab 6.4)
shortcomings 42–3
support for 73–4
theoretical equivalence of Austro-Hungarian monetary union 133–5
unemployment, effect on 160–1, 192
exchange depreciation 114–15
see also nineteenth-century monetary unions
exchange rate pegging 152–3
see also inflation rates
exchange rate policy 161–4, 192
bilateral trade percentages 161(Tab 6.7)
rates
DM/US$ 162(Fig 6.2)
EMU-11/UK£ 166(Fig 6.4)

EMU-11/US$ 164(Fig 6.3)
trends
DM vs. US$ 163(Tab 6.8)
EMU-11 vs. Eastern Europe 169(Tab 6.13)
EMU-11 vs. UK£ 166(Tab 6.11)
EMU-11 vs. US$ 163(Tab 6.9)
exchange rate unions, comparison with monetary unions 29–30
exchange rates
fixed 37–8
fixed but adjustable 11, 15–16, 29
floating 10–11
Flood-Garber models 12–15
Feretti, G-M. M., acknowledgement 135
fiscal policy, relationship with monetary policy 7
fiscal theory of price level determination 7–8, 16, 21, 37
analyses 17–20
bonds 32–4
definition of money 32
implications for monetary unions 34
taxes 33
see also inflation rates
fixed but adjustable exchange rates 11, 29
currency crises 15–16
fixed exchange rates 37–8
Flood-Garber model 13–15
Flandreau, M., overview of paper 1–2, 4–5
floating exchange rates 10–11
Flood-Garber model 12–13
Flood, R.P., currency crisis models 12–14
Friedman, M.
A Monetary History, quote 88
The Case for Flexible Exchange Rates 10–11

Garber, P. M., currency crisis models 12–14
German monetary union 49–50, 143–4
lessons learnt 113–16
obstacles 71
see also national monetary unions
Goodhart, C., comments on 'The future of EMU' 73–5
Great Depression 1890's 85
bank deposits by region 1875–96 87(Fig 4.1)
bank deposits by region 1875–1900 89(Fig 4.2)
bimetallism 86
data sources 99–100
regional split over monetary policy 86–8
Great Depression 1930s 4, 92
data sources 100
deposits by Federal Reserve District 93(Fig 4.4), 94(Fig 4.5), 95(Fig 4.6)
Federal Reserve, lender of last resort 92–3
reserve ratios, raising 93–5
separate currency, consideration of idea 95–6
Greenfeld, R., acknowledgement 100

Habsburg Empire *see* Austro-Hungarian monetary union
Hansson, P., acknowledgement 63

inflation rates
central bank independence 151–3
exchange rate pegging 152–3
national inflation rates 1976–93 148(Tab 6.1)
optimum 26–7
in EMU 75, 146, 182
in monetary unions 30
long-range 28
predicting preferences 147–9, 156, 183–5, 189–91
voter sensitivity 149–152
1976–93 150(Tab 6.2)
cross-section analysis 1976–93 151(Tab 6.3)
see also fiscal theory of price-level determination
International Monetary Conference, Paris (1867) 145
Italian monetary union 47–9, 71
see also national monetary unions
Italy 114–15
see also Latin monetary union

Jonung, L., overview of paper 1–3

Keynes, J.M. 11
Kieghyezés 117
see also Austro-Hungarian monetary union
Koehler, B., acknowledgement 135
Komlos, J., acknowledgement 135

labour market mobility
Europe 44–5, 160–1
United States 77, 84
Latin monetary union 50–2, 114–16, 143–4
dissolution 55, 57(Tab 3.2)
seigniorage issues 71
see also multinational monetary unions
Le Cacheux, J., acknowledgement 135

lender of last resort
EMU 43, 59
United States 47
Great Depression 1930s 92–3, 104

Maastricht Treaty 43–4, 59, 60, 71, 74
McCallum, Bennett T., overview of paper 1–2
McKinnon, R.I.
acknowledgement 100
comments on 'How long did it take the US to become an optimal currency area?' 104–7
Mélitz, J., acknowledgement 135
monetary policy, relationship with fiscal policy 7
monetary unions
CFA Franc Zone 54
comparison with exchange rate unions 29–30
costs/benefits 26–7, 77–8
Obstfeld and Rogoff 8–9
East Caribbean Currency Area 54
fiscal theory of prices, implications 34
inflation problems 30
political cohesion 73
reasons for creation 57–8
reasons for dissolution 58, 71
small/large countries 55
see also currency boards; European monetary union (EMU); multinational monetary unions; national monetary unions
money
definitions 32
taxation of 27
multinational monetary unions 3
creation in C19th 46(Tab 3.1)
definition 45
dissolution 55–6, 57(Tab 3.2)
Latin 50–2
Scandinavian 45, 50, 52–4
see also monetary unions; national monetary unions
Mundell, R. 1, 3, 105
A Plan for a European Currency 106
optimal currency area, introduction of concept 8, 10, 36, 77
Uncommon Arguments for Common Currencies 106
Münzverein see German monetary union

national monetary unions 2–3
centralisation of note issue 71–2
Italy 48–9
creation in C19th 46(Tab 3.1)
definition 45
dissolution 56–7, 57(Tab 3.2), 71
EMU as 58–9, 70
German 49–50, 71
Italian 47–9, 71
United States 46–7, 60, 70–1
see also monetary unions; multinational monetary unions
nineteenth-century monetary unions 113
creation 46(Tab 3.1)
international groupings 113–15
nation-state building 115–17

Obstfeld, M., benefits and costs of common currencies 8–9
ÖNB *see* Austrian National Bank
One Market, One Money (EU publication) 10
one-money country vs. one-money world 28–9
see also optimal currency areas
optimal currency areas 2–3, 7, 20–1, 40
benefits of common currencies 8–9
costs of common currencies 8–9
criteria considerations 9
definition 38–9
Europe 44, 62–3
openness of economy 161
historical perspective 10–11, 36
interior optimum 29
introduction of concept 8, 10, 76–7
loss/gain analysis 38–9
one-money country vs. one-money world 28–9
operationalisation of concept 9–10
size considerations 38–40
United States 108–9
in C19th 4, 83–5
time taken to become 98, 104–5
OUB *see* Austro-Hungarian Bank
overview of text 1–6

Paquentin, C., acknowledgement 135
Pei, D., acknowledgement 100
Perkins, E., acknowledgement 100
Perlman, M., acknowledgement 135

Reichert, B., acknowledgement 174
Rockoff, H. 1–2, 4
Rogoff, K., benefits and costs of common currencies 8–9
Rothschild Syndicate 128–9

see also Austro-Hungarian monetary union

Salmon, M., comments on 'The future of the Euro monetary union' 189–93
Scandinavian monetary union 45, 50, 52–4, 143–4
 dissolution 55–6, 57(Tab 3.2)
 see also multinational monetary unions
Schuler, K., acknowledgement 63
Schwartz, A. 1–2, 63, 88
 A Monetary History, quote 88
 acknowledgements 63, 100
 comments on 'How long did it take the US to become an optimal currency area?' 108–10
seigniorage
 EMU 71, 154(Tab 6.4)
 German monetary union 50, 71
 Latin monetary union 51, 71
 nineteenth-century monetary unions 115
Sinclair, P., comments on 'Theoretical issues pertaining to monetary unions' 26–35
Stability and Growth Pact 74–5, 128–9
Switzerland 115–16
 see also Latin monetary union

Teubner, C., acknowledgement 174
The Case for Flexible Exchange Rates (Friedman, M.) 10–11

Uncommon Arguments for Common Currencies (Mundell, R.) 106
unemployment, effect of EMU on 160–1, 192
United Kingdom, entry to EMU
 exchange rates 164–6, 165(Tab 6.10), 166(Tab 6.11)
 minimum reserve ratios 166–7, 167(Tab 6.12)
 political obstacles 167
 regulation of banks 166
United States as optimal currency area 83–5, 98, 104–5, 108–9
 opposition States post Civil War 83–4
United States monetary union 4, 70–1
 1903/1907 panics 90
  bank deposits by region 1900–14 91(Fig 4.3)
  creation of central bank 91–2
  National Monetary Commission 91
 banking crises 79
 chronology 99(Tab 4.2)
 comparison with EMU 109–10
 creation 46–7
 division by Civil War 80–1
 Great Depression 1890s 85
  bimetallism demands 86, 104
  data sources 99–100
  regional deposits 86, 87(Fig 4.1), 88, 89(Fig 4.2)
 Great Depression 1930s
  case for separate currency areas 94–5, 98, 104, 106–7
  data sources 100
  deposits by Federal Reserve District 93(Fig 4.4), 94(Fig 4.5), 95(Fig 4.6)
  Federal Reserve, failure to act as lender of last resort 92–3, 104
  raising of bank reserve ratios 93–4
 institutional changes aiding union 96–7
 lessons learned 97–8
 National Banks 79–80
 opposition to paper money 78–9
 overcoming problems 60
 post Civil War issues
  agricultural unrest 82–3, 83(Tab 4.1)
  fiscal transfers 84–5
  opposition States as optimal currency areas 83–4
  opposition to gold standard 81–2
  resumption of gold standard 81
  Silver Purchase Act 1890 82
 regional disputes 76
 see also monetary unions

Vaubel, R., overview of paper 2, 5–6
Vilar, P. 133

White, E., acknowledgement 100
Wood, G. E.
 comments on 'Theoretical issues pertaining to monetary unions' 36–41
 introduction to text 1–6

Zampolli, F., comments on 'The future of the Euro monetary union' 182–8
Zollverein 50
 see also German monetary union